SACRAMENTS

AND

GOD'S GRACE

High School Framework Course 5

JOANNA DAILEY AND IVY WICK

saint mary's press

Thanks and Dedication

A very special thank you to our student contributors: Mattias and Karla from Seton Catholic Preparatory School in Chandler, AZ; Victoria and Mike from Red Bank Catholic High School in Red Bank, NJ; and Demetrios from Our Lady of the Hills College Preparatory School in Kerrville, TX.

With gratitude to my parents, who led by example; to the clergy and people of St. Joseph's Parish, Hammond, Indiana, who first introduced me to the wonder and grace of the liturgy; to the Sisters of Providence of St. Mary-of-the-Woods, Indiana, and to the Nuns of Our Lady of the Mississippi Abbey, Dubuque, Iowa, who are continually planting seeds of love in the world through prayer and action.

And with many thanks to Maura Hagarty of Saint Mary's Press, consultant par excellence!

—Joanna Dailey

Thanks to Matthew Wick for your tireless support; and Tomas, Sophia, and Olivia Wick for letting me bounce ideas off you and giving me honest feedback. To all of my former students who have helped in this process in ways you will never know—you rock! And thank you to Steven Ellair and Becky Gochanour, whose guidance and expertise made working on this project a wonderful and empowering experience.

—Ivy Wick

The Subcommittee on the Catechism, United States Conference of Catholic Bishops, has found that this catechetical high school text, copyright 2021, is in conformity with the *Catechism of the Catholic Church* and that it fulfills the requirements of Course 6 of the *Doctrinal Elements of a Curriculum Framework for the Development of Catechetical Materials for Young People of High School Age*.

Nihil Obstat: Dr. John Martens, PhD
                 Censor Librorum
                 November 20, 2020

Imprimatur: † Most Rev. Bernard A. Hebda
               Archbishop of Saint Paul and Minneapolis
               November 30, 2020

The nihil obstat and imprimatur are official declarations that a book or pamphlet is free of doctrinal or moral error. No implication is contained therein that those who have granted the nihil obstat or imprimatur agree with the contents, opinions, or statements expressed, nor do they assume any legal responsibility associated with publication.

The content in this resource was acquired, developed, and reviewed by the content engagement team at Saint Mary's Press. Content design and manufacturing were coordinated by the passionate team of creatives at Saint Mary's Press.

Cover image: © Markus Pfaff / Shutterstock.com

Printed in the United States of America

1169 (PO6881)

ISBN 978-1-64121-112-3

CONTENTS

UNIT 1

An Introduction to Liturgy and the Sacraments

WHY SHOULD THE LITURGY AND SACRAMENTS MATTER TO ME?

LOOKING AHEAD

The liturgy allows me to hear God's word, and the sacraments offer me a way to be forgiven and to receive God. The liturgy and sacraments have helped me find my way to God, and they can bring me back to him if I have strayed. I think they make me a part of the Church and unite me with other people in my faith community.

KARLA
Seton Catholic Preparatory School

CHAPTER 1
Liturgy

HOW CAN THE LITURGY BRING ME CLOSER TO GOD?

SNAPSHOT

Article 1
What Is the Liturgy?

A Roman centurion on horseback rides through a crowded pathway leading to the market. "Make way! Make way! Make way for the *leitourgia!*" he announces. He is followed by a road crew carrying picks and axes. They will remove the large rocks from the path, smooth it out, lay smooth chiseled stones, and make a real road.

This is a *leitourgia*—a liturgy. The literal meaning of *leitourgia* is "the people's work." The Church adopted the word *liturgy* as her own. The **liturgy** is the Church's official, public, communal prayer. It is God's work in which the People of God participate. And, of all the liturgies the Church celebrates, the Eucharist is the most important. When we gather to carry out Jesus' commandment to "do this in memory of me" (Luke 22:19), we are responding to God's invitation and his gracious love.

TAKE IT TO GOD

Lord, today I give thanks.
I am grateful for the resources of the Earth.
I am grateful for the gift of human life.
I am grateful for the ability to share in the work of creation.
Lord, today I give thanks.
I am grateful for the opportunity to know you more intimately in the Mass.
I am grateful for the diversity and unique individuality of my community.
I am grateful to serve others, care for others, and share the gifts you have given me.
Lord, today I give thanks.
Amen.

---

liturgy ➤ The Church's official, public, communal prayer. It is God's work, in which the People of God participate. The Church's most important liturgy is the Eucharist, or the Mass.

Not every public gathering for prayer is liturgy. A group prayer service is public and communal, but it is not liturgy because it is not official—that is, it is not governed by the Church. Private prayer is important, but, because it is not official or public, it is not liturgy. When we say "the liturgy," we mean the liturgy as a whole—all the sacraments, including the Eucharist, as well as liturgies that are not sacraments, such as the Liturgy of the Hours and Catholic funerals. When we say "a liturgy," we mean a particular Mass or liturgical celebration.

An entrance procession is usually part of the Introductory Rites of the liturgy. The Introductory Rites prepare our minds and hearts to fully participate in the celebration.

The Work of God

For decades, teens have told their parents, "I'm not going to church; it's boring and pointless." If you find attending church boring or without purpose, you are not alone! If you enjoy going to Mass, you are truly blessed. You have the good fortune to have been graced with an appreciation for God's great gift to the Church, a little taste of Heaven on Earth. However, many people come to truly appreciate the liturgy as adults, once they find that all the distractions of their daily life—their phones, social media, and work do not satisfy their hunger for meaning and connection with God. It's not that modern technology and media are bad, but their flash and instant gratification can distract us from what is really important. We have to look harder today at what God is offering us in the sacred liturgy to discover its true and eternal value.

Liturgy is primarily the work of God (in Latin, *opus Dei),* in which we participate. It is the public, communal, and official worship of the Church. It is public as a sign of our faith to the local community. It is communal, which means it isn't a prayer that we do alone. It is official, which means the Church governs it. The Eucharist (or Mass) is the central liturgy of the Catholic Church and the foundation for most other liturgical celebrations. The other six sacraments of the Church—Baptism, Confirmation, Penance and Reconciliation, Anointing of the Sick, Holy Orders, and Matrimony—have their own liturgical rites.

The word *liturgy* is taken from the Greek word *leitourgia,* which means "a public work" or "service on behalf of the people." For Christians, *liturgy* means the participation of the People of God in the work of God. So our liturgies aren't something we do, but something God does and we participate in. If you are thinking, "God isn't saying the prayers, singing the songs, and receiving the Body and Blood of Christ. . . that's me!", you are right. But those words and actions are the physical expression of the spiritual work that God is doing in the liturgy to bring us to eternal salvation.

That is why participation in the liturgy is just as important as having faith in Jesus, avoiding sin, and living a moral life. In the liturgy, we learn about the great mysteries of our faith by participating in them. We learn about the mystery of the Trinity by encountering the Trinity in the liturgy. We learn about the Incarnation of Jesus Christ by encountering him as true God and true man. We learn about the Paschal Mystery as we participate in the Passion, death, Resurrection, and Ascension of Christ through the Eucharist.

© Bill Wittman / www.wpwittman.com

Participation in the liturgy is just as important as having faith in Jesus, avoiding sin, and living a moral life.

The liturgy is the focal point of our participation in God's work, but it is not the Church's only way of cooperating in his work in the world. Teaching and preaching the Gospel prepares good soil for the seed of faith and worship to grow in God's people. What we experience through the liturgy, we carry out into the world. Because we participate in God's work through the liturgy, we are strengthened and inspired to share our faith in our everyday lives.

Liturgy, Scripture, and Tradition

All the Church's sacraments and liturgies have Christ as their origin, yet he did not dictate all aspects of the liturgy. So where does liturgy as we know it today come from? The essential elements of the liturgy have been handed on to us through Scripture and Tradition, while other elements that we call traditions (lowercase *t*) have emerged over time. Scripture and Tradition are distinct, yet closely related. Both transmit the Word of God. Together they form a single, sacred Deposit of Faith. The Deposit of Faith, the treasure of the Church handed on from the time of the Apostles and contained in Scripture and Tradition, makes clear the truths that cannot be laid aside because they are part of God's Revelation. Truths like these: Jesus Christ is true God and true man,

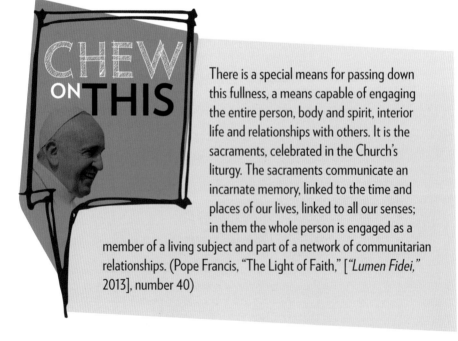

CHEW ON THIS

There is a special means for passing down this fullness, a means capable of engaging the entire person, body and spirit, interior life and relationships with others. It is the sacraments, celebrated in the Church's liturgy. The sacraments communicate an incarnate memory, linked to the time and places of our lives, linked to all our senses; in them the whole person is engaged as a member of a living subject and part of a network of communitarian relationships. (Pope Francis, "The Light of Faith," ["*Lumen Fidei,*" 2013], number 40)

the Pope is the successor of Saint Peter and the visible head of the Church, and the Trinity is one God in three Divine Persons. The Deposit of Faith does not change. The **Magisterium**, the living teaching office of the Church (all bishops in communion with the Pope) is responsible, under the guidance of the Holy Spirit, for interpreting the Deposit of Faith.

The traditions (with a small *t*) that have influenced, and continue to influence, the liturgy are customs, things we do because they are part of our history and culture. They can be incorporated into liturgical celebrations when they express within them the great Tradition of the Church. For example, the priest washes his hands after receiving the gifts of bread and wine at the Preparation of the Gifts. This Christian tradition calls to mind the Old Covenant practice of ritual cleansing before ascending to the altar of sacrifice (see Psalm 26:6). The tradition is preserved in the handwashing ritual in the Eucharist, accompanied by the priest's prayer for purification: "Wash me, O Lord, from my iniquity and cleanse me from my sin" (*Roman Missal*, page 530).

© Renata Sedmakova / Shutterstock.com

The washing of the hands has been preserved in the liturgy even when there is no longer a practical reason for it. Consider the words the priest speaks to understand why the washing of the hands is still symbolically important.

Magisterium ➤ The Church's living teaching office, which consists of all the bishops, in communion with the Pope, the Bishop of Rome. Their task is to interpret and preserve the truths revealed in both Sacred Scripture and Sacred Tradition.

Like the truths of faith, the liturgy is guided by the Magisterium. This is what makes the liturgy the official worship of the Church. Essential elements handed on through Scripture and Tradition are always retained, while aspects of our liturgical celebrations that come from traditions can be kept, modified, or eliminated under the guidance of the Magisterium. Within these guidelines, your parish may make its own decisions about such things as which hymns or songs to sing.

Handed On from Christ

The word *Tradition* is a significant word in our lives of faith and comes from the Latin word *traditio*, which means "to hand on or to give over." Our liturgy has been handed on to us from Jesus, first when he "took bread, said the blessing, broke it, and *giving it* to his disciples said, 'Take and eat; this is my body'" (Matthew 26:26, italics added), and then later, when he died and "*gave up* his spirit" (Matthew 27:50, italics added) to his Father and to us. In Saint Paul's account of Jesus' words at the Last Supper, the earliest account of the words of institution found in Scripture, he notes: "I received from the Lord what I also *handed on* to you, that the Lord Jesus, on the night he was handed over, took bread . . ." (1 Corinthians 11:23, italics added). Our liturgy has been *handed on* to us, as it was to Saint Paul, as the richest inheritance of the Church. ✳

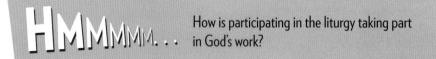

How is participating in the liturgy taking part in God's work?

Tradition ▶ The process of passing on the Gospel message. Tradition, which began with the oral communication of the Gospel by the Apostles, was written down in the Scriptures, is handed down and lived out in the life of the Church, and is interpreted by the Magisterium under the guidance of the Holy Spirit. Both Sacred Tradition and Sacred Scripture have their common source in the Revelation of Jesus Christ and must be equally honored.

Article 2
The Holy Trinity and the Liturgy

The Church's liturgy is Trinitarian. In the liturgy, the three Divine Persons of the **Trinity**—the Father, the Son, and the Holy Spirit—are at work; and through the liturgy, the mystery of the Holy Trinity, the central mystery of the Christian faith, is more deeply revealed. As a sign of this, every liturgy begins, "In the name of the Father and of the Son and of the Holy Spirit." And every liturgy ends with the celebrant's asking for the blessing of the Holy Trinity.

Each Person of the Trinity is involved in the Church's liturgy. We acknowledge the Father as the source of all the blessings of creation, and salvation, especially the gifts of his Son, Jesus Christ, and the Holy Spirit. Jesus Christ, who became incarnate to redeem us, is central in the Church's liturgy. In every liturgy, Christ's gift of himself for the sake of our salvation is made present to us, here and now, by the power of the Holy Spirit. This is a challenging concept. How can Jesus, or any of the three Persons of the Trinity, be present to us in the here and now? How can we feel connected to Christ just by participating in the liturgy? These questions are natural and can be answered only through a deeper understanding of our faith.

I DIDN'T KNOW THAT!

What happens to the bread and wine during the Eucharist? Through the action of Transubstantiation, the ordinary bread and wine change in substance and become the real Body and Blood of Jesus Christ. Though some people suggest that the phrase *hocus pocus* may have come from a corruption of the Latin phrase *"Hoc est enim corpus meum"* ("This is my body"), Transubstantiation is not magic. It is a real and substantial change that takes place through the power of the Holy Spirit in the consecration at Mass.

Trinity ➤ Often referred to as the Blessed Trinity, the central Christian mystery and dogma that there is one God in three Persons: Father, Son, and Holy Spirit.

Let's look at this from an even larger perspective. Something that makes Christ present to us is called a sacrament; thus, we say that liturgy and Christ's work within it are sacramental. However, we can also say that the Body of Christ, the Church, is a sacrament because the Holy Spirit also works through her to make Christ present in the world and to be the instrument of grace and salvation for all. The Church is thus the sacrament of the Holy Trinity's communion with human beings. In every liturgy, especially the Seven Sacraments, the Church encounters God—the Father, Son, and Holy Spirit. Through this encounter and the outpouring of God's grace, we are justified, which means we are freed from sin, and we are sanctified, which means we are made holy and share in the divine life.

When we celebrate the liturgy, we celebrate with not only the people we can see with us but also all the angels, saints, and those who have gone before us in faith. The saving work of Christ extends our liturgy on Earth into Heaven. In the liturgy, the boundaries of time and space are broken, and we are one in Christ. In every liturgy, we participate in and also anticipate the heavenly liturgy that is our ultimate goal. In the liturgy, we remember the saints in Heaven—first of all the holy Mother of God, then the Apostles, the martyrs, and other saints—on fixed days of the Liturgical Year, not for their own accomplishments but for Christ's work of salvation in them. Their trials and final victory encourage us as we journey to the Father in Christ. Thus, the Church on Earth is united with the liturgy of Heaven.

© Cavee / Shutterstock.com

Christ is present in many ways in the liturgy, but in a special way in the Sacrament of the Eucharist. We receive Christ's Body and Blood during Communion.

How, then, is Christ present in the liturgy? He is present in the priest, who acts in the person of Christ. He is present in the assembly because we are the Body of Christ. He is present in the Word of God, the Scriptures. God's Word is an essential element of every liturgy and is proclaimed during the Liturgy of the Word. In the Sacrament of the Eucharist, Christ is present in a special way, in his Body and Blood, which we receive during Communion.

The Holy Spirit is active in the liturgy, preparing us to encounter Christ. The Holy Spirit reveals Christ's presence in the assembly, in Scripture, and in the sacramental actions of liturgical celebrations. By Christ's transforming power, the Holy Spirit makes the saving work of Christ present and active, here and now, for us. When we leave the liturgy, we carry the message of God's love to all we meet, through the work of the Holy Spirit.

It is important to understand what it means to say that "the saving power of Christ is present and active, here and now." In the liturgy and the sacraments, we do not merely remember and celebrate the past because the liturgy and the sacraments are how the saving power of the Risen Christ is made available to us today. Christ is alive and is not limited by time and space. In the liturgy, his power is just as available to us as it was to the Apostles and the disciples. Of course, he is with us at all times, but in the liturgy and the sacraments, in a special way, he keeps his promise to be with us always. ✳

HMMMMM. . .   When does Christ feel most present to you?

Article 3

The Liturgical Year

An underground river, appropriately called the Lost River, can be found in southern Indiana. At several points in its pathway, the river simply disappears. It dips underground and gurgles beneath the surface for miles, only to arise again, sometimes in quiet pools, sometimes in plumes of water, depending on the limestone caves, caverns, and channels underground through which it travels. It has been called one of North America's natural wonders.

For many people, the **Liturgical Year** is like an underground river. The Liturgical Year gurgles beneath the surface of our days, and then, suddenly, it's Advent! or Christmas! or Lent! or Easter! The Liturgical Year rises to the surface of our consciousness, and we catch up to it, at least for a little while.

Look at the liturgical calendar above. What liturgical season is the Church celebrating now? In what season does your birthday usually fall? the birthdays of family and friends? Why are liturgical colors important to the seasons?

Liturgical Year ➤ The Church's annual cycle of feasts and seasons that celebrates the events and mysteries of Christ's birth, life, death, Resurrection, and Ascension, and forms the context for the Church's worship.

But the Liturgical Year is always there and is always *now*. The Liturgical Year celebrates God's time and is therefore timeless. The Liturgical Year provides a structure in which the Universal Church throughout the world celebrates the whole mystery of Christ—from his Incarnation and birth, through his life, suffering, death, Resurrection, and Ascension, to Pentecost—and prays in anticipation of Christ's coming again at the end of time. All these saving events are made present to us now.

Let us follow this calendar—as if following a life-giving river—from season to season. How does it nourish our lives and help us to grow as members of the Body of Christ?

Advent

The Liturgical Year begins in Advent. This season begins on the fourth Sunday before Christmas. Advent is the time of preparation before Christmas and lasts four weeks (the fourth week is typically not a full week). Its liturgical color is purple, to signify waiting. Advent is a time of hope, of waiting, and of preparing. What are we preparing for?

In our culture, preparation in this context often has one dimension: we are preparing for Christmas Day. But as Saint Bernard of Clairvaux (a twelfth-century monk, writer, and teacher) explained, our waiting and preparing have three dimensions: (1) waiting to celebrate the Word Made Flesh at Christmas, (2) waiting to celebrate the birth of the Word of God in our hearts at Christmas, and (3) waiting for the final coming of Christ in glory at the end of time. Our waiting is active. We are preparing to be visited by our Savior. We are waiting and preparing for our Redeemer. We are making room in our hearts and our lives for the One who was sent away because there was no room for him in the inn. And we are waiting for Christ's second coming, his final advent, when all things will be fulfilled in him (see Ephesians 1:7–10).

Christmas

Laney looked around at the chaotic family room. The Christmas tree glittered in the corner, and under it lay mounds of torn wrapping paper and ribbon— the evidence of the successful endeavors of her younger brothers and sisters to

open their gifts in the shortest amount of time possible. Of course, she and her parents had also joined in the fun. Laney smiled a little sadly. It had been a good Christmas, but now it was all over.

But what Laney didn't realize was that the Christmas season begins on December 25 and lasts until the Solemnity of the Baptism of the Lord (the third Sunday after Christmas Day). Its liturgical color is white or gold, signifying joy. During this time, the Church reflects on the wonder and meaning of the Incarnation. The Word of God Made Flesh certainly takes more than one day to celebrate!

One Solemnity of particular note during this season is the Feast of the Epiphany. Originally celebrated on what is now the twelfth day of Christmas (January 6), the Epiphany celebrates the Revelation of the Savior to the Gentiles (the people of the non-Jewish world). In many parts of the world, Epiphany is the day for parties and gift-giving. The Solemnity of the Epiphany is celebrated either on January 6 or, according to the decision of the episcopal conference, on the Sunday between January 2 and January 8.

Ordinary Time

Ordinary Time is not called ordinary because the Church considers it "nothing special." It is called ordinary because its days are numbered with ordinal numbers (that is, the First Sunday in Ordinary Time, Second Sunday in Ordinary Time, and so forth). Two blocks of Ordinary Time occur in the liturgical calendar: The first one is between the Christmas season and Lent, and the second one, which is longer, is between Pentecost and Advent. The liturgical color of Ordinary Time is green, symbolizing hope.

In Ordinary Time, the Church reflects on the life of Jesus Christ—his mission, his miracles, and his teachings. We have the opportunity, day by day and week by week, to know Christ better, to internalize his teachings and values as we encounter him in Word and sacrament.

Lent

Before Christ came into the world, we were like sheep without a shepherd. But Jesus came, redeemed us through his suffering and death, and led us back to the Father. During Lent we recall Christ's Passion—his suffering and death on the cross. Lent, the most solemn and reflective time of the year, begins on Ash Wednesday. Its liturgical color is purple, symbolizing penance. The Church encourages us to perform three Christian practices in a more focused way during Lent: prayer, fasting, and almsgiving. The whole Church, as the Body of Christ, commits to these works together, supporting one another in our efforts to remember Saint Paul's question: "Do you not know . . . that you are not your own? For you have been purchased at a price" (1 Corinthians 6:19–20). During Lent, we recall that Christ redeemed us through his death, and we prepare to celebrate his Resurrection on the most glorious day of the year, the Solemnity of Solemnities: Easter.

Easter Triduum

The week preceding Easter begins on Palm (Passion) Sunday and is called *Holy Week*. During this week, we remember in the most intense way possible the sufferings and death of Christ.

The last days of the week, called the Triduum (meaning "Three Days"), are the most solemn of the entire year. A liturgical "day" always begins at sundown (or Evening Prayer) on the night before. Our liturgical celebration of Sunday really begins at Evening Prayer on Saturday evening. This follows the Jewish custom and is part of our Jewish inheritance. In the same way, the Triduum begins on Thursday evening and ends on Sunday evening.

On Holy Thursday, we celebrate the Mass of the Lord's Supper in the evening, and we commemorate Jesus' gift of himself in the Eucharist. A foot-washing ceremony reminds us that as followers of Jesus, we are to serve one another (see John 13:14–15) On this day, we also recall the institution of the priesthood.

CATHOLICS MAKING A DIFFERENCE

We know much about the early liturgy of the Church through the writings of Egeria, who lived in the fourth century. She was either a nun or laywoman who made a long pilgrimage from her home in Spain or France to the Holy Land. Egeria writes of the liturgical celebrations on Sundays and holy days, like Epiphany and the Feast of the Presentation (February 2). We can recognize our modern traditions in her descriptions. For example, she describes the Palm Sunday procession with the bishop and all the community from the Mount of Olives to Jerusalem like this: "And all the children of the neighborhood, even those who are too young to walk, are carried by their parents on their shoulders, all of them bearing branches, some of palms and some of olives, and thus the bishop is escorted in the same manner as the Lord was of old" ("Egeria's Description of the Liturgical Year in Jerusalem: Translation").

We owe this liturgical pilgrim a debt of gratitude for using her excellent skills of observation and expression to bring our ancient roots alive for us today.

On Good Friday, we remember Jesus' Passion and death. We venerate the cross in some way. We receive Holy Communion, reserved from the Mass of the Lord's Supper, but there is no Mass today. Every Eucharist is a sacrifice because it makes the sacrifice of the cross present. The only sacrifice we offer on Good Friday is the spiritual offering of Jesus' sacrifice on Calvary.

On Holy Saturday, we eagerly prepare for the Easter Vigil, which begins at night. This is the greatest night, the most beautiful night, of the year. "The Church, keeping watch, awaits the Resurrection of Christ and celebrates it in the Sacraments" (Pope Paul VI, *Universal Norms on the Liturgical Year and the General Roman Calendar*, number 21). We celebrate with fire, candles, water, the singing of the Exsultet, readings, and the welcoming of the elect (those preparing to become Catholic) into the Church as they celebrate the Sacraments of Christian Initiation (Baptism, Confirmation, and the Eucharist).

Easter Season

On *Easter Sunday*, we continue our celebration of Christ's Resurrection in all its splendor, with the fullest joy. Easter Sunday begins an entire week of celebration, for each day of Easter week, like Easter Sunday itself, is celebrated as a Solemnity of the Lord. Easter Sunday also marks the beginning of the Easter season, a fifty-day period that ends on Pentecost. The season's liturgical color

is white or gold. During this season, the liturgical readings focus on the Risen Jesus and the growth of the Church in the Acts of the Apostles. In the Northern Hemisphere, the season of Easter coincides with spring. (The word *Easter* is a form of the name of the goddess Eostra, the Greek goddess of spring.) The liturgy and the world itself speak of new life, and the evidence is all around us. Death has been overcome by life, the life of the Risen Christ. His Resurrection is the pledge that our personal lives and the lives of our loved ones will never end. Because of Christ's Resurrection, we live with the hope that one day we will be united with God in Heaven forever.

At Pentecost, the coming of the Holy Spirit seals the work of Jesus Christ in our lives and reminds us of all that Jesus has taught us. We join the Apostles, the disciples, and the Mother of the Lord in the Upper Room, and together we celebrate the gift of the Holy Spirit. With the disciples of Jesus, we are sent into the crowds to proclaim God's salvation in Jesus Christ and to help carry out his mission of love for all humankind. ✳

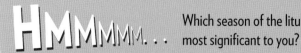

HMMMMM. . .
Which season of the liturgical calendar is most significant to you?

Article 4

Liturgical Rites and Traditions

Art was so excited to be on his spring break trip to Romania. His history and theology teachers had planned the trip together and had a ton of interesting excursions planned. Art knew that not everyone would be jumping at a trip to Romania, but he loved history and architecture and traveling to new places. On their third day there, the group visited a small church in the early morning. Bells clanged as the group entered. Art moved to sit down, but most of the assembly was standing in prayer, and some people were even lighting candles at the front. In the dim light, a deacon carrying a smoking censer walked around the entire space, incensing the icons on the walls. Art looked for the altar, but instead all he could see was a wall of icons. Suddenly, the chandelier above the group burst into light. The middle doors opened, and the deacon emerged. He turned and faced the open doors, through which the priest could be seen, facing the altar. The deacon sang out, "Bless, Master!"

© VladK / Shutterstock.com

Although the Eastern Catholic Church follows its own traditions, liturgical language, and customs, it is still, with the Roman Catholic Church, united under the Bishop of Rome, the Pope.

The priest sang in reply, "Blessed is the Kingdom of the Father, and of the Son, and of the Holy Spirit, now and ever and unto ages of ages." The choir and people sang "Amen" in response.

Art was a little confused. His teachers had told the group that this was a Catholic Church! And it is. It is one of the twenty-three **Eastern Catholic Churches**, which, after the schism of 1054, either chose to remain united with the Catholic Church or later reunited with it. These Churches maintain unity in Apostolic Tradition and Apostolic Succession. To this day, Eastern Catholic Churches follow their own ancient liturgical tradition. All these Churches, with the Latin Church, make up twenty-four Churches united under the Bishop of Rome, the Pope. These Eastern Churches celebrate the liturgy according to one of these various liturgical rites: the Antiochene Rite, the Chaldean Rite, the Byzantine Rite, the Alexandrian (Coptic or Ethiopian) Rite, or the Armenian Rite.

Also found within the Catholic Church are other Latin Rites (besides the Roman Rite), which are celebrated in various places, according to ancient customs. Of course, the Roman Rite is celebrated by most of the Roman (Latin) Church. These other Latin Rites celebrated alongside the Roman Rite are the Ambrosian Rite (in and around Milan, Italy); the Mozarabic Rite (in the Cathedral of the Archdiocese of Toledo, Spain, and six surrounding parishes); the Bragan Rite (in the Archdiocese of Braga, Portugal); and three rites associated with religious orders: the Dominican, the Carmelite, and the Carthusian Rites.

All these diverse rites, in both the East and the West, are legitimate expressions of the liturgy of the Universal Catholic Church. They all make present the saving power of God and the saving mysteries of Christ. Because they make present and express the same mystery of Christ, they show us that the Catholic Church is truly catholic (universal). Therefore, even in diversity, the Church remains one body. This is because we follow the teachings of Christ as we have received them from the Apostles and their successors, the bishops. Our unity, amid the diversity of rites, is assured by Apostolic Succession. ✳

HMMMMM... How comfortable would you be in a church with a different liturgical tradition? Why would you feel this way?

Eastern Catholic Churches ➤ The twenty-three Churches of the East, with their own liturgical and administrative traditions, which reflect the culture of Eastern Europe and the Middle East. Eastern Catholics are in union with the Universal Catholic Church and her head, the Bishop of Rome.

Article 5
Celebrating the Liturgy

The first World Youth Day was instituted on December 20, 1985, at the request of Pope Saint John Paul II (1920–2005). Since then, convocations of youth have been held in Rome and also in several cities and countries around the world—cities like Buenos Aires, Argentina; Denver, Colorado; Manila, Philippines; and Paris, France. Pope Benedict XVI hosted World Youth Day in 2005 in Cologne, Germany. And in 2008, over three hundred thousand young people traveled to Sydney, Australia, for the worldwide meeting. For the meeting in Madrid, Spain, in 2011, the Spanish capital hosted 1.5 million young people!

© Dzurek / Shutterstock.com

These young people are taking part in one of many celebrations and liturgies that happen during World Youth Day each year. World Youth Day was established by Pope Saint John Paul II, and the activities actually take place over several days!

Unquestionably, a liturgy with the Pope and 1.5 million young people would probably be the most exciting and wonderful liturgy imaginable. Yet, in essence, this liturgy is no different than the liturgy available to you every Sunday morning (or Saturday night).

How can this be? How can a liturgy celebrated by the Pope and attended by so many people be the same as one that is celebrated in our parish churches every day? It is the same because Jesus Christ is the same, yesterday, today, and forever. It is Jesus Christ whom we encounter in every liturgy; no matter if there is music or not; if there are crowds of people or just a few; or if it is celebrated in a great cathedral, a stadium, or a small chapel. Jesus Christ died and rose for us, and it is always him we meet in the liturgy.

That being said, the Church, through its documents and directives, encourages all her members to help make the liturgy as beautiful and as meaningful as possible. We cannot be satisfied with the minimum needed for a celebration. We must make every effort to make the liturgy the best it can be.

But what if you are not on the parish liturgical committee or in the choir? How can you contribute to the celebration of the liturgy? Let us speak particularly of the Eucharist for the moment, as that is the sacrament we celebrate most frequently and the one that unites us in a special way with Christ and with others. Consider these ways to contribute:

1. Make every effort to be present and accounted for, mentally and spiritually as well as physically. Prepare in advance by examining your conscience in light of the Word of God. Once Mass begins, pay attention to what is going on.

2. Pray to the Holy Spirit. We have learned that the role of the Holy Spirit is to help us fully participate in the liturgy. Ask him to help you focus and give thanks for Jesus Christ and all the good things in your life.

One way to contribute to the celebration of the liturgy is by praying. Regardless of the distractions you may face, you can always ask the Holy Spirit to help you center yourself in prayer to focus on the Mass.

The best way to pray with the Church's seasons is to participate in Mass. You may also try some of the following seasonal prayers and practices.

Advent: Help your family set up an Advent wreath at home and light one more candle each week.

Christmas: Each day after Christmas, choose a Christmas card your family has received and pray for its sender.

Ordinary Time: Choose a Scripture reading from the next Sunday's liturgy to pray with and to focus on as you prepare for Sunday Mass.

Lent: Give up something for Lent, or choose one way to *give* during Lent. Each week do something positive, individually or with others, to help those in need.

Easter: Go to the Easter Vigil! Each day of the Easter season (until Pentecost), find one way to bring joy to a person in your life.

Pentecost and Ordinary Time: Make plans to share the gifts the Holy Spirit has given you, especially during the summer.

3. Listen to the prayers. In some cases, they have survived thousands of years. Put yourself in the prayers. Find their value.

4. Listen to the readings. Try (with the help of the Holy Spirit) to allow the words to touch your mind and heart.

5. Pray during the General Intercessions. Pray for the Church, the world, and those who suffer. Pray for your family and friends. Pray for yourself, particularly if you are going through a challenging time.

6. Sing. Music opens up our hearts and our spirits. It opens us up to God. As Saint Augustine (354–430) said, "He who sings prays twice." There is no need for embarrassment or pride. We do not sing at the Eucharist to show off our voices, but rather to give glory to God with whatever voice he gave us!

7. Say the responses and think about the meaning of the words you say.

Concentrating on Christ's presence in the Eucharist can strengthen you to live your faith in an active way.

8. Use your body. When you make the Sign of the Cross, make it thoughtfully. When you kneel, hold yourself up straight. When you stand or walk, stand up straight. Our bodies help us to pray when we truly participate in the action asked of us.

9. When you receive Communion, concentrate on the reality of Christ's presence in the Eucharistic species and the gift of grace you are receiving, which gives you strength to lead a moral life. Pray that you may have the grace to give of yourself for others as Jesus did.

10. When you are dismissed from Mass, resolve to go forth to live in a way that is pleasing to God. Strive to do what is good and avoid what is evil. This includes carrying out works of mercy, loving actions that help others with their physical and spiritual needs.

The liturgy is a two-way street: God communicates with us, and we communicate with him. Communication is difficult if one of us (and guess which one that might be) is missing in action!

HMMMMMM. . . Which of the suggested ways to more fully participate in the liturgy is the most challenging for you? Which one would you be most apt to try?

1. What is the original meaning of the word *liturgy*?

2. What does the Church mean by the word *liturgy*?

3. What is the Magisterium of the Church?

4. What is Tradition?

5. What does it mean when we say that the Church's liturgy is Trinitarian?

6. How are we in union with the Trinity?

7. What is the Liturgical Year?

8. How does the Holy Spirit help us to celebrate the liturgy?

9. Explain why every liturgy is a participation in, and anticipation of, the heavenly liturgy.

10. What are Eastern Catholic Churches?

11. What are two of the ways listed in this chapter to contribute to the liturgy?

UNIT 1

ART STUDY

Fresco of Last Supper of Christ, by Leopold Kupelweiser

1. What strikes you most about this artwork? Why?

2. In what way does the painting depict Christ as both human and divine?

3. What elements of the liturgy today do you see in the painting?

UNIT 1

CHAPTER 2
Sacraments

HOW CAN THE LITURGY HELP ME TO GROW SPIRITUALLY?

SNAPSHOT

Article 6
Symbols and Rituals

If you are like most Catholics, the sacraments have been part of your life for as long as you can remember. You probably don't remember your Baptism, but you will likely never forget the excitement of your First Communion! If you've celebrated Confirmation, you have affirmed the faith you were given as a gift in Baptism and received the fullness of the Gifts of the Holy Spirit.

But you may have questions about these and the other sacraments. Where did they come from? How do they work? Why do we have them? These are excellent questions, because they keep us from taking the great gift of the sacraments, "God's masterpieces" (*Catechism of the Catholic Church [CCC]*, number 1091), for granted.

In understanding the sacraments, it helps to look first at the importance of symbols and rituals. We use symbols and rituals every day, almost without realizing it. One good example of a set of symbols we use every day is language. When people have a shared language, they have a shared understanding of what words mean. If we share the meanings of words, we can communicate our thoughts and ideas. Through language, we can turn what is within us (our thoughts and feelings) into something outside us that can affect or influence others. It is hard to imagine how different our lives would be without language.

Yet, however wonderful language is, sometimes words are not enough. Where our deepest thoughts and feelings are concerned, we all sometimes need to be *shown* the meaning of words. And this is not a bad attitude to have. Saint John, the beloved disciple of Christ, wrote to his community in the first century, "Children, let us love not in word or speech but in deed and truth" (1 John 3:18). Love is a verb. Love is not only thinking and feeling but also *doing*.

A sign conveys a message: Go. Stop. Caution. A symbol conveys a web of meaning, often without words. Think of some symbols we often see and use that convey deep meaning.

TAKE IT TO GOD

Use the symbols in this hymn to help you envision your relationship with God.

> Peace is flowing like a river,
> flowing out from you and me,
> flowing out into the desert,
> setting all the captives free.

> Love is flowing like a river,
> flowing out from you and me,
> flowing out into the desert,
> setting all the captives free.

> Hope is flowing like a river,
> flowing out from you and me,
> flowing out into the desert,
> setting all the captives free.
> Amen.

Making Symbols, Doing Rituals

Because we have a need to act out our deepest thoughts and feelings, we are naturally symbol-makers and ritual-doers. On Valentine's Day, saying "I love you" is not enough for us. We want to share something tangible like a card and flowers or a box of candy. When we meet someone, we use both words and gestures (a handshake or another kind of ritual) to show our friendliness. When we have finished a course of studies, we could just receive a certificate in the mail that says our studies are complete, but instead we have a graduation ceremony, complete with songs, speeches, invited guests, and a personal handing over of a beautifully printed diploma (probably with a handshake as well). Words are not always enough. We are human. We need action. We need symbols and rituals to act out what we really mean.

© Brent Hofacker / Shutterstock.com

What are some tangible ways you convey your feelings, such as caring, love, forgiveness, or sorrow?

Symbols and Rituals Defined

Symbols and rituals are related, but they are not exactly the same thing. The word **symbol** comes from a Greek word meaning "to throw together." A symbol "throws together" the literal meaning of an object or action with other meanings that it evokes. For example, in the Sacrament of Baptism, water is water. It is a combination of hydrogen and oxygen. But it also evokes other meanings, like washing, cleansing, and purifying. Thus, water becomes a symbol of something more than itself. The symbol of water invites us to look beyond the liquid to its deeper meanings.

A **ritual** is an established pattern of actions, usually including words. The words and actions have symbolic meaning, so "symbolic action" is another way to refer to a ritual. Rituals can be simple, such as a handshake, a wave, or the Sign of the Cross. They can also be more complex, such as the opening ceremonies of the Olympic Games or the inauguration of a president. Because the liturgy and the sacraments involve symbols with words and actions, we call them rituals.

Sacraments, Symbols, and Rituals

Why are we symbol-makers and ritual-doers? Because God made us this way. When God communicates with us, he does not use words alone. And when we respond to him, we do not use words alone. The fact that God communicates with us and we respond through everyday life in the world makes life itself sacramental. The Church holds a sacramental view of all reality. Yet one of God's best ways of communicating with us is through liturgical celebrations, especially in the Seven Sacraments. And our participation in these sacraments is one of the best ways we can respond to him. ✳

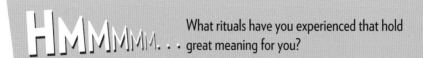

HMMMMMM. . . . What rituals have you experienced that hold great meaning for you?

---

symbol ➤ An object or action that points to another reality and leads us to look beyond our senses to consider a deeper mystery.

ritual ➤ The established form of the words and actions for a ceremony that is repeated often. The actions often have a symbolic meaning.

UNIT 1

Article 7

Sacraments: Sign and Mystery

The sacraments are signs of God's love. They are signs of his presence in our lives. They are rituals, instituted by Christ and handed down to us through Scripture and Tradition, by which God gives us his very life of grace. In order to appreciate their richness and to define the meaning of *sacrament*, we need to define a few related terms.

What is the difference between this arrow as a sign and a sacrament as a sign?

The first term is *sign*. In everyday language, *sign* has a definite and limited meaning. A red, eight-sided sign with the letters S-T-O-P written on it means "stop." This command is its entire meaning. A sign pointing down a road to a nearby town says "To Riverdale." The sign gives you directions to Riverdale.

However, when we say that "a sacrament is a sign of God's love," we mean that this sign, this sacrament, is much more than a pointer or a command. The word *sign* in this instance means "symbol," a sign that points beyond itself, a sign that invites us to consider the deeper meaning present within it.

Signs in the Gospel of John

In the Gospel of John, the miracles of Jesus are called signs not because they are commands or directions, but because they point to a deeper reality: that God is here among us. The Gospel account of the miracle at Cana, when Jesus turns water into wine, ends with, "Jesus did this as the beginning of his signs in Cana in Galilee and so revealed his glory, and his disciples began to believe in him" (John 2:11). In fact, the Gospel of John contains seven signs. The changing of water into wine at Cana is just the first of the signs. These miracles, or "signs" as they are referred to in John's Gospel, include:

The Seven Signs in the Gospel of John	
John 2:1-11	The changing of water into wine at Cana
John 4:46-54	The healing of the royal official's son in Capernum
John 5:1-15	The healing of the paralytic at Bethesda
John 6:5-14	The feeding of the five thousand
John 6:16-24	Jesus' walking on water
John 9:1-7	Healing the man blind from birth
John 11:1-45	The raising of Lazarus

These seven signs are presented to show Jesus' divinity. Together as a group, they prefigure the greatest demonstration of Jesus as the Son of God in his death and Resurrection. The signs in John's Gospel help us to understand the deeper meaning that each sacrament can hold for us. Though the sacraments are different from Jesus' miracles, they are signs because they call us to faith in a deeper reality: God is here among us. They are signs through which Christ acts sacramentally to bring about what they signify: They communicate to us the grace of Christ and bring us into deeper relationship with him.

Sacrament and Mystery

The words *sign* and *symbol* have shaped our understanding of the sacraments for centuries. In the fifth century, when the New Testament was translated from its original Greek into the then-common language of Latin, the Greek word for *sign* was translated into *sacramentum*. It is from this word that we get our English word *sacrament*. In the Eastern Catholic Churches, the sacraments are called mysteries. This focuses on the sacraments as the way we enter into the greatest mystery: the mystery of Christ. Through the sacraments, or mysteries, we encounter Christ's life-giving presence in our lives.

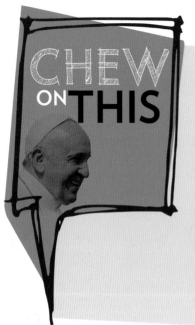

CHEW ON THIS

Every encounter with Christ, who in the Sacraments gives us salvation, invites us to "go" and communicate to others the salvation that we have been able to see, to touch, to encounter and to receive, and which is truly credible because it is love. In this way, the Sacraments spur us to be missionaries, and the Apostolic commitment to carry the Gospel into every setting. . . . (Pope Francis, "General Audience," November 6, 2013)

The core of every sacrament is the **Paschal Mystery** of Christ—his Passion, death, Resurrection, and Ascension into Heaven—and his promise to be with us always. (You may recall that *Paschal* refers to Passover, when the angel *passed over* the houses of the Israelites and spared their firstborn sons, and, centuries later, when Jesus, the Son of God, *passed over* from death to life, and spared us from eternal death.) The Paschal Mystery is most evident in the Eucharist, when we offer bread and wine and receive it back, by the words and actions of the priest and by the power of the Holy Spirit, as Christ's own Body and Blood, given up for us.

Yet in every sacrament, empowered by the grace of the Holy Spirit, we die with Christ to our "former selves" (the stubborn, sniping, or indifferent selves) and come to a new, risen life with him by embracing in faith the life of grace and love he offers us. In every sacrament, in every one of these signs of God's love, we enter into the mystery of Christ's death and Resurrection and then allow him to enter into our lives. How does this work for us in our everyday lives? Do we die a small death in every sacrament? What does the "new life" we receive feel like?

Paschal Mystery ➤ The work of salvation accomplished by Jesus Christ mainly through his Passion, death, Resurrection, and Ascension.

Try to recall your First Reconciliation. As you prepared for the celebration of this sacrament, you were likely encouraged to examine some questions, such as: What kind of person am I? What kind of person do I want to be? What changes do I need to make to be the person Jesus created me to be? When we truly examine our conscience, we often identify what we need to let go of. We identify which parts of our former selves we need to release or change to embrace God's grace and love in our lives. By letting go of these behaviors or aspects of ourselves, we are "dying with Christ." We can then rise to "new life" with him by replacing those "dead" behaviors with words and actions that bring joy, healing, and love into our lives and the lives of others.

At the words of the consecration, bread and wine become the Body and Blood of Christ. This is the "mystery of faith" that we proclaim at every Eucharist.

How Do the Sacraments Work?

We have already seen that the sacraments work because God—Father, Son, and Holy Spirit—is at work in them. Through the centuries, questions arose as to the validity of the sacraments under various circumstances. Is it "better" to receive a sacrament from a priest known to be holy? Are people really baptized or married if the priest is not as holy as he could be? What if the recipients are not known for their overall goodness—do the sacraments still work for them? These kinds of questions were pondered by scholars and theologians until finally the Council of Trent, in 1547, declared that the sacraments act *ex opere operato*—literally, "by the work worked," or, as the *Catechism of the Catholic Church* translates, "by the very fact of the action's being performed" (number 1128). In this, the Council of Trent agreed with the statement of Saint Thomas Aquinas: "The sacrament is not wrought by the righteousness of either the celebrant or the recipient, but by the power of God" (*Summa Theologica, part* III, question 68, article 8).

None of us is in a position to judge another person's holiness or "righteousness" or closeness to God. The power of Christ and the Holy Spirit acts in the sacraments independently of the personal holiness of the person administering the sacrament. Grace can neither be seen nor quantified; each of the sacraments works whether we feel it or not. However, the fruits (or effects) of the sacrament do depend on the disposition of the one who receives it.

The Sacraments Are . . .

Understanding the meaning of *sign*, *symbol*, *sacrament*, and *mystery*, we can now approach the exact definition of a **sacrament**:

> The sacraments are efficacious signs of grace, instituted by Christ and entrusted to the Church, by which divine life is dispensed to us. The visible rites by which the sacraments are celebrated signify and make present the graces proper to each sacrament. They bear fruit in those who receive them with the required dispositions. (*CCC,* number 1131)

Let's break apart this definition. First, the sacraments are "*efficacious*" signs. This means they are *effective* and they actually *work* because Christ is at work in them. They are not empty words and gestures, but words and gestures that carry with them the power of God.

The sacraments are signs of *grace*. Grace is divine favor, the free and undeserved help that God gives us so that we might become his adopted children and share his divine life. We sometimes talk about grace as a gift from God. Each of the Seven Sacraments has a particular grace, or spiritual gift, that is given to the person receiving the sacrament. Sacramental grace is the grace of the Holy Spirit by which we are healed and transformed, and through which we become united in Christ.

The sacraments were "*instituted by Christ and entrusted to the Church.*" The sacraments originate in Christ. In the Gospels, we see Christ at work—healing, forgiving, serving, and giving of himself. In his earthly life, he provided the words and gestures for several of the sacraments, such as the Sacrament of Baptism and the Sacrament of the Eucharist. Guided by the Holy Spirit, the Church over several centuries discerned how Christ's work continues in the Church through the Seven Sacraments. Through these sacraments, Christ works in his people today.

---

sacrament ➤ An efficacious and visible sign of God's grace, instituted by Christ and entrusted to the Church, by which divine life is dispensed to us. The Seven Sacraments are Baptism, the Eucharist, Confirmation, Penance and Reconciliation, Anointing of the Sick, Matrimony, and Holy Orders.

HOLY ORDERS

BAPTISM

CONFIRMATION

ANOINTING OF THE SICK

MATRIMONY

PENANCE AND RECONCILIATION

EUCHARIST

The Seven Sacraments are tangible signs of God's grace. They are not empty words and gestures but words and gestures that carry with them the power of God.

The visible rites (the symbols and rituals) by which the sacraments are celebrated "*signify (symbolize) and make present*" the graces that belong to each sacrament. The sacraments bear fruit in those who receive them with the "*required dispositions.*" A sacrament gains us entry into the mystery of Christ, the life of grace and love. But we need to have the required disposition. This means that our attitude and readiness matters. We must be prepared for and actively participate in the sacraments for the grace given by God in them to have an effect on our lives. For example, to receive the Sacrament of Penance and Reconciliation, we must be truly sorry for our sins, committed to not repeating them, and willing to make reparation for the harm we have caused. To receive the Sacrament of the Eucharist, we must be in a state of grace, free from mortal sin. If someone has committed a mortal sin, they must not receive the Eucharist until they have been absolved from their sin in the Sacrament of Penance and Reconciliation.

The Catholic Church has Seven Sacraments. The *Sacraments of Christian Initiation* are Baptism, Confirmation, and the Eucharist. The *Sacraments of Healing* are Penance and Reconciliation and Anointing of the Sick. The *Sacraments at the Service of Communion* are Holy Orders and Matrimony. ✳

HMMMMMM. . . What sign, symbol, or ritual has helped you to understand something on a much deeper level?

Article 8

Sacraments: Signs of Christ

Andra looked down at the sleeping face of her new baby brother. She had been more than a little surprised when her parents told her they were having another baby. She already had a younger sister, Zola, who was five! Andra knew having a new baby in the house would change everything. She would have more responsibilities. Money would be tight. Her parents would be tired. It would be harder to go to school activities, the movies, or even to eat out as a family. But during her mother's pregnancy this time, Andra noticed things she was too young to notice when her mom was pregnant with Zola. Her dad was really attentive—not just to her mom, but to Andra and Zola too. He wanted to be sure they each got some special time with him.

Money was tight because they had to get new things for the baby, but Andra could see that they were working together as a team. Her parents wanted her and Zola to be part of picking out the crib and the colors for the baby's room. They started meal planning together to save money when grocery shopping. And most important, Andra's parents seemed really, truly happy.

Just as a new addition to a family can be considered a gift, Jesus is also a gift. Jesus is the primary sign of God's love for us.

They weren't just going through the motions of a day-to-day routine. They were more loving toward each other, and even to Andra and Zola. Finally, the day came and little Diamonte arrived. Once Andra's parents and the baby got home, her mom asked if Andra wanted to hold him. And Andra realized she had never wanted anything more in her whole life! Andra appreciated what a gift she and her whole family were given with the birth of Diamonte.

Have you ever thought of Jesus as a gift? Have you ever thought of Jesus Christ as the living, ever-present sacrament of God? Jesus Christ, the Son of God, is the great sign of God's love for us and of how we are to love God. God sent his Son as the culmination of a long history of salvific events that have revealed his presence and actions. Perhaps it is time to think of Jesus as a gift, not only for what he sacrificed for us but also for how he continues to save us today, especially through the Seven Sacraments of the Church.

Jesus is the Father's final answer to our sin and suffering. When the Word became flesh and God became man, the world changed. Even those who kept the Old Law to the best of their ability would find new life in Jesus. As the Apostle John wrote: "While the law was given through Moses, grace and truth came through Jesus Christ. No one has ever seen God. The only Son, God, who is at the Father's side, has revealed him" (John 1:17–18). In other words, Christ—the Second Person of the Holy Trinity Incarnate—is the living, ever-present sacrament of God. Through him, we encounter the fullness of God's saving love.

The Sacramental Economy

Christ commissioned the Church to carry on his work, to carry on his very presence in the world, through the sacraments. All the sacraments signify and make present the work of Christ in our lives, through grace. This is called the **sacramental economy**.

We are all familiar with the monetary system, the economy that runs on money. Through work (physical or intellectual), we make goods and services. We sell our goods and services to others. We get money, and then we spend our money on other goods and services that other people offer. This is how our economy works. We do not trade or barter. We receive and spend money as a substitute for trading and bartering.

In the sacraments, we encounter the Risen Christ. Jesus enters our hearts and our lives to heal us and guide us. A sacrament is a meeting with Jesus Christ himself.

---

sacramental economy ➤ The communication or dispensation of the fruits of Christ's Paschal Mystery in the celebration of the Church's sacramental liturgy.

In this way, we can provide ourselves and others with everything we need to live. Under ordinary circumstances, in order to eat, to clothe ourselves, to have shelter, to live, we must be in the flow of money. Without money, we are stuck. (It is said that money is a good servant but a terrible master.)

The sacramental economy runs on grace. Try to remember that grace is not a thing; rather, grace is a relationship with God and a participation in his life. So it is not *exactly* like money. That being said, other comparisons work. To live to the fullest, to share God's life, to participate in the mystery of Christ, we must be in the flow of grace. Without grace, without God's life, we are stuck.

Through the Sacrament of Baptism, we were adopted as God's sons and daughters, and we have been living "in grace" (as long as we have steered clear of mortal sin) since that moment. Grace has made us God's children and, in Christ, has brought us into the life of the Trinity.

What Is Grace?

Sanctifying grace is the free gift of God's life, first given to us at Baptism and renewed in us in all the sacraments. Sanctifying grace orients us toward God. We might say it "tilts us" in his direction. It helps us to live according to his call. Through the Holy Spirit, sanctifying grace heals our souls of sin and makes us holy.

Sanctifying grace gives us a stable and supernatural disposition that enables us to live with God. This type of grace is distinct from **actual graces**, which are God's interventions in our lives. His initiative in the work of grace both prepares us to respond and demands that we respond, but it does not limit our freedom. Instead grace "responds to the deepest yearnings of human freedom, calls freedom to cooperate with it, and perfects freedom" (*CCC*, number 2022).

---

sanctifying grace ➤ The grace that heals our human nature wounded by sin and restores us to friendship with God by giving us a share in the divine life of the Trinity. It is a supernatural gift of God, infused into our souls by the Holy Spirit, that continues the work of making us holy.

actual graces ➤ God's interventions and support for us in the everyday moments of our lives. Actual graces are important for conversion and for continuing growth in holiness.

I DIDN'T KNOW THAT!

The popular hymn "Amazing Grace" was written by an Englishman, a former sea captain and slave trader named John Newton (1725–1807). Newton wrote the song from personal experience. He was not a religious man. Eventually, he became a sailor and then a slave trader. He was notorious for his profanity, his insubordination, his mockery of believers, and his denunciations of God. One night, a terrible storm battered his vessel. Exhausted, Newton called out, "Lord, have mercy upon us!" This was the beginning of his conversion. He began to think about his life and his relationship with God. A few years later, he quit the sea and began to study theology.

Newton would go on to write the verses to "Amazing Grace" for a prayer meeting on New Year's Day in 1773. During the twentieth century, the song's popularity surged.

Here are the words of the first verse of the hymn:

> Amazing grace! How sweet the sound,
> That saved a wretch like me!
> I once was lost but now am found,
> Was blind, but now I see.

Freedom

When we freely respond to and cooperate with God, we open ourselves to even more grace and more freedom. We sometimes imagine that sin will make us free or happy. "If I could only do *that*," we think, "I'd really feel good. I'd really be free and happy!" But this could not be further from the truth. True happiness and true freedom come from responding to grace.

For example, imagine you have a friend who struggles with math, but math comes fairly easily to you. You suggest that you could help. After only one tutoring session, your friend is beginning to get it and is so grateful for your help! You feel good. You feel happy. Whose idea was this to help your friend? God's. Who gave you "the gift of math" so that you *could* help your friend? God. Who helped you to say yes to the idea of helping? God. You responded to grace, and if you continue to respond to grace, you will freely choose to help your friends, and others, in the future.

UNIT 1

Doorways to Life

Without this flow of God's life, grace, we are stuck. But we have hope because Christ founded the Church to be the ordinary channel of his grace, his life, for his followers. Christ wants to be accessible and available through the Church and the sacraments, especially the Eucharist, in which he is really and substantially present. This was his plan of salvation for us. We need not be stuck in our sin. Through the sacraments, we were given a door, a way in, to the life of grace, the life of relationship with God. This life is what we are made for. It is only through God that we are able to live a fully human life and find true happiness.

The Church communicates the grace she signifies, and so we can say that the Church is a sacrament. She is the sign and instrument of communion between God and human beings, and the means of bringing about that communion. Thus, the Church in this world is the sacrament of salvation. All salvation comes from Christ through the Church.

The coming of Christ to be present among us continues through the ministry of the Church. Being a sacrament of the communion of human beings and God also means that the Church is the sign of unity among all people. As Jesus said, "This is how all will know that you are my disciples, if you have love for one another" (John 13:35). Jesus intended the Church, which includes all who are members of the Body of Christ, to be that sign of love. He intended the sacraments to be those doorways to divine life, open to all people of all times and in all places. ✳

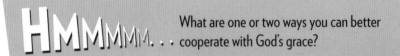

HMMMMMM. . . What are one or two ways you can better cooperate with God's grace?

Article 9

Sacraments: Signs of Redemption

We do not often use the word *redeem* in ordinary life, but it has its moments. We *redeem* coupons at a store. We might say something like, "This old table was *redeemed* from the scrap heap," or "This afternoon I am going to the dry cleaner to *redeem* my shirts." What can we learn from these uses of the word *redeem*?

Generally, we can say that *to redeem* something implies taking something from one state of being to another. A coupon is just another piece of paper until we *redeem* it and get some value in return. An old table is doomed until someone with a good eye *redeems* it and makes it useful and valuable again. Shirts will stay at the dry cleaner forever unless their owner comes and *redeems* them—gets them back to his closet where they belong.

© Tootles / iStockphoto.com

Have you ever purchased a raffle ticket? If you have the winning ticket drawn in a raffle, you have to redeem your ticket for the prize. Redemption can have deeper meanings as well, such as buying back, deliverance, or rescue.

CATHOLICS MAKING A DIFFERENCE

Not all saints were originally saint material! Saint Augustine was born to his mother, Monica, a devout Christian, and his father, Patricius, a pagan, Roman official. Augustine lived his life as a testament to pagan beliefs and practices of excess. He admitted to stealing food, not because he was hungry, but because it was forbidden. He confessed to enjoying the sinful behavior. Much to his mother's distress, he continued to live a lifestyle of hedonism and sexual impropriety. He was incredibly bright, and his thirst for knowledge led him to commit himself to a variety of philosophical and heretical groups. His mother prayed every day for his conversion of heart and lifestyle. During this time, he took a lover and had an illegitimate son. Under pressure to marry, he abandoned them and fled to Milan. Monica never stopped praying for Augustine's redemption. Her prayers were answered when he came under the tutelage of Ambrose. He eventually converted to Christianity at the age of thirty-one, and went on to become a priest, a bishop, and an author! You can read his own account of struggle and redemption in his autobiography, *Confessions*.

To Buy Back

The word *redeem* comes from a Latin word meaning "to buy back" or "to purchase." Meanings for the word *redemption* include "deliverance" or "rescue." At the time of Jesus, this is what many of the People of God were looking for. They were a conquered people, being ruled by the Romans. Faithful Jews were awaiting the Messiah who would deliver them from their oppression. It was at this time that God chose to send his Son into the world as its rescuer, its deliverer, and its redeemer, not just for the Jews but for all people.

As Jesus himself said, he did not come to destroy the Old Law but to fulfill it. When people were tithing their harvests of herbs and spices to give one tenth to the Temple, as the Law directed, he did not object. He commended them. But he also warned them not to neglect the bigger things, like mercy and fidelity. Jesus accused the leaders of being blind guides who were straining out gnats but swallowing camels (see Matthew 23:23–24)! In the New Law, Jesus gives us the grace of the Holy Spirit to reform our hearts to love as he does and to carry out God's commandments.

The People of God at the time of Jesus definitely needed **redemption**. They needed to be brought back to the truth about God and about themselves and into a graced relationship with God, freed from the burden of sin. So that was the mission of Jesus: to conquer sin and death, to redeem his people, and to bring them back to God, in freedom and in truth.

What About Us?

Are love and faithfulness gaining ground in our time, in our lives? Are we concentrating on the bigger things in our lives and in our world? Or are we straining out gnats while swallowing camels? You may have heard the saying "Don't sweat the small stuff." Keep the bigger picture—what life is really about—in mind. How are you doing on that?

Fortunately for us, the teachings of Jesus and his work of redemption did not die in the tomb. His work of redemption reaches people of all times and all places.

The Paschal Mystery (the Passion, death, Resurrection, and Ascension of Jesus Christ) is a real, historical event; its saving power transcends history, making Christ's saving work available to all people throughout all time. When Christ rose from the dead, he destroyed death. He conquered sin. His saving power is available to us in our time, especially in the liturgy and the sacraments. And that is not all. When we participate in the liturgy, we are given a participation in his divine, eternal life. Christ invites us to experience a small foretaste of Heaven, made present in the liturgy. ✳

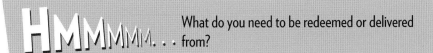

HMMMMM. . . What do you need to be redeemed or delivered from?

---

redemption ➤ From the Latin *redemptio*, meaning "a buying back," referring, in the Old Testament, to Yahweh's deliverance of Israel and, in the New Testament, to Christ's deliverance of all Christians from the forces of sin. As the agent of redemption, Jesus is called the Redeemer.

Article 10

The Praying Church

Iris unfolded her towel and sat cross-legged facing the ocean. She could feel the warmth when she closed her eyes and tipped her face upward. Iris loved coming to the beach, but most of the time, she didn't come to swim. She came to wiggle her feet in the sand and listen to the ocean. She watched the waves roll in and slide up the sand, sometimes all the way up to her feet. In a few hours, the beach would be full of people—little kids chasing seagulls and digging in the wet sand, teenagers strolling and carrying their sandals, grandparents under umbrellas doling out juice boxes and snacks. Yet, none of that was a distraction to Iris. At the beach, no chores had to be done, no bickering, no homework. At the beach, the waves approached and then drew back in a rhythm all their own.

If you have ever watched waves crash upon a beach and then recede, in a beautiful and mysterious rhythm, you have some idea of the reciprocal relationship of prayer. "Prayer unfolds throughout the whole history of salvation as a reciprocal call between God and man" (*CCC*, number 2591). God is always calling each of us to this mysterious encounter with him. His call surges into our lives, sometimes like a wave's mighty crash or a quiet ripple, and then recedes, giving us time and space to respond. When we do, prayer unfolds, in our lives and in the Church.

© Lynne Carpenter / Shutterstock.com

Do you have a favorite place to pray? It doesn't need to be a physical place. It can be somewhere in your imagination. Take time to go there often.

Prayer in Scripture

If prayer is an encounter with God, where do we learn how to pray? We need only look directly to God's Revelation in Scripture. The word *pray*, in its various forms, is used almost four hundred times! In even more instances, prayer is inferred but not mentioned specifically. One example of this is James 1:5, which reads, "But if any of you lacks wisdom, he should ask God who gives to all generously and ungrudgingly, and he will be given it." If prayer is our direct line of communication with God, the Gospel of Matthew gives us some tips on how to pray and how *not* to pray!

How to Pray	
Matthew 6:9-13	"This is how you are to pray: Our Father in heaven, hallowed be your name. Your kingdom come, your will be done, on earth as in heaven. Give us today our daily bread; and forgive us our debts, as we forgive our debtors; and do not subject us to the final test, but deliver us from the evil one."
How *Not* to Pray	
Matthew 6:5-8	"When you pray, do not be like the hypocrites, who love to stand and pray in the synagogues and on street corners so that others may see them. Amen, I say to you, they have received their reward. But when you pray, go to your inner room, close the door, and pray to your Father in secret. And your Father who sees in secret will repay you. In praying, do not babble like the pagans, who think that they will be heard because of their many words. Do not be like them. Your Father knows what you need before you ask him."

Many verses can encourage our daily communication with God and give us direction for prayers of healing, strength, protection, petition, devotion, and more.

The earliest monks and nuns lived in the desert. They were following an inner call to seek God and to live the Gospel more closely. In your life, you too may need a "desert time" when you can seek God in prayer and reflection. Here are a few ideas:

1. Take a short time each day to read God's Word and to meditate on it. Look over the readings for the coming Sunday. Let the Word of God speak to you through them.

2. Use a short form of Morning or Evening Prayer from the Liturgy of the Hours, and pray with the Church.

3. Choose a Scripture verse to meditate on for the day or the week.

4. Pray the Rosary.

5. Draw a peaceful scene. Mentally place yourself and Jesus within it. What is Jesus saying to you?

6. Start and keep a "prayer and life journal." Make up your own prayers.

The Liturgy of the Hours

As we have learned, the liturgy, the public prayer of the Church, is our greatest prayer. In the liturgy, we lift up our hearts to the Lord as we pray in the name of Jesus, in the power of the Holy Spirit. The Liturgy of the Hours, prayer designated for certain hours of the day, is part of the public prayer of the Church. The **Liturgy of the Hours** originated with the Jewish practice of meeting several times a day for prayer. The first Jewish Christians continued this practice as they met daily in the Temple (see Acts of the Apostles 2:46). This practice evolved into the basic structure of the Liturgy of the Hours we know today: an opening hymn, psalms, a reading from Scripture, the Lord's Prayer, and the prayer of the day from the liturgy.

Liturgy of the Hours ➤ Also known as the Divine Office, the official, public, daily prayer of the Catholic Church. The Divine Office provides standard prayers, Scripture readings, and reflections at regular hours throughout the day.

The Liturgy of the Hours is the prayer of the whole People of God. It is prayed (or chanted in the ancient melodies of Gregorian chant) most completely by the contemplative orders of the Church. The **ordained** members of the Church are also obliged to pray the Liturgy of the Hours each day. Laypeople are also encouraged to pray regularly and to include at least the major hours (Morning and Evening Prayer) in their daily prayer. This is, of course, in addition to the celebration of the Sunday Eucharist and the feasts of the Liturgical Year. If there is a monastery or convent of monks or nuns near you, it would be worthwhile to visit them and pray with them. In the Liturgy of the Hours, the entire Church prays in the Holy Spirit and opens its heart to God.

Communal and Private Prayer

When we pray outside of liturgy, either alone or with others, our **prayer** is a small, quiet stream flowing into the great river of living waters, the liturgical prayer of the Church. When we raise our minds and hearts to God (see *CCC*, number 2559), we do so as individuals, yet as members of Christ's Body. United with Christ in Baptism, we are heard as beloved children of God in Christ. United with others in prayer, we have been assured by Jesus himself that "where two or three are gathered together in my name, there am I in the midst of them" (Matthew 18:20). And when we pray alone, we are not really alone, because we are in communion with Christ and with the Church (see Ephesians 3:18–21).

Some ways we pray with others spring from particular cultures or local traditions. These expressions of faith are called popular piety. *Piety* means religious reverence or devotion. These expressions are called popular because they are "of the people." They include customs like novenas (nine days of prayer) requesting the intercession of a saint; processions in honor of Our Lord, Our Lady, or particular saints; and the crowning of a statue of Our Lady during the month of May. Although these popular expressions of faith are not part of the official liturgy, the Church encourages them as long as they express the spirit of the Gospels and offer sound guidance in living a Christian life.

---

ordained (ministries) ➤ Refers to ministries that require ordination, such as presiding at the Eucharist, hearing confessions, administering Confirmation, and so on. Ordained ministers may also perform other ministries that can be performed by laypeople, such as distributing Communion, reading the Scriptures at the liturgy, and teaching theology.

prayer ➤ Lifting up of one's mind and heart to God or the requesting of good things from him. The six basic forms of prayer are blessing, adoration, praise, petition, thanksgiving, and intercession. In prayer, we communicate with God in a relationship of love.

Personal prayer is a living relationship with God and is essential for a believer and a follower of Christ. No relationship can survive without communication, and that is what prayer is. It may not even need words. Sometimes deep thoughts and feelings are communicated in a glance, a gesture. It is the same with you and God. He knows you, loves you, and can read you like a book. Saint Thérèse of Lisieux (1873–1897), a young woman living an obscure life in a Carmelite monastery, described it this way: "For me, prayer is a surge of the heart; it is a simple look turned toward heaven, it is a cry of recognition and love, embracing both trial and joy."

Thérèse was a young nun in a Carmelite monastery in France. After her death, her writings were circulated. Saint Thérèse, who is now recognized as a Doctor of the Church, taught "Do little things out of great love."

Prayer of the Heart

Since ancient times, Christians have practiced "the prayer of the heart." In the Semitic view, the heart is the center of the body. From the heart springs both good and evil thinking, as well as what we call feelings or emotions. Thus, according to the fathers and mothers of the desert (the first monks and nuns), if you can direct and control your thoughts, you can direct and control your heart, your desires, and your prayer.

In simplest terms, "the prayer of the heart" is repeating a phrase—a Scripture verse or a short prayer—over and over again, calmly and sincerely, until it becomes part of you. Some choose a different Scripture verse each day. Others may choose the Jesus Prayer: "Lord Jesus Christ, Son of the living God, have mercy on me, a sinner." Still others choose just one word: *God*, *love*, or *peace*. This prayer becomes our foundation, something we fall back on amid the demands of our lives. For example, you can be listening in class or waiting in a checkout line or stopped at a stoplight, and your prayer word or phrase will come to mind. In this one simple word or phrase, God is reaching out to you and you are reaching out to him.

So try it. In your Scripture verse or prayer word, you will find that God is with you, every minute, every hour, every day of the week.

Forms of Prayer

Through the inspiration of the Holy Spirit, various forms of prayer have arisen in the Church: blessing or adoration, petition, intercession, thanksgiving, and praise. The Holy Spirit continues to teach the Church, recalling all that Jesus has taught and helping her to pray, inspiring new expressions of these ancient forms.

In prayers of *blessing (or adoration)*, we bless God because he has first blessed us: "Blessed be the God and Father of our Lord Jesus Christ, who has blessed us in Christ with every spiritual blessing in the heavens" (Ephesians 1:3). We *adore* God for his greatness, his power, and his holiness. We marvel at his creation, and wonder that he has made us as part of it. In prayers of *petition*, we pray for our needs, most especially our need for forgiveness. We also pray for the coming of the Kingdom, and for what we need to cooperate with the mission of Christ on Earth. Through prayers of *intercession*, we pray for the needs of others. We ask on behalf of another, just as Jesus continually intercedes with the Father for us.

In prayers of *thanksgiving*, we acknowledge God as the Creator and thank him for his goodness. The Eucharist is our primary prayer of thanksgiving; from it flows thanksgiving for all God's gifts, in every circumstance. Prayers of *praise* erupt in joy and express our love for God, recognizing above all that he is God. Praise "embraces the other forms of prayer" (*CCC*, number 2639), for in it we acknowledge not only what God does but also who he is—the source and goal of our lives, the One in whom "'we live and move and have our being'" (Acts of the Apostles 17:28).

You might evaluate your relationship with God by thinking about these forms of prayer. Are you always petitioning for your needs and hardly ever praising or thanking? Do you bless God and praise him? Consider whether your relationship with God may benefit from a greater variety of prayer.

© wavebreak media / Shutterstock.com

A rosary is an example of a sacramental. Sacramentals hold no power in themselves. But we can use them to assist us in deepening our faith, prayer life, and relationship with God.

Three Expressions of Prayer

In the Christian tradition, three major expressions of the life of prayer have come down to us. In the following chart, each expression of prayer is presented with corresponding characteristics.

Expressions of Prayer	
Vocal Prayer	• uses words to speak to God • words can be spoken aloud or silently • can be prayed alone or in a group • includes memorized prayer and spontaneous prayer
Meditation	• uses thoughts, imagination, and emotions to get in touch with God • uses Scripture, rosary, pictures or creation as a way to focus our minds and hearts
Contemplation	• described as "resting in God" • wordless prayer • listening for God's movement in our lives • enter into union with God through peaceful silence

Sacramentals

Sacramentals are sacred signs instituted by the Church that prepare us to receive God's grace and to cooperate with it. They include blessings; actions, such as blessing ourselves with holy water while making the Sign of the Cross; and objects, such as blessed ashes or holy cards. Sacramentals occupy an important place in the life of the Church. They prepare us for the sacraments and contribute to our holiness, our closeness to God, in varying circumstances of our lives.

Among all sacramentals, blessings come first. The Church blesses persons, meals, objects, and places. Every blessing includes praise of God for his works and gifts. Blessings also lift up the Church's intercessory prayer for us, that we may be able to use God's gifts in the spirit of the Gospel.

Because every baptized person is called to both be a "blessing" and to bless, the Church derives its power to bless from Baptism. In certain circumstances, laypeople can bless: Parents can bless their children, for example. When a blessing concerns Church and sacramental life, it is usually reserved for the ordained—bishops, priests, or deacons. Blessings of certain ministers in the Church, like lectors, altar servers, and catechists, are sacramentals.

Some blessings are consecrations to God, like the blessing of an abbot or an abbess or the rite of religious profession.

Some objects that can be blessed are familiar to us: a crucifix, rosary beads, palms, and holy cards with pictures of Jesus, Mary, or the saints. These objects are also sacramentals. We treat them with respect because they are part of our spiritual inheritance. They are not jewelry or magic. They have no power in themselves, but their power comes from the faith of the Church, which blesses them and offers them to us as helps and supports in our journey to God. ✳

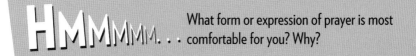

HMMMMMM. . . What form or expression of prayer is most comfortable for you? Why?

1.   How are a symbol and a ritual related?

2.   What is a sacrament?

3.   What is the Paschal Mystery?

4.   What do we mean by sacramental economy?

5.   What is grace?

6.   Explain the difference between sanctifying grace and actual grace.

7.   How do the sacraments fulfill Christ's plan of redemption for us?

8.   Describe each of the three expressions of prayer: vocal prayer, meditation, and contemplation.

9.   What is the Liturgy of the Hours?

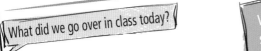

What did we go over in class today?

We talked about the sacramental economy.

I was asking about religion class, not economics.

That was in religion class!

Not helpful. What do you mean?

OK, so our economy runs on money, right?

We sell our goods and services to other people and we get money.

Yeah, where's the religion part?

Well the sacramental economy runs on grace.

So how is that like our economy?

To live to the fullest, we have to be in the "flow of grace." Like in the regular economy we need a "cash flow."

So how do we get the cash? I mean . . . grace?

As soon as we are baptized! We receive grace through the sacraments. The sacraments are the way Christ enters our life. If we don't have him, we're stuck.

SACRAMENTAL ECONOMY
TEXT EXCHANGE

UNIT 1 HIGHLIGHTS

CHAPTER 1   Liturgy

Where Does the Liturgy Come from?

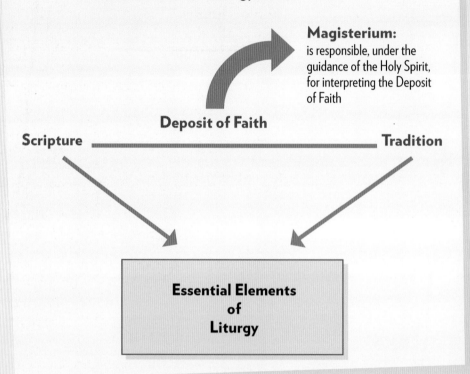

Magisterium:
is responsible, under the guidance of the Holy Spirit, for interpreting the Deposit of Faith

Deposit of Faith

Scripture ———————————————————— **Tradition**

**Essential Elements
of
Liturgy**

The Trinity Is Present in the Liturgy

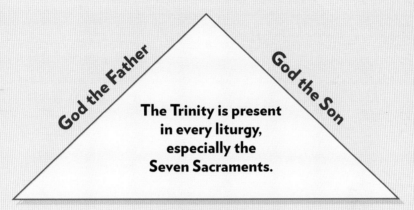

God the Father

God the Son

**The Trinity is present
in every liturgy,
especially the
Seven Sacraments.**

The Holy Spirit

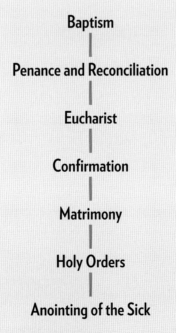

Baptism

Penance and Reconciliation

Eucharist

Confirmation

Matrimony

Holy Orders

Anointing of the Sick

Liturgical Calendar

CHAPTER 2   Sacraments

Symbols and Rituals

Symbol

An object or action that points to another reality.

Example = Water

Meaning = washing, cleansing, purifying

Ritual

A symbolic action, often including words.

Example = Handshake

Meaning = sign of welcome or sharing peace

Signs or Miracles in the Gospel of John

Seven signs
to show
Jesus'
divinity

Seven Sacraments—Three Categories

Sacraments of Christian Initiation

Baptism   Confirmation   Eucharist

Sacraments of Healing

Penance and Reconciliation
Anointing of the Sick

Sacraments at the Service of Communion

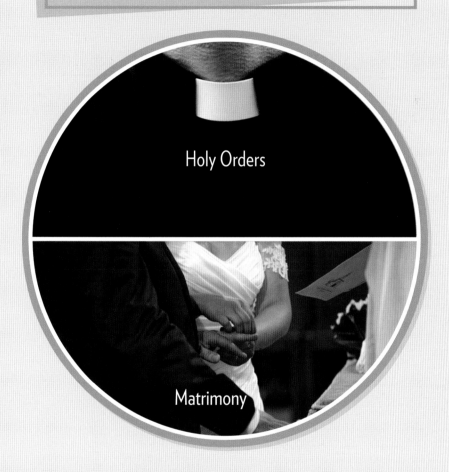

Holy Orders

Matrimony

UNIT 1

BRING IT HOME

WHY SHOULD THE LITURGY AND SACRAMENTS MATTER TO ME?

FOCUS QUESTIONS

CHAPTER 1   How can the liturgy bring me closer to God?

CHAPTER 2   How can the liturgy help me to grow spiritually?

KARLA
Seton Catholic Preparatory School

The liturgy should matter to me because when I celebrate with my community, I am in the presence of God. I can come together with others as a community to share in the liturgy. All of the sacraments allow me to be close to God, and help me to know and understand him better. By participating in the liturgy and sacraments, I am reminded of the history of my faith, and I can also see how I am part of a universal community of faith.

REFLECT

Take some time to read and reflect on the unit and chapter focus questions listed on the facing page.

- What question or section did you identify most closely with?

- What did you find within the unit that was comforting or challenging?

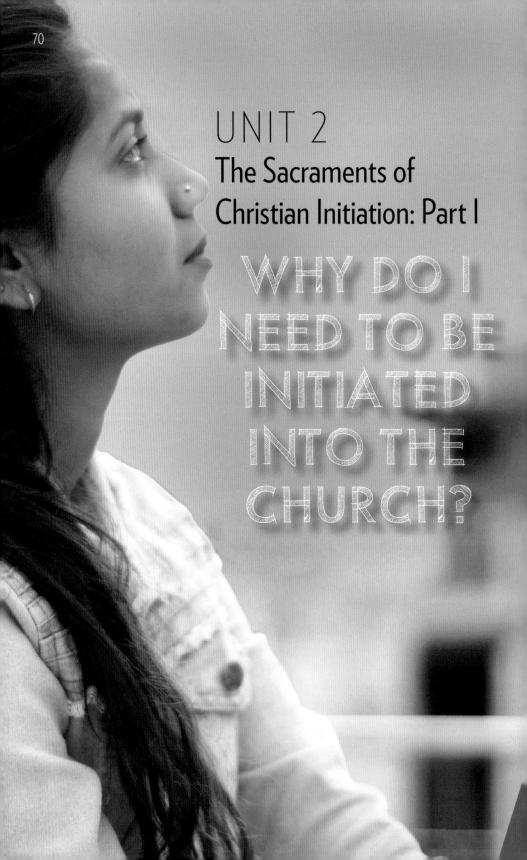

UNIT 2
The Sacraments of Christian Initiation: Part I

WHY DO I NEED TO BE INITIATED INTO THE CHURCH?

LOOKING AHEAD

UNIT 2

I think it is necessary to be initiated into the Church so I can fully experience God. Being initiated into the Church through Baptism means that my parents and godparents confirmed their trust and belief in God, and promised to raise me in the Catholic faith. Through all of the Sacraments of Initiation, we truly become children of God. We are freed from the burden of Original Sin and are given the opportunity for salvation. Through the Sacraments of Initiation, we enter into a relationship with God.

MIKE
Red Bank Catholic High School

CHAPTER 3
Baptism

IS BAPTISM REALLY NECESSARY?

SNAPSHOT

UNIT 2

Article 11
Introduction to Baptism

Elaina and Jeff sat in Mass with their parents. They were bored. The priest who celebrated the Mass usually geared his homilies toward the adults and elderly members of the congregation. Elaina fiddled with the hem of her dress. She wished she could check her messages, but her mom made them leave their phones at home when they went to church. Jeff was just as bored. He looked around and counted how many women were wearing hats and how many men had mustaches.

Then, Father McGowan did something different that caught the attention of both Elaina and Jeff. He called up a young family sitting in the front pew. Elaina recognized them. She had been watching as the wife's pregnancy progressed. She always noticed the loving way the husband looked at his wife. And here they were, right in front of the whole church, holding their new baby! Father McGowan asked for the godparents to join them, and they stepped up to the baptismal font. He talked about the commitment the parents and godparents were making to raise this child in their faith tradition. He talked about the responsibility of the entire community in *caring* for the new baby named Elijah.

TAKE IT TO GOD

Open my eyes, Lord!
I am reminded of the promises made in Baptism . . .
promises to raise me and keep me, protect me and teach me.
Open my eyes to the community that surrounds me with love.
Let me see with fresh perspective those who have helped to
support my parents in their endeavors to make a home in my
    parish for me.
Open my eyes to the sacredness of family and community,
and how blessed I am to be part of this family.
Amen.

Elaina and Jeff strained to see what was happening. They were completely engrossed in the actions and words of baby Elijah's Baptism. Elaina and Jeff started wondering about their own Baptisms when Father McGowan encouraged the congregation to renew their baptismal promises. The whole car ride home, the kids peppered their parents with questions about their Baptisms. Where are their white gowns? Who are their godparents? Why did their parents decide to baptize them?

The Sacraments of Christian Initiation are the three sacraments that initiate us into the life of Christ and the life of the Church: Baptism, Confirmation, and the Eucharist. These three sacraments begin our lives as followers of Christ. The **Sacrament of Baptism**, the first Sacrament of Christian Initiation, is the foundation of the entire Christian life. In Baptism, we become members of Christ and of the Church and sharers in her mission to bring the Good News of Jesus Christ to the world.

The word *baptism* comes from the Greek word *baptizein*, which means "to plunge." In Baptism, we are plunged into the water, symbolizing burial into Christ's death, from which we rise to new life in Christ. Baptism is also called "the bath of enlightenment," for through Baptism we are enlightened by the Word that is Christ and receive "the true light" (John 1:9) that enlightens every follower of Christ.

The next time you witness a Baptism, either in your own family or at a parish celebration, try to think about its meaning as plunging into death in order to rise into life, and as the bath of enlightenment.

© likingthings / Shutterstock.com

What are some ways that water symbolizes something positive? negative?

Baptism, Sacrament of ➤ The first of the Seven Sacraments and one of the three Sacraments of Christian Initiation (the others being Confirmation and the Eucharist) by which one becomes a member of the Church and a new creature in Christ.

The Waters of Life: Creation

The Sacrament of Baptism finds its roots in the Old Testament, the Old Covenant with God, the Old Covenant that Jesus came "not to abolish but to fulfill" (Matthew 5:17). These roots begin in the Book of Genesis.

"Since the beginning of the world, water . . . has been the source of life" (*Catechism of the Catholic Church [CCC]*, number 1218). At the beginning of Creation, the Holy Spirit hovered over the waters, breathed on them, and brought life from them (see Genesis 1:1).

This is what the Church remembers at every Baptism: The Holy Spirit hovers over the possibility of every human life and brings wonderful gifts to fruition in it. In Baptism, a human being becomes a new creation in the Father, the Son, and the Holy Spirit.

The Great Flood

But water can be deadly. Among all the natural disasters possible in this world, human life is most frequently lost not through earthquakes, fires, or tornadoes, but through flooding. Again, we find in the Book of Genesis, chapters 6–9, a picture of that kind of flood. Human life had been overtaken by sin. In the account of Noah's ark, we are told that God was so grieved with the human state of affairs that he wanted to start over. He wanted to save a remnant of his people and of his creation so that eventually all could be saved.

Noah's ark, and all the people and animals in it, survived the waters of the Flood. A dove (a symbol of the Holy Spirit) brought evidence that land (a symbol of the Promised Land) was near. This is why the story of Noah's ark is considered a foreshadowing of Baptism. At every Baptism, a human being is "buried" in water as a symbol of death and at the same time is brought through those same waters into new life, life in Jesus Christ and in his Church.

From Death to Life: The Exodus

Another foreshadowing of Baptism in the Old Testament is the account of the Israelites' passage through the Red Sea (see Exodus, chapter 14). The People of God, with their leader Moses, were led from slavery to freedom, from certain death to new life, by passing through the waters of the Red Sea. At first, Pharaoh agreed to let the People of God leave peacefully, but then he changed his mind. He sent his chariots and charioteers to chase them and bring them back. The Red Sea loomed ahead. They were caught! How would they cross? Moses lifted his rod, the waters parted in great walls to the left and right, and God's people marched through on dry land.

UNIT 2

© vlastas / Shutterstock.com

At every Easter Vigil, the Israelites' passage through the Red Sea is proclaimed in the beautiful song of the Exsultet and in the third reading (Exodus 4:15–15:1). When you hear these proclamations, thank God for your Baptism.

The Church remembers all this at every Baptism. The waters of Baptism are the waters that part for *us* so we can be freed from sin and can continue our journey to the Promised Land of eternal life. The image of the Israelites' safe passage through the waters of death is an image of the freedom that is ours through Baptism.

The Waters of the Jordan

The River Jordan is a symbol of Baptism that leads us from the Old Testament to the New. To reach the Promised Land, God's people had one more river to cross: the Jordan River. When they did, they knew they were "home free." Centuries later, in the same River Jordan, John the Baptist offered a baptism of repentance to the people. He was offering them a chance to prepare themselves to recognize and follow the Messiah, the Anointed One, when he should appear. Of course, we know that John was the first to recognize Jesus as this very Messiah. The writer of the Gospel of John, when recounting this important moment of recognition, notes carefully that "this happened in Bethany across the Jordan, where John was baptizing" (1:28). In this Messiah, in Jesus, is true freedom.

When the water is blessed for Baptism, these four great events of salvation history—creation, Noah's ark, the crossing of the Red Sea, and the crossing of the River Jordan—are remembered. They prefigure the mystery of the

Sacrament of Baptism. Because these events are part of the Church's memory and understanding of salvation, they illuminate our own understanding of what the Sacrament of Baptism does for us.

Poor, Wayfaring Strangers

An old folk song illustrates one of the symbolic meanings of the River Jordan. The song goes like this:

> I'm just a poor, wayfaring stranger
> A-travelin' through this world of woe
> There is no sickness, no toil or danger
> In that fair land to which I go.
> I'm goin' home to see my mother
> I'm goin' home no more to roam
> I'm just a-goin' over Jordan
> I'm just a-goin' over home.

In the song, the wayfaring stranger is near death. He is going "over Jordan" to the Promised Land—that is, to Heaven. He is going to a land free from sickness, toil, and danger. He is going home.

I DIDN'T KNOW THAT!

Did you know that you could be the celebrant of a sacrament? It's true! In certain circumstances, if a priest or deacon is not present, you could baptize any person. In case of an emergency, anyone, even someone not baptized, can baptize another person. The main requirement is that they have the correct intention to baptize the person as a follower of Christ and member of his Body, the Church. If you are ever in a dire situation and a person with you requires Baptism, all you must say is: "[Name], I baptize you in the name of the Father, and of the Son, and of the Holy Spirit" (*CCC*, number 1284) while pouring water over their head three times. Then make the Sign of the Cross over the person receiving the sacrament. If you forget to do the Sign of the Cross, the sacrament is still valid. This type of Baptism might be necessary in some scenarios, such as parents wanting to baptize their very sick baby before a priest can come, baptizing someone who desires the sacrament on the battlefield, or perhaps in a situation of quarantine.

But what if we see the River Jordan as a symbol of the waters of Baptism? Then going "over Jordan" would mean being baptized into Christ. The "fair land" is the Promised Land, here a symbol of the Church itself. In the Church, through the waters of Baptism, we poor, wayfaring strangers find our true home.

The Baptism of Jesus

When Jesus was baptized in the waters of the River Jordan, the heavens opened. The Holy Spirit, who had hovered over the waters of creation, descended upon Jesus as "the firstborn among many" (Romans 8:29) and the beloved Son of the Father (see Mark 1:11). Even though, as the Son of God, Jesus had no need to repent, he asked to be baptized. He wanted to show his solidarity with us. Think back to the accounts of Jesus' Baptism detailed in each of the Gospels. It was at this event that the Father's voice was heard, saying, "This is my beloved Son, with whom I am well pleased" (Matthew 3:17, see Mark 1:11, Luke 3:22). At this Baptism, the Father acclaimed his Son. At our own Baptism, we are adopted as the Father's sons and daughters in Christ.

© Adam Jan Figel / Shutterstock.com

"This is my beloved Son, with whom I am well pleased" (Matthew 3:17).

The Holy Spirit appeared in the form of a dove at Jesus' Baptism (see Matthew 3:16, Mark 1:10, Luke 3:22, John 1:32). The presence of the Holy Spirit prefigures the presence of the Holy Spirit at the Baptisms of the followers of Christ that were to come. John the Baptist himself compared his Baptism with the Baptism to be brought about by Jesus: "The one who sent me to baptize with water told me, 'On whomever you see the Spirit come down and remain, he is the one who will baptize with the holy Spirit'" (John 1:33).

Did John realize that when he baptized Jesus, the heavens would open to reveal the presence of the Holy Trinity? Probably not. But ever since, whenever someone is baptized in the name of the Father, and of the Son, and of the Holy Spirit, the "heavens are opened," and the Holy Trinity is present.

UNIT 2

Fulfilled in Jesus Christ

All these events of salvation history are fulfilled in Jesus Christ. When Jesus was baptized, the Holy Spirit was with him. On the night before he died, Jesus celebrated the Passover, the passing over of the Jews from slavery into freedom. He spoke of his Passion as a "baptism" with which he was to be baptized (see Mark 10:38, Luke 12:50). When Jesus died and was raised from the dead, he passed from death to life and brought us out of the slavery of sin into the "glorious freedom of the children of God" (Romans 8:21). Jesus, then, is the true ark in which we have been saved.

When the Jewish leader Nicodemus came to Jesus by night, Jesus told him, "No one can enter the kingdom of God without being born of water and Spirit" (John 3:5). After his Resurrection, Jesus entrusted this mission of baptizing all nations to his Apostles (see Matthew 28:12). In the Acts of the Apostles, we find that Peter is following Jesus' instructions, for in Peter's address to the crowd immediately after Pentecost, he tells them, "Repent and be baptized, every one of you, in the name of Jesus Christ for the forgiveness of your sins; and you will receive the gift of the holy Spirit" (2:38). The same promise holds true for us today. ✳

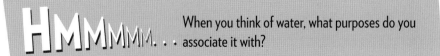

HMMMMMM. . . When you think of water, what purposes do you associate it with?

Article 12

Baptism: The Source of Christian Living

A Question of Why

Ryan leaned into the doorway of the walk-in closet that his dad fondly called his "home office."

"Dad," he said.

"Hmm," said his father, staring intently at the computer screen.

"I have a question."

"Okay," his dad said, still staring at the screen. "Just a second." He jiggled the mouse and clicked a few times. "Come on," he urged the computer. Ryan wondered why people talked to their electronics. It made no sense.

"Okay," his dad said, and twirled around in his chair to face his son. "What's this about?"

"It's a question for school," said Ryan. "Why did you have me baptized?"

"Oh. Well." His dad tipped back in his chair until his head almost touched the bookcase behind him. "Let's see. We wanted you to grow up Catholic, that's for sure."

"Okay," said Ryan. "Thanks."

Who can be baptized? Every person who has not yet been baptized is able to be baptized; you are never too old or too young to be baptized. **Can a person be baptized twice?** The only way for someone to be baptized twice would be if the original Baptism was not valid. And this would not be considered to be a "second Baptism" because the "first Baptism" was not a real Baptism. **What would make a Baptism invalid?** A Baptism would be invalid if the person baptizing does not use the correct Trinitarian formula or have the correct intention. If a person is baptized without water, this would be invalid. **Does the Catholic Church accept Baptisms from another church?** Yes, the Catholic Church recognizes any Baptism that uses water and in which the person was baptized with the Trinitarian formula.

"Wait," his dad said. "There's something else."

Ryan waited. His dad tipped forward, back again, closed his eyes, opened them, and looked at Ryan and said, "We wanted to give you the best we had: our faith in God."

"After that," he continued, as he gave his son a look that was a mixture, as usual, of love, pride, and concern, "we made a promise to God and to you—that we would help you to live that faith to the best of our ability—and yours."

The Effects of Baptism

All through our lives, the gifts of Baptism keep giving. However, it is up to us to open these gifts each and every day. The theological term for the gifts of Baptism is *effects*. The effects of Baptism are what Baptism does for us. These effects are:

- We die and rise with Christ.
- We are freed from Original Sin and all personal sins.
- We become adopted children of God.
- We become members of the Church and sharers in the priesthood of Christ.
- We receive a permanent or indelible sacramental character; therefore, the Sacrament of Baptism can never be repeated.
- We are empowered by the Holy Spirit for discipleship.

Dying and Rising with Christ

At Baptism, we are united with Christ and we share in his Paschal Mystery: the Passion, death, Resurrection, and Ascension of Jesus through which we are saved from sin and death. This dying and rising is what the waters of Baptism symbolize. Because the Paschal Mystery of Christ saves us from our sins, we say that it brings us the gift of justification. We become just in God's sight through God's mercy. Baptism holds the promise that at our death, if we have been faithful to Christ, he will take us up into a new and resurrected life. This is the ultimate way we participate in the Paschal Mystery.

In the meantime, the dyings and risings that are part of our lives right now can help us to understand and participate in the Paschal Mystery more deeply. We face experiences in life in which we "die" a little: the loss of a friend, unfair treatment, an illness or other physical suffering, the hurt of a divorce. As part of our spiritual progress, we also learn to die to ourselves in order to love and serve others and to overcome sinful habits. But because of Baptism, we face these little deaths in Christ, with Christ, and through Christ. And because of Christ, we can look beyond our earthly sufferings, traveling through the way of the cross, to resurrection in him.

UNIT 2

The image of Christ on the cross brings to mind his ultimate sacrifice for us. Yet, it is the Risen Christ that brings us salvation.

Freedom from Original Sin

Picture yourself tied up in chains, weighed down by their iron weight. You cannot move. You are stuck. You have a feeling you will never get free. This is a picture of Original Sin. We inherit it as part of our human condition. But when we choose Christ (or when our parents choose Christ for us) and are baptized, our chains are broken. All sins—personal sin as well as Original Sin—are forgiven. We are free! We are graced! We are sons and daughters of God in Christ!

Although Baptism frees us from the state of Original Sin, some of its effects remain in our lives even after Baptism. Ignorance, suffering, and death remain, and we continue to be attracted to sin. But with God's grace, we have the strength to resist this inclination, and sin cannot harm us if we fight against it. Baptism requires an ongoing conversion, a continual turning toward God amid our everyday lives. And we know that in Christ the final victory over sin, suffering, and death is ours.

Children of God

Our understanding of adoption by God can be deepened by looking briefly at the writings of Saint Paul. In Galatians, chapter 4, he describes the situation of an heir that is too young to make decisions about his inheritance, supervised by guardians, and "no different from a slave" (verse 1).

Saint Paul compares the heir's situation with our own before Christ came to redeem us: we were enslaved by sin and death. But after our redemption in Christ, Saint Paul explains, our situation changed radically: we were ransomed by Christ and adopted in him as children of God. Paul calls on the Holy Spirit, the fountain of prayer within us, as evidence of this adoption: "As proof that you are children, God sent the Spirit of his Son into our hearts, crying out, 'Abba, Father!' So you are no longer a slave but a child, and if a child then also an heir, through God" (Galatians 4:6–7).

As children of God, we become members of Christ, partakers in the divine nature, and temples of the Holy Spirit. At Baptism, we are given sanctifying grace, the grace that enables us to believe in God, to hope in him, and to love him. We are given the power to live and act under the inspiration of the Holy Spirit, and to use his gifts in our lives. We are also given the grace to grow in goodness and to turn away from sin and selfishness.

Members of the Church

Baptism makes us members of the Church, the People of God, the Body of Christ. We are not alone anymore: "We are members one of another" (Ephesians 4:25). We have been baptized into one Spirit, and we share our spiritual gifts with one another, for "to each individual the manifestation of the Spirit is given for some benefit" (1 Corinthians 12:7). Paul is talking about spiritual gifts (like hospitality and preaching), and he emphasizes that of all these gifts, the greatest is love (see 1 Corinthians, chapter 13).

© Rawpixel.com / Shutterstock.com

Friendship is one of God's greatest gifts. Sharing ourselves with others is part of belonging to the Body of Christ. Each friendship is unique and should always seek to include, not exclude others.

UNIT 2

As members of the Church, we no longer belong to ourselves but to Christ. The rights and duties of a baptized person flow from belonging to Christ. Paul teaches in First Corinthians that we are one body with many parts. Yet all the parts, though many, are still one body. Each part of the Body of Christ has its own role and responsibility. However, each of those roles means nothing unless we are functioning as part of the whole (see 1 Corinthians 12:12–26). As part of the Body of Christ, we find our places in the community of faith by serving others and by showing respect, love, and obedience to Church leaders. Participating in the spreading of the Gospel through apostolic and missionary work is also a duty of Baptism and an opportunity to share the great gifts we have received. In return, we, as baptized persons, have certain rights: to receive the sacraments, to be nourished with the Word of God, and to be guided by other spiritual helps the Church provides. Anointed as sharers in the priesthood of Christ, we are called together to worship, especially on Sundays and holy days, and so to support one another in following Christ. For we are now included among those true worshippers who, as Jesus said, "will worship the Father in Spirit and truth" (John 4:23).

Through Baptism, we are also united with all who have been baptized, even if they were not baptized in the Catholic Church. These are our fellow Christians, and we see them as our brothers and sisters in Christ. Baptism is *"the sacramental bond of unity"*[1] (*CCC*, number 1271) among all those who, through it, are reborn into Christ.

Sacramental Character of Baptism

In Baptism, we receive an anointing with Sacred Chrism. This is a sign of the gift of the Holy Spirit. Eventually, the holy oil disappears but not so the indelible character of Baptism that comes with it! The character is an invisible mark on the soul. We are chosen and sealed for Christ, and consecrated for Christian worship. This invisible mark can never disappear, and Baptism can never be repeated.

The seal of Baptism both "enables and commits Christians to serve God"[2] (*CCC*, number 1273) by participating in the liturgy, living holy lives, and serving others in love. In the Eucharist, we pray for those who have died "with the sign of faith" (*Roman Missal*, Eucharistic Prayer I). This sign of faith, the character of Baptism that we share with them, gives us hope that they live eternally and that we also will share eternal life with them one day.

Empowered for Discipleship

The word *christ* means "anointed." In the Sacrament of Baptism, we are anointed and incorporated into Christ as Priest, Prophet, and King. Our anointing empowers us to be disciples, to share in Christ's priestly, prophetic, and kingly ministry. Through sharing in his priestly ministry, we are empowered to worship. Through our sharing in his prophetic ministry, we are empowered, as Jesus said, to "hear the word of God and act on it" (Luke 8:21). Through our sharing in his kingly ministry, we are to use our gifts in the service of others. We do not usually think of kings as servants. Jesus himself explained the nature of his kingship: "I am among you as the one who serves" (Luke 22:27). This is the pattern of discipleship we are to follow.

UNIT 2

The Common Priesthood of the Faithful

Baptism gives us a share in the priesthood of Christ. This is called the **common priesthood of the faithful.** The word *common* means "for all," as in for all those who are baptized. From this word, we get the words *communal* and *community.* As we are incorporated into Christ, who is Priest, Prophet, and King, so we are given the gift of proclaiming the praises of God, "who called you out of darkness into his wonderful light" (1 Peter 2:9). "The faithful exercise their baptismal priesthood through their participation, each according to his own vocation, in Christ's mission as priest, prophet, and

Through Baptism, we belong to the common priesthood of the faithful. Being a part of this faith community gives us a sense of belonging and deepens our relationship with our family, community, and Christ.

© Mike Kuhlman / Shutterstock.com

king" (*CCC*, number 1546). This common priesthood is, of course, different from the ministerial priesthood, which we will look at in unit 5, when we study the Sacrament of Holy Orders. ✳

HMMMMM. . . Which of the effects of Baptism do you see most clearly in your daily life?

common priesthood of the faithful ➤ The name for the priesthood shared by all who are baptized. The baptized share in the one priesthood of Jesus Christ by participating in his mission as priest, prophet, and king.

Article 13

The Baptism of Children

Baptizing infants and young children is an ancient tradition of the Church. Today, when infants and young children are baptized, we celebrate rites of Baptism. Baptisms celebrated in this manner include the same elements as those celebrated according to the *Rite of Christian Initiation of Adults* (RCIA); however, the celebration of Baptism compresses a number of elements into one liturgy. As the baptized child progresses in age and understanding, appropriate instruction and involvement in the Christian way of life is offered so that the life of faith nourished by the grace of Baptism can also grow.

God's Life Is Pure Gift

God's life is a generous gift. Thus, from the earliest times, Baptism, with its gifts of entry into Christian life and true freedom, has been administered to children. This is because Baptism, a grace and gift of God, does not depend on any human merit. By this the Church fulfills the words of Jesus, that "no one can enter the kingdom of God without being born of water and Spirit" (John 3:5). By bringing a child to the Sacrament of Baptism, parents and godparents share their most precious possession, their faith and the faith of the entire Church, with this child. In doing so, they truly nurture this little one at the deepest level.

Baptism frees us from **Original Sin**—the sin of the first man and woman, who disobeyed God's command by choosing to follow their own will and so lost their original holiness and became subject to death, which is passed on to us. Because of this sin, the Church baptizes even those who haven't committed personal sin—infants and young children.

Original Sin ➤ From the Latin *origo*, meaning "beginning" or "birth." The term has two meanings: (1) the sin of Adam and Eve, who disobeyed God's command by choosing to follow their own will and thus lost their original holiness and became subject to death, (2) the fallen state of human nature that affects every person born into the world, except Jesus and Mary.

Asking questions is critical to understanding the teachings of the Church. What questions do you have about Church doctrine that you might like to ask your parents, a teacher, or a youth minister?

UNIT 2

The gift of Baptism must be affirmed throughout life, in our everyday choices to live by faith, hope, and love. And even if we say no, God never gives up. He will always try to find us and bring us back to him. As we read in the Letter to the Romans:

> What will separate us from the love of Christ? Will anguish, or distress, or persecution, or famine, or nakedness, or peril, or the sword? . . . No, in all these things we conquer overwhelmingly through him who loved us. For I am convinced that neither death, nor life, nor angels, nor principalities, nor present things, nor future things, nor powers, nor height, nor depth, nor any other creature will be able to separate us from the love of God in Christ Jesus our Lord. (8:35,37–39)

Celebrating Baptism

Before the Baptism of a child, pastors have the responsibility of preparing parents for the celebration of Baptism with full understanding. Often parents of infants and young children are gathered in groups to be prepared by pastoral counsel and prayer for the coming celebration.

The Sacrament of Baptism is celebrated amid the community simply because, in Baptism, the child becomes a child of God and a member of the community. The community will be the "village of faith" in which the child will be raised.

It is preferable that the Sacrament of Baptism be celebrated on a Sunday, the day of the Lord's Resurrection. Ideally, it is celebrated at the Mass, as this underlines the child's incorporation into the Body of Christ, the community of faith. The ordinary minister of the Sacrament of Baptism is a bishop or priest. In the Latin Church, a deacon may also celebrate the sacrament.

Whether celebrated within the Mass or not, the celebration of Baptism begins with the reception of the child. First, the celebrant greets the family and asks for the child's name. He then asks the parents,

> What do you ask of God's Church for [N.]?
> Parents: Baptism.

(The Order of Baptism of Children, number 76)

It is entirely possible that you may someday be asked to be a godparent to a niece or nephew, cousin, or friend's child. It's a serious responsibility to accept an invitation to be a godparent. Being a godparent means that you will be a consistent source of support to the parents and child, and also be a strong spiritual guide. You can prepare to be a godparent by modeling the example of living out your faith. This means attending Mass regularly, encouraging others, and modeling service. If you are asked to be a godparent, remember to celebrate the milestones in the Church year and in your godchild's everyday life. Treat their Baptism as their birthday in the Church by sending a card or gift. Make Christmas and Easter extra special. Reach out to them and answer any questions they may have. Pray for them. You may find that supporting and encouraging someone in their faith journey can also make your faith life more meaningful!

The parents may use other words: e.g., *Faith* or *The grace of Christ* or *Entry into the Church* or *Eternal life.*

Both parents and godparents agree to help the child grow up in the faith, loving God and neighbor. Just as the catechumens were welcomed into the order of catechumens, the celebrant continues, saying:

> N., the Church of God receives you with great joy. In her name I sign you
> with the Sign of the Cross of Christ our Savior; then, after me, your parents
> (and godparents) will do the same. (*The Order of Baptism of Children,*
> number 79)

The Liturgy of the Word follows. After the Homily, the prayer of the faithful is offered for the child, the godparents, and the family. Then, as in the scrutinies of the Rite of Christian Initiation of Adults, the celebrant prays a prayer of exorcism. He prays that this child may be set free from Original Sin and that the Holy Spirit may dwell within this child.

The celebrant then anoints the child on the chest with the oil of the catechumens, "the oil of salvation," as a strengthening before Baptism. The family, with the child, and celebrant go to the font. Following a brief prayer for the child, the celebrant blesses the water, if it is not already blessed. The parents and the godparents then renew their baptismal promises.

UNIT 2

© StockPhotoArt / Shutterstock.com

In Baptism, water is poured three times over the head in the name of the Father, Son, and Holy Spirit.

In Water and the Holy Spirit

Finally, the celebrant asks the parents and godparents if it is their will that the child (and he says the name of the child) should be baptized in the faith of the Church. When they answer, "It is," the celebrant baptizes the child as follows:

> N., I BAPTIZE YOU IN THE NAME OF THE FATHER,
> *(He immerses the child or pours water over him [her] a first time.)*
>
> AND OF THE SON,
> *(He immerses the child or pours water over him [her] a second time.)*
>
> AND OF THE HOLY SPIRIT.
> *(He immerses the child or pours water over him [her] a third time.)*
>
> *(The Order of Baptism of Children,* number 97)

After Baptism, the child is anointed on the crown of the head with the chrism of salvation, **Sacred Chrism**. This newly baptized child is now a child of God, a priest (joining in worship), prophet (listening to and living God's Word), and king (responsible to serve) in Jesus Christ!

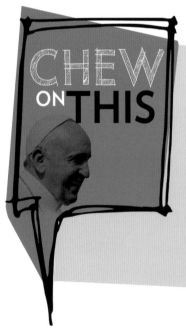

CHEW ON THIS

Each one of us, in fact, through Baptism . . . is incorporated into Christ and united to the entire community of believers. . . . It is the Sacraments that "make" the Church, that build her up, by generating new children, by gathering them into the holy people of God, by strengthening their membership. (Pope Francis, "General Audience," November 6, 2013)

Sacred Chrism ➤ Perfumed olive oil consecrated by the bishop that is used for anointing in the Sacraments of Baptism, Confirmation, and Holy Orders.

Symbols of New Life

The clothing in the white garment is next. This is the outward sign of Christian dignity, as the white color is the symbol that the new Christian has put on Christ and has risen with Christ. With the help of friends and family, the child is to bring this dignity "unstained into eternal life" *(The Order of Baptism of Children*, number 99).

The celebrant then takes the Paschal candle and says, "Receive the light of Christ" *(The Order of Baptism of Children*, number 100). A parent or godparent carries and lights this candle for the child. This candle is brought home and can be lit on significant days in the child's life, such as a birthday or baptismal anniversary.

The garment and the candle carry the same significance as in the Rite of Christian Initiation of Adults. But, in the case of a child, the "light of Christ" is entrusted to the parents and godparents. It is their responsibility to keep the light of Christ burning brightly in the life of the newly baptized child (see *The Order of Baptism of Children*, number 100).

If Baptism is celebrated at the Eucharist, the Mass continues with the preparation of the altar and the gifts. If Baptism is celebrated outside the Mass, it continues with the Lord's Prayer and blessings of the mother, the father, and the assembly.

The rite ends with the following:

> Celebrant: Go in peace.
> All: Thanks be to God.
>
> *(The Order of Baptism of Children*, number 105)

Holy Water

The holy water, blessed by a priest or bishop for use at Baptism and for private use as a sacramental, is a reminder of our Baptism. We find a holy water font at the entrance of every church. It is customary to dip our fingers in the holy water and bless ourselves with the Sign of the Cross as we enter the church.

The entire assembly may be sprinkled with holy water at Sunday Mass. This is often done during the Easter season. This replaces the penitential act, and reminds us that we are a holy people, ready to worship God as we share in the priestly, kingly, and prophetic mission of Christ.

UNIT 2

We use holy water to make the Sign of the Cross when entering a church to bless ourselves and be reminded of our Baptism.

Many families keep a small bottle of holy water at home to use in small holy water fonts. Sometimes, following ancient custom, it is sprinkled through the house during storms or even amid a family crisis. Parents may also bless the family with holy water before bedtime.

Holy water has been penetrated by the power of the Holy Spirit. It is no longer "ordinary water." It is a tangible sign that carries with it the presence of God.

Baptism of Blood and Desire

Baptism, birth into new life in Christ, and the Church itself, which we enter through Baptism, are necessary for salvation and are the ordinary means to reach salvation. However, because God is not bound, a person can be saved, in certain circumstances, without having been baptized. Those who die because of their faith in Christ but have not received the Sacrament of Baptism are baptized by that very death suffered in, with, and for Christ. This is called the *Baptism of blood* (see *CCC*, number 1258).

Catechumens who die before they are baptized are understood to have *Baptism by desire*. This means that they can still be saved. In fact, everyone who may have been ignorant of the Gospel through no fault of their own, and may have been seeking God by doing his will according to the best of their ability and understanding have the potential to be saved. It is possible that had they known Baptism was necessary, they would have desired it (see *CCC*, number 1260).

For infants who die without Baptism, the Church entrusts them to the mercy of God and to the tenderness of Jesus, who said, "Let the children come to me; do not prevent them" (Mark 10:14). ✳

HMMMMMM. . . Which of the symbols of Baptism has the most meaning for you?

UNIT 2

1. Why do we use a word that comes from the Greek word *baptizein*, meaning "to plunge," to describe our rise to a new life in Christ?

2. Name four events in salvation history associated with water that help us to understand the meaning of the Sacrament of Baptism.

3. Describe how to baptize in an emergency.

4. Choose one of the six effects of Baptism and explain its meaning.

5. What is the common priesthood of the faithful, and why is it connected to Baptism?

6. Why has Baptism been administered to children from the earliest times of the Church?

7. What are we freed from during Baptism, and why must we baptize even those who haven't committed personal sin yet?

8. Who are the ordinary ministers of Baptism?

ART STUDY

1. What key elements of Baptism can you identify in this image?

2. How do the facial expressions and body language of those represented in the artwork make you feel about Baptism?

3. What elements of the artwork remind you of the Baptism of Jesus?

CHAPTER 4
The Rite of Christian Initiation of Adults

HOW DO YOU JOIN THE CHURCH AS AN ADULT?

SNAPSHOT

Article 14
Christian Initiation in the Early Church

When Gia and her friends walked into theology class, they immediately noticed that the room looked different. Ms. Liddle had the lights off and some twinkle lights strung around the room, which gave it a warm glow. Gia noticed a sound machine playing quiet nature sounds. Ms. Liddle asked the students to put their bags and backpacks away and to sit down and make themselves comfortable. Gia liked Ms. Liddle. She always had a unique way of presenting material that was interesting. Most of Gia's other teachers just made the class take notes or review a slide presentation.

UNIT 2

In Baptism, we are called from darkness into light. How can you be light for the world?

The class quieted down and Ms. Liddle stood at the back of the room. She asked the group to use their imagination, and then she began to speak: "It is the third century in Rome. It is the night before Easter Sunday. It is early evening, just before dark. You are gathered with other men and women, some old, some young like yourself, near a gurgling stream that feeds into the Tiber River. You are a **catechumen**. You have been learning the Christian faith and living, as best you can, as a follower of Jesus for the past three years. Now,

---

catechumen ➤ An unbaptized person who is preparing for full initiation into the Catholic Church by engaging in formal study, reflection, and prayer.

tonight, you will be baptized. Your catechist is here, and your sponsor is by your side. The priest is standing up to his knees in the water, with the deacon at his side ready to help him and the catechumens during the ritual."

Ms. Liddle continued to speak: "The men stand in one group, the women in the other. One by one, you are called by name and walk into the water. You are immersed three times, in the name of the Father, and of the Son, and of the Holy Spirit. You come up dripping. You are anointed with Sacred Chrism, wrapped in a towel, dried off, and then given a new white garment. It is dark now, and a glowing candle is placed in your hands as you and the others begin to walk toward the assembly. They have been gathered for some time, listening to the readings from the prophets and the Apostles. They are waiting for you to join them, for the first time, in the Prayers of the Faithful."

Ms. Liddle invited the class to stand in two lines, the boys in one and the girls in the other. She handed them each a small candle and draped a scarf of white cloth over each of their shoulders. Gia looked around at her classmates. None of them were talking or giggling. Ms. Liddle had everyone's undivided attention.

Ms. Liddle continued: "The bishop greets you at the door, seals you in the Holy Spirit with the seal of Sacred Chrism, and leads you into the assembly. As the prayers begin, you realize that you can now pray with your brothers and sisters; no one has dismissed you, and soon you will receive the Eucharist, the Body and Blood of Christ. For this is the night of celebration of the Resurrection of Jesus Christ. This is the night of new life and new beginning. 'Yes,' you say to yourself, 'this is the night of my resurrection too, my resurrection in Christ and my new beginning in him. Alleluia!"

Ms. Liddle explained that the class had just experienced what Baptism was like for those entering the early Church. She asked the students to place their candles in a basket in the front of the room and put their white scarves in a pile on the table. When they took their seats, she didn't ask them to take out their notebooks; she asked them questions about believing and belonging. Ms. Liddle had given them a taste of the wonder of an early Baptism ceremony.

TAKE IT TO GOD

God,
Today I ask for your help.
Help me to worship you with an undistracted heart.
Deepen my faith, and let me bask in the glories of your goodness.
Reveal your message to me as I hear your Word.
Lead me to build up others with the gifts you have given me.
Protect me from all evil.
Guide the leaders of your community and empower me to faithfully
    follow their guidance.
Give me strength for my mission to share the Good News with others.
And thank you, Lord.
Thank you for bringing me to this faith community where you are
    always present.
Amen.

Three Special Sacraments

Ms. Liddle walked her students through a rough approximation of the receiving of a catechumen into the Church in the early centuries. In this vignette, we can recognize the **Sacraments of Christian Initiation**: Baptism, Confirmation, and the Eucharist. These three sacraments have been linked from the beginning. Receiving all three of them at the Easter Vigil or the Vigil of Pentecost was the usual way of becoming a Christian in the early Church.

The Sacraments of Christian Initiation involved much preparation. The vignette told us that the catechumens had been studying and learning for three years! The early Christians realized that change is not easy, and that a commitment to a way of life requiring love, forgiveness, and service to others took time. This "learning" was not simply hearing information about Jesus and the truths of the faith; it involved active learning and practicing a new way of life

Christian Initiation, Sacraments of ➤ The three sacraments—Baptism, Confirmation, and the Eucharist—through which we enter into full membership in the Church.

amid the Christian community—the Christian way of life. During the process of preparing, the catechumen was supported by the liturgy and the personal involvement of the community and was provided with **catechesis**, or oral instruction, aimed at education and formation in the Christian life. ✳

HMMMMM. . .

What do you think are the benefits of having a long preparation period before receiving the Sacraments of Initiation?

catechesis, catechists ➤ Catechesis is the process by which Christians of all ages are taught the essentials of Christian doctrine and are formed as disciples of Christ. Catechists are the ministers of catechesis.

Article 15

The Rite of Christian Initiation of Adults I

Aspects of the catechumenal process followed in the early centuries of the Church eventually fell away as circumstances changed and Baptism was more commonly administered in infancy. However, throughout the centuries, the process of becoming a fully initiated member of the Church has always involved the following essential elements: the proclamation of the Word, acceptance of the Gospel and conversion to a new way of life, the profession of faith, Baptism, the outpouring of the Holy Spirit, and reception of the Eucharist (see *CCC*, number 1229).

Today, as always, Baptism is the first Sacrament of Christian Initiation. We use two different but closely related rites when celebrating this sacrament. As discussed earlier, we celebrate the rite of Baptism when baptizing children who have not reached the age of reason (age seven). Those baptized as young children usually complete their initiation (with the Sacraments of Confirmation and the Eucharist) later in childhood or during their teen years. When baptizing older children (seven and older) and adults, we celebrate the **Rite of Christian Initiation of Adults (RCIA)**. Those celebrating according to the RCIA are fully initiated during the same liturgy of their Baptism.

The Restoration of the Catechumenate

The Second Vatican Council's *Constitution on the Sacred Liturgy* (*Sacrosanctum Concilium*, 1963) called for the restoration of the catechumenate, the process of initiation known and practiced in the early Church (see number 64). This beautiful communal process was recovered and reestablished as the normative process for an adult (or a child who has reached the age of reason) to become a Catholic. In 1972, the *Rite of Christian Initiation of Adults (RCIA)* was published.

Who Are the Candidates for the Sacraments?

The Rite of Christian Initiation of Adults is first of all intended for catechumens, those who have not been baptized. Those who have already been baptized do not participate in the baptismal rites of the RCIA, as they are already members of the faith. The Rite of Christian Initiation of Adults can

UNIT 2

Rite of Christian Initiation of Adults (RCIA) ➤ The process by which an unbaptized person, called a "catechumen," and those who were baptized in another Christian denomination, called "candidates for full communion," are prepared to become full members of the Church.

UNIT 2

The candidates for RCIA should have the support of a sponsor who is an example of a person living faith in their everyday life.

also include those who have already been baptized as a Christian but not in the Catholic Church. The individual would not need to be baptized again as long as their Baptism was valid. If there was any question about the validity of the Baptism, the individual could receive what is called a "conditional Baptism." Someone who was baptized in the Catholic Church but never practiced the faith would also not be baptized again but would also be a candidate for the Sacraments of Confirmation and the Eucharist. A Catholic who was never confirmed may also, in some instances, join the catechumens and other candidates in formation sessions while preparing for Confirmation.

The Stages of the Rite of Christian Initiation of Adults

An unbaptized person who is thinking of becoming a Catholic has a wonderful and life-changing journey ahead. But it is not a journey taken alone. The Rite of Christian Initiation of Adults involves a journey within a community. Certainly, catechumens will have times of solitary decision-making and individual reflection, but the process is in itself an introduction to life within the Church. The process involves the local parish and also the local diocese. By examining the process, we will see how a person is welcomed, catechized, chosen (or "elected") for Baptism, and then admitted to the Sacraments of Baptism, Confirmation, and the Eucharist—all in the midst of, and with the help and support of, the local Church.

CATHOLICS MAKING A DIFFERENCE

Not all Catholics were born into the faith and baptized as babies. The famous Italian singer Andrea Bocelli was agnostic in his youth. His conversion and Baptism as an adult provides him with daily support, and he hopes that his music will bring people together in prayer. Actor Gary Sinise was baptized Catholic but had never been confirmed. The acts of courage and selflessness he witnessed during crisis events such as 9-11 led the actor to appreciate his Catholic faith and eventually be confirmed. This commitment became a turning point for the actor toward a life of service. Often when people make the choice to become Catholic as adults, they are compelled to live out their faith in their everyday lives, making a difference in the lives of others and being the face of Christ for others.

The process is structured to include seven stages—four distinct periods of preparation and three steps, as follows:

- Period of Inquiry (Period of Evangelization and Precatechumenate)
- First Step: Rite of Acceptance into the Order of Catechumens
- Period of the Catechumenate
- Second Step: Rite of Election or Enrollment of Names
- Period of Purification and Enlightenment
- Third Step: Celebration of the Sacraments of Initiation
- Period of Postbaptismal Catechesis or Mystagogy

Period of Inquiry

A person interested in being baptized in the Catholic Church begins by becoming an "inquirer." The official name for this time of inquiry is the period of **evangelization** and precatechumenate. *Evangelization* means "the proclamation of the Gospel of Jesus through word and witness." During this time, the inquirer listens to the Good News, learns about the Catholic faith, and discerns a call to live the Gospel life as a Catholic. This process of evangelization unfolds through meetings with priests, deacons, the religious education or

---

evangelization ➤ The proclamation of the Gospel of Jesus Christ through word and witness.

catechumenate director, catechists, and often other inquirers and parishioners. The duration of this inquiry time is flexible.

First Step: Rite of Acceptance into the Order of Catechumens

The Rite of Acceptance into the Order of Catechumens follows the period of the precatechumenate. In this rite, the inquirers publicly declare their intention to follow Christ and are accepted as catechumens. The celebrant greets them (preferably at the door of the church) and asks:

> "What is your name?"
> The candidate gives his or her name.
> "What do you ask of God's Church?"
> The candidate answers: "Faith."
> Celebrant: "What does faith offer you?"
> Candidate: "Eternal life."
> (*RCIA*, section 50)

The faith required for Baptism is a "beginning" faith, a faith that will develop within the community of believers, the Church. Sponsors must be ready to help the new believers on the road of Christian life, and the entire Church community is responsible to some extent for the development of the gift of faith given at Baptism.

The priest greets the catechumens at the door of the church when they declare their intention to follow Christ and become part of the Church.

The celebrant tells the candidates that because they have followed God's light, the way of the Gospel lies open before them. He encourages them to continue to walk in the light of Christ and to commit their lives each day to his care. The celebrant then asks the candidates if they are prepared to begin their journey. When they answer that they are, the celebrant asks the sponsors and the community if they are ready to "help these candidates find and follow Christ" (*RCIA*, section 53). The assembly answers: "We are" (section 53).

The celebrant then signs the foreheads of the candidates with the Sign of the Cross. The celebrant may also sign other parts of the body (ears, eyes, lips, and so on). Then the candidate's sponsor does the same. The celebrant then prays a concluding prayer, asking for grace, protection, and perseverance for those who have been accepted into the order of catechumens.

The Rite of Acceptance always includes the Liturgy of the Word and often takes place during the Eucharist. Here, for the first time, the catechumens have assembled together and, in most cases, will be dismissed together after the Homily.

UNIT 2

Throughout the RCIA process, the catechumens meet with their sponsors and as a community to learn about Church teachings and the liturgy, to develop their spiritual life, and to find ways to share the Gospel with others.

Period of the Catechumenate

The catechumenate is a time of formation. The catechumens are gradually introduced to the Catholic faith. They are also guided in the Christian way of living in love for God and neighbor and in gratitude for Christ's salvation. Catechumenal formation is carried out in these ways:

1. **Catechesis:** Catechesis, gradual and complete, aims not only to help the catechumens understand the Church's teaching but also to introduce them to the mystery of Christ. This catechesis is generally coordinated with the Liturgical Year and incorporates celebrations of the Liturgy of the Word (see *RCIA*, section 75, number 1).

2. **Spiritual development:** The spiritual life of the catechumens deepens through their participation in the life of the community. Gradually, their views and actions reflect more and more the Christian way of life. They learn to pray, to witness to the Gospel through words and actions, and to live rooted in the hope that Christ makes possible (see *RCIA*, section 75, number 2).

3. **Liturgy:** The catechumens are supported by liturgical rites, especially celebrations of the Word, during Sunday Mass with the community and at other times when celebrations of the Word are planned for the catechumens, as well as blessings and anointings (see *RCIA*, section 75, number 3).

4. **Apostolic witness:** The catechumens learn to work with others to share the Gospel and to build up the Church through the witness of their actions and profession of faith (see *RCIA*, section 75, number 4).

We noted that the catechumens baptized in the early Church in Rome spent three years preparing for initiation. Today, the duration of the catechumenate varies according to the faith development of the individual catechumen.

Catechumens are considered "part of the household of Christ" (*RCIA*, section 47). Although not yet baptized, a catechumen who dies during the catechumenate is given a Christian burial. ✴

HMMMMMM. . .   What do you think would be the most challenging or rewarding part of the process of the catechumenate?

Article 16
The Rite of Christian Initiation of Adults II

The next step in the Rite of Christian Initiation of Adults is the **Rite of Election** or Enrollment of Names. The word *election* implies a choice. The Church has *elected* to accept the catechumens for the Sacraments of Christian Initiation. They are no longer called catechumens. They are given a new title: the **elect**.

Second Step: Rite of Election or Enrollment of Names

The Rite of Election is usually held on the first Sunday of Lent. It is the bishop of the diocese, or his delegate, who admits the candidates to the Rite of Election and to the sacraments. The rite takes place at the cathedral; however, in dioceses that cover vast distances, regional groupings of parishes often celebrate the Rite of Election together at a centrally located parish church.

Godparents

Sometime before the Rite of Election, those preparing for Baptism choose godparents. A godparent must be a practicing Catholic, over the age of eighteen, who can support this person in their faith journey—formally from the

© Bill Wittman / www.wpwittman.com

Who do you know that would be an excellent choice to fulfill the role of a godparent?

Rite of Election ➤ The Rite, which takes place on the first Sunday of Lent, by which the Church elects or accepts the catechumens for the Sacraments of Christian Initiation at the Easter Vigil. The Rite of Election begins a period of purification and enlightenment.

elect ➤ In the Rite of Christian Initiation, the title given to catechumens after the Rite of Election, while they are in the final period of preparation for the Sacraments of Christian Initiation.

Rite of Election through reception into the Church and beyond. "It is the responsibility of godparents to show the candidates how to practice the Gospel in personal and social life, to sustain the candidates in moments of hesitancy and anxiety, to bear witness, and to guide the candidates' progress in the baptismal life" (*RCIA*, section 11). Godparents are chosen for their good qualities, their example, and their friendship. This choice is made with the consent of the pastor or priest, and sometimes with the consultation of the catechists.

In the Rite of Election, the godparents are asked to attest to the candidates readiness for the sacraments by answering the following questions:

- Have they faithfully listened to God's Word proclaimed by the Church?
- Have they responded to that Word and begun to walk in God's presence?
- Have they shared the company of their Christian brothers and sisters and joined with them in prayer?

These questions set out the basics of the Christian life: listening to God's Word, responding to that Word, and joining in Christian community with others. You may find these questions to be valuable guidelines on your journey with Christ. Ask yourself: How well have I listened and responded to the Word of God? How regularly do I pray with the members of my community of faith through liturgical prayer and devotions?

Called and Chosen

The Rite of Election begins after the Homily when the catechumens are presented. The godparents are asked to affirm that the catechumens are worthy and prepared to be admitted to the ranks of the elect and to look forward to receiving the Sacraments of Baptism, Confirmation, and the Eucharist at Easter.

The catechumens are asked if they wish to enter fully into the life of the Church through the Sacraments of Baptism, Confirmation, and the Eucharist. After they respond, "We do," they are asked to offer their names for enrollment (see *RCIA*, section 132). As one option, they may inscribe their names, usually in a special book. After all have offered their names, the Act of Admission or Election takes place. The bishop turns to the candidates and says:

> "I now declare you to be members of the elect, to be initiated into the
> sacred mysteries at the next Easter Vigil."
> The candidates respond, "Thanks be to God."
>
> (RCIA, section 133)

After the Act of Election, the liturgy continues with intercessions for the elect. Then the bishop, with outstretched hands, prays a prayer over the elect, asking that they may be helped and strengthened in the coming days. After this, if the Eucharist is being celebrated, the elect are dismissed.

Period of Purification and Enlightenment

The Rite of Election begins a period of what the Church calls purification and enlightenment. This time is intended to purify and enlighten the minds and hearts of the elect. This involves an examination of conscience and doing penance as well as deepening one's knowledge of, and relationship with, Jesus Christ. The period customarily coincides with the season of Lent, which is a time of purification and enlightenment for the whole Church. The elect participate in reflection that helps them to prepare for Baptism while the others in the community reflect on the meaning of their Baptism.

Scrutinies

During this period, the elect participate in three **scrutinies**, liturgical rites celebrated on the third, fourth, and fifth Sundays of Lent. These rites aid in self-examination and repentance, and have the spiritual purpose of healing any weakness or sin. These rites also strengthen what is good, and help the elect to "hold fast to Christ" (*RCIA*, section 141).

The scrutiny takes place after the Homily. As the elect stand with bowed heads or kneel, the assembly prays several petitions directly for them as they prepare to receive the sacraments at Easter.

The scrutiny is followed by an exorcism, a prayer that the elect will acknowledge their weaknesses and put their trust in God. The celebrant lays hands on each of the elect if it can be done easily. Then, with hands outstretched over all the elect, he prays that their hearts may be touched by the Holy Spirit. The laying on of hands and the outstretched hands of the celebrant are both signs of the presence of the Holy Spirit, who is called on to

scrutinies ➤ Rites within the Rite of Christian Initiation of Adults that support and strengthen the elect through prayers of intercession and exorcism.

UNIT 2

purify the hearts of the elect and to make them ready for all the graces God is preparing for them. After the Liturgy of the Word, the elect are dismissed as usual.

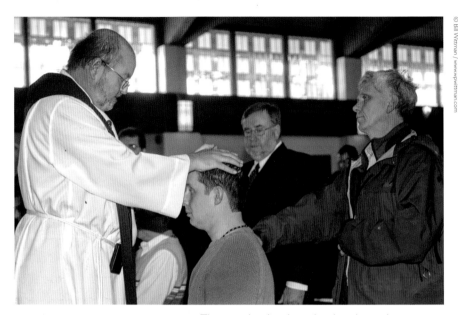

© Bill Wittman / www.pwittman.com

The priest lays hands on the elect during the scrutinies.

The Creed and the Lord's Prayer

The period of purification and enlightenment also includes two presentations: the Apostles' Creed (or Nicene Creed) and the Lord's Prayer. The presentations take place on weekdays during the third week of Lent (Creed), and the fifth week of Lent (Lord's Prayer).

Ideally, the key elements of the Christian faith are not presented on paper. Instead, in each instance, the elect are asked to stand and *listen* as the Creed and the Our Father are recited for them. This represents the personal, spoken handing on of the faith. This kind of learning explains Saint Paul's words that we receive the Spirit from faith in what we hear (see Galatians 3:2). In handing over the Creed and the Lord's Prayer to the elect, the Church asks the elect not only to learn them by heart but to *live* them by heart. ✳

Based on the qualities of a godparent, whom would you choose, and why, if you were to go through the process of RCIA?

Article 17

The Rite of Christian Initiation of Adults III

As the end of Lent nears, the elect, with the entire Church, are focused on the saving events of Holy Week and the Paschal Mystery of Jesus Christ, the mystery into which they will soon be immersed through the Sacraments of Baptism, Confirmation, and the Eucharist. For the elect, Holy Saturday is a special day of preparation, and they are urged to use it as a day of reflection in preparation for the Easter Vigil, when they will celebrate the Sacraments of Christian Initiation.

UNIT 2

Third Step: Celebration of the Sacraments of Christian Initiation

© Brianna Arambula / CatholicStock.com

Imagine this: It is the Easter Vigil. We are gathered in assembly, with the elect in our midst. The new fire has been lit. The church is dark. Out of the darkness, a voice sings out, "Light of Christ!" We respond, "Thanks be to God!" We turn and see a flame marching slowly toward us, a flame at the top of a tall white candle. As smaller candles are lit from this flame, light slowly overcomes the darkness. Now it is your turn to light your small candle and to pass the light on.

The tall candle (the **Paschal candle**, the symbol of the Risen Christ in our midst) has reached the front of the church. All eyes are upon it as the deacon sings these ancient words excerpted from the Exsultet (named after its first word, *Exult!* or *Rejoice!*):

The Paschal candle is a symbol of the Risen Christ, who overcomes all darkness, sin, and death. It is lit at the Easter Vigil and remains lit for the entire Easter season. It is also lit at Baptisms and funerals as a sign of new life in Christ.

Paschal candle ➤ Also called the Easter candle, this is the large, tall candle lit at the Easter Vigil by a flame from the new fire; the symbol of the Risen Christ.

These, then, are the feasts of Passover,

in which is slain the Lamb, the one true Lamb,

whose Blood anoints the doorposts of believers.

This is the night,

when once you led our forebears, Israel's children,

from slavery in Egypt

and made them pass dry-shod through the Red Sea.

This is the night

that with a pillar of fire

banished the darkness of sin.

This is the night

that even now, throughout the world,

sets Christian believers apart from worldly vices

and from the gloom of sin,

leading them to grace

and joining them to his holy ones.

(*Roman Missal,* pages 354–355)

I DIDN'T KNOW THAT!

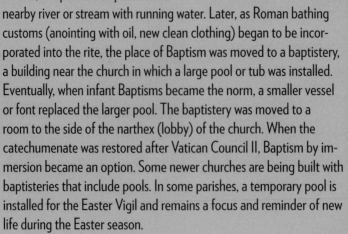

© TheBiblePeople / Shutterstock.com

The location for Baptism changed and developed through the centuries. At first, the place of Baptism was a nearby river or stream with running water. Later, as Roman bathing customs (anointing with oil, new clean clothing) began to be incorporated into the rite, the place of Baptism was moved to a baptistery, a building near the church in which a large pool or tub was installed. Eventually, when infant Baptisms became the norm, a smaller vessel or font replaced the larger pool. The baptistery was moved to a room to the side of the narthex (lobby) of the church. When the catechumenate was restored after Vatican Council II, Baptism by immersion became an option. Some newer churches are being built with baptisteries that include pools. In some parishes, a temporary pool is installed for the Easter Vigil and remains a focus and reminder of new life during the Easter season.

The Exsultet sets the context for the entire Easter Vigil. It prepares us for the Liturgy of the Word, which reacquaints us with the history of our salvation. It reminds us that this night is our passover feast, and, in a special way, is the passover feast of the elect, when they will pass through the waters of Baptism, will be washed clean of sin, and, with Christians everywhere, will be restored to grace and holiness. In Baptism, Confirmation, and the Eucharist, Christ will rise in them and will bring them "out of darkness into his wonderful light" (1 Peter 2:9). For all these reasons, the **Easter** Vigil is the most appropriate time for the Celebration of the Sacraments of Christian Initiation.

Baptism

As the elect come forward for Baptism, we pray for them in the Litany of the Saints. The water is then blessed. The blessing recalls the meaning of water as God's creation and its use in the sacraments. It also recalls the wonderful works of God throughout the history of our salvation (see *RCIA*, section 210). Near the end of the blessing, the Paschal candle is lowered into the water (either once or three times) as a sign that it is Christ himself who gives life and power to the waters of Baptism.

The profession of faith, in the form of the baptismal promises, follows. The elect promise to reject sin and profess their belief in God the Father, God the Son, and God the Holy Spirit.

The water of Baptism is a sign of new life. Water can be poured three times over the head, or the entire body can be immersed three times in a pool of water.

Easter ➤ The day on which Christians celebrate Jesus' Resurrection from the dead; considered the most holy of all days and the climax of the Church's Liturgical Year.

Then the elect come forward, one by one, to be buried with Christ in Baptism and to rise with him to new life. The celebrant may baptize the candidate either by immersion three times or by pouring water over the head three times, saying the following:

> (Name), I baptize you in the name of the Father,
> *(The celebrant immerses or pours water the first time.)*
>
> and of the Son,
> *(The celebrant immerses or pours water the second time.)*
>
> and of the Holy Spirit.
> *(The celebrant immerses or pours water the third time.)*
> (RCIA, section 226)

Saying these words and pouring the water, or immersing in water, are the essential elements of the Sacrament of Baptism.

White garment: Immediately after Baptism, the new Christian is given a new white garment. New life, new clothes! We all know the wonderful feeling of hopping out of the shower or bathtub and putting on fresh, clean clothing. For the new Christians given a new white garment, it is the same thing, only multiplied eternal times. This garment symbolizes that the newly baptized have clothed themselves in Christ.

Lighted candle: The godparents of the newly baptized are called forward. They are given a candle, which they light from the Paschal candle and present to the newly baptized, who are urged to "keep the flame of faith alive in your hearts" (*RCIA*, section 230).

Confirmation

In the absence of the bishop, the same priest who baptized the candidates is authorized to confirm the newly baptized. The Holy Spirit will strengthen them to be active members of the Church "and to build up the Body of Christ in faith and love" (*RCIA*, section 233).

After the Sacrament of Confirmation, the priest then leads the entire assembly in renewing their baptismal promises. This reminds the community of believers that faith must continue to grow after Baptism. After renouncing sin and affirming belief in God, the assembly is sprinkled with the newly blessed baptismal water.

And then we prepare to receive the Sacrament of the Eucharist, when the new Catholics in our midst (both those who have just been baptized and confirmed, and those who made a profession of faith and received Confirmation) will receive the Body and Blood of Christ for the first time. Thus, their Christian initiation will be complete.

The Eucharist

The Liturgy of the Eucharist continues as usual. Before saying, "Behold the Lamb of God," the celebrant may have a few words to say to the newly baptized and confirmed. He may remind them that the Eucharist will complete their Christian initiation and that with Jesus in the Eucharist, they will continue their journey "from here to eternity."

Period of Postbaptismal Catechesis or Mystagogy

UNIT 2

Mysta-what? Mystagogy! This is a Greek word meaning "study of the mysteries." Another term for this RCIA period is *Period of Postbaptismal Catechesis*—that is, catechesis after Baptism.

After the Easter Vigil, the newly initiated Catholics are called by the Greek term *neophytes*, meaning "beginners." The time of **mystagogy** is "a time for the community and the neophytes together to grow in deepening their grasp of the paschal mystery and in making it part of their lives through meditation on the Gospel, sharing in the eucharist, and doing the works of charity" (*RCIA*, section 244). The neophytes' godparents, pastors, catechist, and entire parish community help them to do this.

During mystagogy, the neophytes are helped to reflect on their recent celebration of the Sacraments of Christian Initiation and on their being incorporated into Christ and into the Church. Through this reflection and new understanding, they can perceive the faith more fully, and their vision of the Church and the world is renewed and expanded.

An appropriate celebration close to Pentecost Sunday, marking the end of the Easter season and the immediate postbaptismal catechesis, might be held for the neophytes. In some parishes, neophytes continue to gather monthly during the year for continued support and guidance in their new lives as Catholics. ✳

HMMMMMMM. . .

Why do you think it is meaningful for members of the community to renew their baptismal promises?

---

mystagogy ➤ A period of catechesis following the reception of the Sacraments of Christian Initiation that aims to more fully initiate people into the mystery of Christ.

1. What are the three Sacraments of Christian Initiation?

2. What is the Rite of Christian Initiation of Adults (RCIA)?

3. What are the four periods and three steps of the RCIA?

4. Describe the four aspects of formation presented in the catechumenate.

5. Why are the catechumens given the new title of "the elect" during the second step of the RCIA process?

6. What are the essential elements of the Sacrament of Baptism?

7. What is mystagogy?

The Stages of RCIA

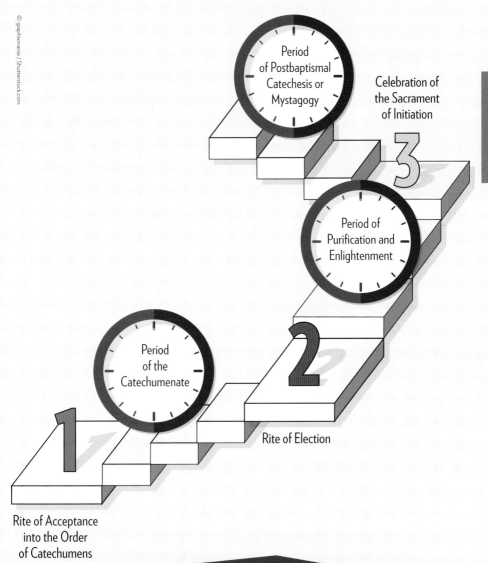

Period of Postbaptismal Catechesis or Mystagogy

Celebration of the Sacrament of Initiation

Period of Purification and Enlightenment

Period of the Catechumenate

Rite of Election

Rite of Acceptance into the Order of Catechumens

© graphixmania / Shutterstock.com

UNIT 2

Period of Postbaptismal Catechesis or Mystagogy

1. Why do you think there are periods of waiting and processing between each step?

2. In what ways do you think this process is both communal and individual?

UNIT 2

CHAPTER 5
Confirmation

WILL I FEEL DIFFERENT AFTER I'M CONFIRMED?

SNAPSHOT

Article 18
The Holy Spirit among Us

The Holy Spirit is with us. As followers of Jesus and members of the Church, we know this. Our study of the Sacrament of Confirmation gives us the opportunity to learn more about the Holy Spirit, the Third Person of the Trinity, who lives within the heart of the Church and within the heart of every Christian. The Holy Spirit is with us and in us, for "You are in the spirit, if only the Spirit of God dwells in you" (Romans 8:9).

The prophet Ezekiel was one of the most influential prophets in the history of Israel and in the history of our salvation. When the Jews were exiled to Babylon, Ezekiel went with them and prophesied the fall of Jerusalem. Yet, amid this great loss, Ezekiel prophesied a renewal of life and a new covenant with God that has only come about through Jesus Christ. Think back to the pre-read section from Ezekiel, chapter 37. One of Ezekiel's most profound visions demonstrates what the Holy Spirit does. Through his recounting of dry bones rattling together—standing joined together but without life—we understand that he could prophesy to the bones (the people), but nothing would change if they weren't filled with the Holy Spirit. But when the Lord tells Ezekiel to prophesy to the bones (the people) and call on the Holy Spirit to breathe life into them, they come alive!

Why is the image of dry, rattling bones helpful for the Israelites to understand the effect of being filled with the Holy Spirit?

[The Lord] said to me: "Son of man, these bones are the whole house of Israel! They are saying, 'Our bones are dried up, our hope is lost, and we are cut off.' Therefore, prophesy and say to them: Thus says the Lord God: Look! I am going to open your graves; I will make you come up out of your graves, my people, and bring you back to the land of Israel. . . . You may come to life, and I will settle you in your land. Then you shall know that I am the Lord. I have spoken; I will do it—oracle of the Lord." (Ezekiel 37:11–14)

In English, the words *wind*, *breath*, and *spirit* have three different meanings. Hebrew has only one word for all three meanings: *ruah*. In the passage from Ezekiel, we see all three meanings of the word *ruah* come into play. Ezekiel cries out, "Thus says the Lord God: From the four winds come, O breath, and breathe into these slain that they may come to life" (verse 9). In the prophet's vision, the bones scattered across the battlefield are the exiled People of God, who have experienced the "death" of defeat and humiliation. God promises that the Spirit *(Ruah)* of God (see verse 14) will bring the people of Israel back from the Exile and restore them to their land.

Where death abounds, the Holy Spirit brings life. Where there is loss and confusion, the Holy Spirit guides and clarifies. Where despair settles in, the Holy Spirit brings hope—not a vain and empty hope, but a hope based on the sure promises of the Lord.

TAKE IT TO GOD

Heavenly King, Consoler Spirit, Spirit of Truth, present everywhere and filling all things, treasure of all good and source of all life, come dwell in us, cleanse and save us, you who are All-Good. Amen. (CCC, number 2671)

The Promise of a Messiah

Another significant prophet, Isaiah, prophesied that from the family of David would come a Messiah upon whom the Spirit of God would rest:

But a shoot shall sprout from the stump of Jesse,
and from his roots a bud shall blossom.
The spirit of the LORD shall rest upon him:
a spirit of wisdom and of understanding,

A spirit of counsel and of strength,
    a spirit of knowledge and of fear of the LORD,
    and his delight shall be the fear of the LORD.
                     (Isaiah 11:1–3)

Centuries passed. Then an angel, a messenger of God, visited a young woman, Mary of Nazareth, and told her she had been chosen to be the mother of the Messiah, the Son of the Most High God. The angel said: "The holy Spirit will come upon you, and the power of the Most High will overshadow you. Therefore the child to be born will be called holy, the Son of God" (Luke 1:35). Jesus was conceived of the Holy Spirit and was in total communion with the Holy Spirit throughout his entire life and mission.

UNIT 2

The angel Gabriel visits Mary. This is called the Annunciation.

After the baptism of Jesus in the Jordan River, John the Baptist said of Jesus: "I saw the Spirit come down like a dove from the sky and remain upon him. I did not know him, but the one who sent me to baptize with water told me, 'On whomever you see the Spirit come down and remain, he is the one who will baptize with the holy Spirit.' Now I have seen and testified that he is the Son of God" (John 1:32–34).

John the Baptist knew the prophecies of Isaiah and Ezekiel. He recognized that Jesus was the Son of God and the hoped-for Messiah because the Holy Spirit came down from the Father, rested upon Jesus, and remained upon Jesus. After Jesus' Resurrection, the Father and the Son would send the Holy Spirit, the Giver of Life, upon the Church.

The Promise of the Holy Spirit

At the Last Supper, Jesus prepared his Apostles for what was to come. He promised that he would not leave them orphans. Jesus said, "I will ask the Father, and he will give you another Advocate to be with you always, the Spirit of truth" (John 14:16–17). An *advocate*, Jesus' word for the Holy Spirit, is someone who speaks up for you, someone who is on your side in conflict, someone who is a trusted helper and advisor.

In the Gospel of Luke, immediately before the Ascension of Jesus, the disciples were gathered in Jerusalem. Jesus appeared among them, and told them, "And [behold] I am sending the promise of my Father upon you; but stay in the city until you are clothed with power from on high" (Luke 24:49). Here Jesus names the Holy Spirit in two ways: "the promise of my Father" and "the power from on high."

You read the account of this promise and the demonstration of the power of the Holy Spirit in the pre-read Scripture excerpt Acts 2:1–41. This account describes how the Holy Spirit came upon the Apostles and disciples, with Mary, the Mother of the Lord, as they were gathered in prayer on the fiftieth day after Passover, the day called Pentecost. (*Pente* is the Greek word for "fifty.") The sound of a strong, driving wind filled the entire house. Tongues as of fire came to rest on each of them. And they were all filled with the Holy Spirit.

The Holy Spirit had an immediate effect upon the small group of believers. They left the house and began to proclaim the Good News in different tongues. Because Pentecost was a harvest festival, many Jews had come from different areas to celebrate the feast in Jerusalem. Noticing this group of people that was speaking in tongues, they were "confused because each one heard them speaking in his own language" (Acts of the Apostles 2:6). Those who believed and were baptized received the same Holy Spirit that had been given to the Apostles.

Wind, fire, and "different tongues" are all signs of the presence of the Holy Spirit. Like wind, the presence of the Holy Spirit can be strong or gentle. Like wind, the Holy Spirit is not seen, but his effects can be powerful. Like fire, the Holy Spirit purifies us and leads us through darkness by his eternal light. Like ecstatic tongues of prayer, the Holy Spirit can be heard in many languages and in many ways. At Pentecost, the Holy Spirit led the Church, then a small band of believers, into the mission mandated by Jesus Christ: to bring the Good News of salvation to the entire world.

The Charismatic Renewal

In the last half-century, a movement characterized by an openness to the *charisms*, or Gifts, of the Holy Spirit documented in the New Testament has grown among Catholics. These included the gift of miracles and the gift of tongues (see *CCC*, number 2003)—that is, the gift of praising God in a language unknown to the speaker. Other charismatic gifts are the interpretation of tongues, prophecy, discernment of spirits, and healing.

Pope Benedict XVI, addressing international leaders of the Catholic Charismatic Movement in 2008, spoke of charisms as "visible signs of the coming of the Holy Spirit" and noted that a positive element of the movement is its emphasis on the outpouring of the Spirit's gifts in the world today. Pope Benedict spoke also of the need for the authenticity of charisms to be discerned by pastors and for charismatic communities to safeguard their Catholic identities and remain closely bonded to the bishops and the Pope.

At a charismatic prayer meeting, you will find spontaneous prayer, readings from Scripture, prayer in tongues, and spontaneous song. Yet, the process of the meeting is free-flowing and orderly. Many find that charismatic prayer helps them to live their lives with more joy and peace.

The purpose of every gift of the Holy Spirit, including the charismatic gifts, is to build up the Church. We can be sure that the Holy Spirit works in each of us for a good purpose, no matter what our own particular gifts might be (see 1 Corinthians 12:7). And, as Saint Paul reminds us, of all the Gifts, "the greatest of these is love" (13:13). ✳

Charismatic prayer can include spontaneous prayer and songs, praying in tongues, and praise motions such as raising hands in prayer.

UNIT 2

© aldomurillo / istockphoto.com

HMMMMMMM. . . Which image of the Holy Spirit speaks more strongly to you: fire or wind?

Article 19

Confirmation: East and West

"The wind blows where it wills, and you can hear the sound it makes, but you do not know where it comes from or where it goes; so it is with everyone who is born of the Spirit" (John 3:8).

These words of Jesus, spoken to Nicodemus, a religious leader, sum up the way the Holy Spirit works. Under the influence of the Holy Spirit, the Church has grown and developed throughout history, influencing and transforming the complicated web of human cultures, and from within those diverse cultures, bringing humanity into a sacred encounter with Christ.

The history of the **Sacrament of Confirmation** reflects this involvement in different cultures that accounts for differing practices in the Eastern Churches and the Western (Latin) Church. You will recall that Christian initiation is accomplished in the three Sacraments of Christian Initiation (Baptism, Confirmation, and the Eucharist) together. Baptism begins new life, Confirmation strengthens that new life, and the Eucharist nourishes new Christian life through the transforming power of the Body and Blood of Christ.

I DIDN'T KNOW THAT!

In the early centuries, a "double anointing" after Baptism was the custom in the Roman Church. The priest who baptized also anointed the neophyte upon coming out of the baptismal pool. This anointing was followed by a second anointing from the bishop. The first anointing with Sacred Chrism, by the priest, is still part of the Baptism of children. This anointing is the sign of the participation of the newly baptized in the prophetic, priestly, and kingly office of Christ. Today, when an adult is baptized and confirmed, the first anointing is omitted and only the postbaptismal anointing, that of Confirmation, is performed (see CCC, number 1291).

Confirmation, Sacrament of ➤ With Baptism and the Eucharist, one of the three Sacraments of Christian Initiation. Through an outpouring of the special Gifts of the Holy Spirit, Confirmation perfects and strengthens the graces received in Baptism and gives a unique outpouring of the Spirit for Christian witness.

In the first centuries of the Church, Confirmation was celebrated following Baptism in the same liturgy, and the bishop was the ordinary minister of Confirmation. Gradually, due to the increased number of infant Baptisms, the distance between parishes, and the growth of large dioceses, it became more and more difficult for the bishop to be present at every Baptism. The response to this situation differed in the East and the West. In the West, Confirmation ("the completion of Baptism" [*CCC*, number 1290]) was delayed until the bishop could be present. This remains the usual practice today in the Latin Church. In the Churches of the East, the three sacraments were never separated. Because the sacred oil used at Confirmation, called *myron*, which means "chrism," had been consecrated by the bishop, the link to the bishop was maintained. And so today, in the Eastern Churches, Confirmation immediately follows Baptism and is administered by the priest. Reception of the Eucharist follows (even for infants).

This child was baptized and chrismated (or confirmed) and is receiving the Eucharist. All communicants in the Eastern Churches receive the Body (a small piece) and Blood of Christ together from a spoon.

The Age of Confirmation

The Church mandates that a candidate for Confirmation must have reached the age of reason (age seven). In the United States, the age of Confirmation has been set by the United States Conference of Catholic Bishops as between the age of discretion (about seven) and about sixteen years of age. An individual bishop can set a specific age within this range for his diocese. Some dioceses have adopted the "restored order" of receiving the sacraments: first Baptism, then Confirmation, and last, the Eucharist. In this order, a baptized child who has reached the age of reason will receive Confirmation followed by First Communion in the same liturgy. Administering the sacraments in this order emphasizes the Eucharist as the culmination of Christian initiation.

How old were you when you were confirmed?

The Bishop as Sign

Both the Western (Latin) Church and the Eastern Churches, in their practice of the Sacraments of Christian Initiation, reflect profound truths about the Church. The practice of the Eastern Churches emphasizes the unity of Baptism, Confirmation, and the Eucharist. The practice of reserving Confirmation to the bishop in the Latin Church emphasizes that the sacrament strengthens the communion of the newly confirmed with the bishop and highlights the connection of the sacrament with the apostolic origins of the Church. Why is this communion with the bishop so important? The bishop is a sign that the Church is truly one (unified), catholic (universal), and apostolic (descended from the Apostles). Every bishop was ordained by a bishop who was ordained by a bishop who was ordained by a bishop and so on. This line can be traced back to the Apostles, the ones whom Jesus chose to lead his Church at the beginning. This is called *Apostolic Succession*. **Apostolic Succession** is sacramental, handed on through the laying on of hands in the Sacrament of Holy Orders.

The Minister of Confirmation

In the Latin Church, as we have seen, the Sacraments of Baptism and Confirmation became separated. With the restoration of the catechumenate, when adults and children who have reached the age of reason are baptized, Confirmation is administered immediately after Baptism, followed by reception of the Eucharist. In the Latin Church, the bishop is the ordinary minister of Confirmation; however, when the need arises, he may grant a priest permission to administer the sacrament. This is often the case at the Easter Vigil. If someone is in danger of death, however, any priest can administer Confirmation: "Indeed the Church desires that none of her children, even the youngest, should depart this world without having been perfected by the Holy Spirit with the gift of Christ's fullness" (*CCC*, number 1314). ✳

Every bishop is ordained by a bishop. Bishops are the ordinary ministers of Confirmation.

UNIT 2

HMMMMMM. . .

Which makes more sense to you, celebrating Confirmation and First Eucharist together or having them separated? Why?

Apostolic Succession ➤ The uninterrupted passing on of apostolic preaching and authority from the Apostles directly to all bishops. It is accomplished through the laying on of hands when a bishop is ordained in the Sacrament of Holy Orders as instituted by Christ. The office of bishop is permanent, because at ordination a bishop is marked with an indelible, sacred character.

Article 20
Confirmation

In the Book of the Prophet Joel, we find a wonderful description of the work of the Holy Spirit:

> It shall come to pass
> > I will pour out my spirit upon all flesh.
> Your sons and daughters will prophesy,
> > your old men will dream dreams,
> > your young men will see visions.
> Even upon your male and female servants,
> > in those days, I will pour out my spirit.
> I will set signs in the heavens and on the earth.
> > (Joel 3:1–3)

© Paolo Gallo / Shutterstock.com

This stained-glass window portraying the Holy Spirit is the window over the main altar at the Basilica of Saint Peter in Rome. Why do you think this window is appropriate for this papal basilica?

This prophecy, fulfilled at Pentecost, is again fulfilled at every Confirmation. The effects of the Holy Spirit, which we discuss in more detail in the next article, are not always dramatic. But they are real, for, as Jesus told his disciples, the Father in Heaven will always give the Holy Spirit to those who ask (see Luke 11:13).

Who, then, is eligible to receive the Sacrament of Confirmation? We have already discussed that a candidate for Baptism must be within the required age range. The candidate must also do the following:

- profess the faith
- be in the state of grace
- desire to receive the sacrament
- intend to live as a disciple of Christ and a witness to the faith, both within the Church and in the world

Preparing for Confirmation

If you have been confirmed, think back to the time of preparation before receiving the sacrament. The preparation sessions, retreat, and activities with your sponsor were meant to lead you into a deeper relationship with Christ and encourage a "lively familiarity" with the Holy Spirit (see *CCC*, number 1309).

Why do you think prayerful discernment is an important part of the process of being confirmed?

UNIT 2

© Freedom Studio / Shutterstock.com

Perhaps you or some of your fellow candidates were uncertain as you began the preparation process. Receiving the Sacrament of Confirmation is a big commitment, so you were encouraged to spend time reflecting and praying about taking this important step. This process of prayerful decision-making is called **discernment**. The leaders of your preparation classes were there to encourage you in your discernment process, and explain that learning about the teachings of the Church is key in making the commitment to be confirmed. You were likely encouraged to receive the Sacrament of Penance and Reconcil-iation in order to be prepared for the Gift of the Holy Spirit. By the time you were confirmed, you were expected to know what you were saying yes to. You were also encouraged to know the Holy Spirit, recognize him at work in his actions and gifts, and be willing to follow his inspirations. The world we live in does not make following Christ easy. Thankfully, the Holy Spirit is there to help us with his gifts of grace, courage, and love.

Do you remember how you decided to ask someone to be your sponsor? Though many times candidates choose a relative or family friend, it is also appropriate for the sponsor to be one of the candidate's godparents if possible. The connection between godparent and sponsor helps to emphasize the unity of Baptism and Confirmation. Whomever you chose as a sponsor, their role was to be an important part of guiding you through the process, supporting you and answering any questions that came up outside the preparation sessions. Your sponsor is called to continue to be a model for how to live out your faith in your everyday life, as well as participate in weekly Mass and the sacraments.

Celebrating the Order

In a sense, Confirmation begins before the actual celebration of the sacrament. At the Chrism Mass celebrated during Holy Week, the bishop consecrates the Sacred Chrism and shares it with all the parishes in his diocese. This is in itself a significant action that is, in a certain way, a part of the Sacrament of Confir-mation.

The celebration of the actual Order of Confirmation is as follows: "As a rule, Confirmation takes place within a Mass so that the fundamental connec-tion of this Sacrament with all of Christian Initiation, which reaches its culmi-nation in the Communion of the Body and Blood of Christ, may stand out in a clearer light" (*The Order of Confirmation*, number 13). The celebration includes the following elements.

---

discernment ➤ From a Latin word meaning "to separate or to distinguish between," the practice of listening for God's call in our lives and distinguishing between good and bad choices.

Introductory Rites

As does every other liturgy, the Sacrament of Confirmation begins with the gathering of the assembly. Candidates, sponsors, families, and other members of the community gather in the designated church. Candidates often process into the church with the bishop, the parish priests, and the other liturgical ministers.

The Liturgy of the Word

The explanatory notes for *The Order of Confirmation* inform us that the celebration of the Word should be given a lot of emphasis because it is through the Word of God that the Holy Spirit flows out upon the Church and upon each one of the baptized and confirmed (see number 13). Through the hearing of God's Word, we learn his will for us, and in the Holy Spirit, we are strengthened to carry it out.

Presentation of the Candidates

The pastor, deacon, or catechist presents the candidates to the bishop, usually by the calling of names. Each candidate stands or, if possible, comes individually to the sanctuary. (If the candidates are children, they are accompanied by one of their sponsors or parents.)

UNIT 2

MAKE IT SO

"If we live in the Spirit, let us also follow the Spirit" (Galatians 5:25).

Here are a few ideas to help you follow the Spirit.

Helpfulness: The Holy Spirit is our Advocate or Helper.
Openness: How can you open your life to the Holy Spirit today?
Love: Which kind of love can you live today?
Youth: How can your life be an example for others to follow?

Scriptures: Find a Scripture passage that gives you hope. Write it down and put it where you will see it often.
Prayer and praise: Pray Psalm 150. Try setting it to music!
Indwelling: Be open to the leading of the Holy Spirit today.
Righteousness, justice: What does the Lord ask of you today?
Intercession: What is your need today?
Truth: What truth can you live by today?

UNIT 2

Homily or Instruction

The bishop gives a brief Homily. *The Order of Confirmation* suggests that the following ideas, among others, be included in these remarks:

> Therefore, you who are already baptized will now receive the power of his Spirit and be signed with his Cross on your foreheads. And so, you must always bear witness to his Passion and Resurrection before the world, so that your manner of life, as the Apostle says, may be in every place the pleasing fragrance of Christ. His Mystical Body, which is the Church, the People of God, receives from him diverse graces, which the same Holy Spirit distributes to individuals for the building up of that Body in unity and love. (Number 22)

Renewal of Baptismal Promises

When Confirmation is celebrated separately from Baptism (which is usually the case in the Latin Church), the liturgy includes the renewal of baptismal promises. The renewal of baptismal promises helps to express the close relationship between Confirmation and Baptism. In these promises, the candidates renounce Satan and sin, and profess their faith in God.

What does it mean to respond "I do" to rejecting Satan, all his works, and empty promises? It means rejecting sin. Like the early Christians, we promise to turn away from the darkness of sin and to turn toward the light—the light of Christ. This decision must be affirmed daily because the opportunities—temptations—to cooperate with Satan, his works, and his empty promises are endless.

Rejecting Satan does not mean we will never sin, but it does mean that each day we must make an effort to live as a disciple of Christ. With the help of God's love and grace, we will realize when we are heading into the darkness and turn around once again to walk in the light of Christ.

In addition to the rejection of sin, the renewal of baptismal promises addresses other core aspects of our faith and asks us to affirm our belief. It ends this way:

> Bishop: This is our faith. This is the faith of the Church. We are proud to profess it in Christ Jesus our Lord.
>
> The gathering of the faithful gives its assent by replying: Amen.
>
> *(The Order of Confirmation*, number 23)

The Laying On of Hands

The laying on of hands has been a sign of the descent of the Holy Spirit since the time of the Apostles. This laying on of hands communicates the grace of Pentecost in the Church. The bishop extends his hands over the candidate and alone sings or says a prayer, asking the Father to send the Holy Spirit upon the candidates to be their guide and helper. He prays: "Give them the spirit of wisdom and understanding, the spirit of counsel and fortitude, the spirit of knowledge and piety; fill them with the spirit of the fear of the Lord" (*The Order of Confirmation*, number 25).

This laying on of hands is significant, even though it is not the action by which Confirmation is conferred. It is a vital expression of the Church's prayer. It also makes Confirmation more complete and contributes to a deeper understanding of the sacrament (see *The Order of Confirmation*, number 9).

UNIT 2

During Confirmation, the bishop makes the Sign of the Cross on the forehead of each candidate with Sacred Chrism.

The Anointing with Sacred Chrism

Early in the development of the Sacrament of Confirmation, the anointing with Sacred Chrism was added to the laying on of hands. You may remember that the title Christ means "anointed one." So does the derivative title that we bear, Christian.

In the East, with the anointing, the formula for the words is, "The seal of the gift of the Holy Spirit." The sacrament is called, from the name of this anointing, Chrismation.

In the West, the formula for the words is "Be sealed with the Gift of the Holy Spirit." The Western term, *Confirmation*, defines this sacrament as confirming and strengthening baptismal grace. Thus "the essential rite of Confirmation is anointing the forehead with sacred chrism (in the East other sense-organs as well), together with the laying on of the minister's hand and the words" (*CCC*, number 1320).

In the celebration of the sacrament, the candidate stands before the bishop. The sponsor of the candidate stands near, with their right hand on the candidate's shoulder. Either the candidate or the sponsor says the name of the candidate. The bishop dips his right thumb into the Sacred Chrism and makes the Sign of the Cross on the forehead of the candidate. The celebration then continues as follows:

> The bishop dips the tip of the thumb of his right hand in the Chrism and, with the thumb, makes the Sign of the Cross on the forehead of the one to be confirmed as he says:
>
> N., be sealed with the GIFT OF THE HOLY SPIRIT.
>
> The newly confirmed responds: Amen.
>
> The bishop adds: Peace be with you.
>
> The newly confirmed: And with your spirit.
>
> (*The Order of Confirmation*, number 27)

The Holy Spirit is poured out, with all his gifts, once again.

The Prayer of the Faithful

After all have been confirmed, the Prayer of the Faithful follows. In this prayer, we pray for the newly confirmed, for their parents and godparents, for the Church, for all people of every race and nation, and that the work of the Holy Spirit, begun in the Church at Pentecost, be continued in the hearts of all who believe (see *The Order of Confirmation*, number 30).

The Liturgy of the Eucharist

When the Sacrament of Confirmation is celebrated within the Mass, the celebration continues with the Liturgy of the Eucharist. The Profession of Faith (the Creed) is omitted, as this profession was made in the renewal of baptismal promises. Some of the newly confirmed may be asked to join in bringing the gifts of bread and wine to the altar.

Great importance is attached to the praying of the Lord's Prayer, "because it is the Spirit who prays in us and in the Spirit the Christian says, 'Abba, Father'" (*The Order of Confirmation*, number 13).

Celebrating the Sacrament of Confirmation within the Mass links Confirmation to Christian initiation as a whole, which "reaches its culmination in the Communion of the Body and Blood of Christ" (*The Order of Confirmation*, number 13). At the end of the Eucharistic celebration, a special blessing is prayed over the people, asking the Father, the Son, and the Holy Spirit to give special gifts of love, courage, and faith to the newly confirmed and to the entire assembly. The bishop then blesses the entire assembly.

The Character of Confirmation: Marked for Life

Like Baptism, the Sacrament of Confirmation imprints a spiritual mark, an indelible character, on the soul. This means that this sacrament is so unique that, like Baptism, it can be received only once in a lifetime. This character is permanent.

Another term for this mark or character is seal of the Holy Spirit. A seal is an identifier. It is like a brand mark, like a seal on a letterhead or diploma, or like the embossed seal you find on documents that have been certified by a notary public. These seals show that the documents are real and authentic. Jesus Christ marks us with the seal of the Holy Spirit so that we may be his witnesses through the power of the Holy Spirit. The Sacred Chrism is the sign of this seal.

UNIT 2

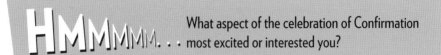

HMMMMM. . . What aspect of the celebration of Confirmation most excited or interested you?

Article 21
Life in the Holy Spirit

The Prophet Elijah was afraid for his life. He had spoken out against the false god Baal, and the prophets of that god were seeking to kill him. He hid in a cave on Mount Horeb, where the Lord found him and said, "Go out and stand on the mountain before the Lord; the Lord will pass by." The account continues:

> There was a strong and violent wind rending the mountains and crushing rocks before the LORD—but the LORD was not in the wind; after the wind, an earthquake—but the LORD was not in the earthquake; after the earthquake, fire—but the LORD was not in the fire; after the fire, a light silent sound.
>
> When he heard this, Elijah hid his face in his cloak and went and stood at the entrance of the cave. (1 Kings 19:11–13)

Elijah recognized the Lord in "a tiny whispering sound." Yes, the Holy Spirit can come in wind and earthquake and fire—but most of the time, we can recognize the Holy Spirit in the tiny whisperings of our hearts, in the inspirations for good that come to us and will not let us rest until we act on them. The Holy Spirit is with us, as baptized and confirmed Christians, as we strive to be "imitators of God, as beloved children, and live in love, as Christ loved us" (Ephesians 5:1–2).

© Brian Singer-Towns / Saint Mary's Press

The prophet Elijah brings down fire from Heaven. This mural is found in the Elijah Chapel in the Church of the Transfiguration in Israel. There is also a Moses Chapel in this church. Do you know why?

Gifts and Responsibilities

The greatest and overarching effect of Confirmation is "the special outpouring of the Holy Spirit as once granted to the apostles on the day of Pentecost" (*CCC*, number 1302). At Confirmation, we gather in prayer, with the Apostles; with Mary, the Mother of God; and with all the angels and saints. In answer to that prayer, the Holy Spirit comes to us in the anointing, the laying on of hands, and the words of the bishop. The Sacrament of Confirmation strengthens and confirms the graces and Gifts of the Holy Spirit received in Baptism. And with the sacrament come its effects and responsibilities, which will last the rest of our lives. What are these effects and responsibilities? The Sacrament of Confirmation does the following for us:

- It gives us the Holy Spirit to root us more deeply in the divine filiation— that is, in our adoption as sons and daughters of God. The Holy Spirit will lead and guide us: "For those who are led by the Spirit of God are children of God. For you did not receive a spirit of slavery to fall back into fear, but you received a spirit of adoption, through which we cry, '*Abba,* Father!'" (Romans 8:14–15).
- It unites us more firmly to Christ.
- It increases the Gifts of the Holy Spirit in us.
- It strengthens our relationship with the Church.
- It involves us more deeply in the Church's mission of bringing the Good News of salvation to all people.
- It helps us to bear witness to our faith through our words and actions.

(See *CCC*, number 1303)

UNIT 2

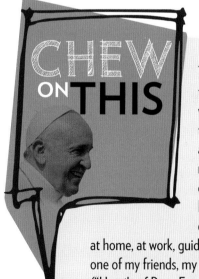

CHEW ON THIS

The Holy Spirit is truly transforming us, and through us he also wants to transform the world in which we live. Let us open the doors to the Spirit, let ourselves be guided by him, and allow God's constant help to make us new men and women, inspired by the love of God which the Holy Spirit bestows on us! How beautiful it would be if each of you, every evening, could say: Today at school, at home, at work, guided by God, I showed a sign of love towards one of my friends, my parents, an older person! How beautiful! ("Homily of Pope Francis," Saint Peter's Square, April 28, 2013)

UNIT 2

Gifts and Fruits of the Holy Spirit

All the Sacraments of Christian Initiation are great gifts and carry great responsibilities. Saint Paul asks us, "Do you not know that your body is a temple of the holy Spirit within you, whom you have from God, and that you are not your own?" (1 Corinthians 6:19). We are not to be sponges, simply absorbing all the graces and blessings of the sacraments; we are to be fountains, spreading the gift of life we have received—in service to others, and ready to give an answer in defense or explanation of our faith (always gently) when that is asked of us.

But we always have the help of the Holy Spirit. Throughout our lives, we are sustained by the Seven Gifts of the Holy Spirit:

Gifts of the Holy Spirit	What Do They Mean Today?
Wisdom	This gift helps us to make choices and give leadership according to God's will.
Understanding	This gift helps us to know and comprehend the mysteries and teachings of our faith more clearly. Understanding inspires us to a more active faith life.
Right Judgment (Counsel)	This gift helps us to learn how we can best please God. It is especially necessary for those in positions of leadership, such as parents, teachers, political leaders, and even just as citizens.
Courage (Fortitude)	This gift is the courage to do what we know is right. We can overcome our fear, anxiety, and shyness to do what we know is God's will.
Knowledge	The gift to have a comprehensive understanding of spiritual issues or circumstances. Guided by the gift of Knowledge, we value our relationship with God beyond all else.
Reverence (Piety)	This gift infuses reverence for God into our souls. In piety, we are moved to love others as children of God.
Wonder and Awe (Fear of the Lord)	This gift allows us to take in the greatness of God and his creation; and in doing so, we are filled with the desire to honor God. Our hearts are filled with the desire to be sure our words and actions are pleasing to God.

These are messianic gifts that Christ has in all their fullness, and, in the Holy Spirit, they are shared with us (see Isaiah 11:1–2.) These gifts are not to be kept unopened on a shelf. Instead, they are to be opened and used every day, in every need and every situation that affects ourselves or others.

When we "live by the Spirit" (Galatians 5:16), the fruits of the Holy Spirit begin to show up in our lives. These fruits are charity, joy, peace, patience, kindness, goodness, generosity, gentleness, faithfulness, modesty, self-control, and chastity. These qualities or characteristics are called fruits because they are the results of growth in Christ, the results of following the Holy Spirit's "tiny whispering sound" each day. They are also called fruits because they are the "firstfruits" of eternal life: They are a small taste of what Heaven will be like, and as such, they give us a bit of Heaven on Earth.

What do these gifts and fruits look like in our everyday lives? And when the fruits of the Holy Spirit grow in us, how can we share them with others? In cooperating with the grace of the Holy Spirit, you might find yourself being more joyful, more peaceful, less judgmental, or more patient with others.

When we allow the Holy Spirit to work through us, we might find some untapped compassion for our classmates who are difficult to get along with, or siblings who might usually annoy us. Because you are taking time to pray a little more sincerely, you might be surprised when your kindness helps someone else through a rough moment. Asking the help of the Holy Spirit might mean you grow in controlling your temper, and you may discover that a little self-control on your part can keep a situation from escalating or getting out of hand. Little by little, with the grace of the Holy Spirit, you are being transformed. You are becoming more true to yourself. You are becoming all that God meant you to be. And he will say of you:

What do the fruits and Gifts of the Holy Spirit look like in your everyday life?

> See, I am doing something new!
> Now it springs forth, do you not perceive it?
> In the wilderness I make a way,
> in the wasteland, rivers.
>
> (Isaiah 43:19)

Walk, therefore, in newness of life! ✳

UNIT 2

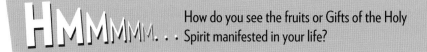

HMMMMMM. . . How do you see the fruits or Gifts of the Holy Spirit manifested in your life?

Article 22

Discernment of God's Will

All through life, we discern (or find) the will of God for us. We want to know his will in big things, such as our choice of a **vocation** in life, and in smaller things too, such as whether to allow a friendship to grow, which part-time job to take, or whether to try out for a sports team or the school play or something else altogether. But first, let's stop and ask: Does God really care?

Of course God cares. He created you with gifts and talents, and he wants you to use them. God wants you to be happy in this life, as well as in the next. Often you may find that the way is clear. You are able to go from one decision to another in peace and with no regrets. At other times, however, things can get cloudy. You may feel stuck and not know what to do in a particular situation. At those times especially, the help of the Holy Spirit can clear a path for you and help you to see your way to the right decision—one that is right for your life and for your relationship with God.

What decisions are you discerning, if not now then in the immediate future? Who can help you sort out the possibilities you will meet on the road ahead?

As we seek to discern what is right for our lives, the Church offers us certain helps, or guiding principles, to lead us. If we use these principles, or practices, we are more likely to find the right path, to "walk in the Holy Spirit," and to discover God's will for us. Let's explore four of these practices:

---

vocation ➤ A universal call from God, rooted in our Baptism, to all members of the Church to embrace a life of holiness. Specifically, it refers to a call to live the holy life as an ordained minister, as a vowed religious (sister or brother), or in a Christian marriage. Single life that involves a personal consecration or commitment to a public, permanent, celibate gift of self to God and one's neighbor is also a vocational state.

1. **Know and pray with the Sacred Scriptures.** One of the best ways to learn Scripture is to listen carefully during the liturgy. The liturgy is a scriptural treasury, and anyone who listens well at the Mass and the other sacraments, to the readings and the Homily, will find that their knowledge of the Word of God will grow, with the help of the Holy Spirit. As you listen, try to catch a few words or phrases you can take with you. Saint Jerome (345–420), one of the Fathers and Doctors of the Church, once wrote, "Ignorance of the Scriptures is ignorance of Christ." In other words, the more we know Scripture, the more confident we can be that we are following the way of Christ.

2. **Live the sacraments.** Participate regularly in the Eucharist and in the Sacrament of Penance and Reconciliation in a conscious and active way. Your involvement in the liturgy will lead to renewed life in the Holy Spirit, fuller participation in the mission of the Church, and more dedicated service to all in a spirit of unity and love.

3. **Love the Catholic Church, the Church that Christ began.** In his Letter to the Ephesians, Saint Paul urges husbands to love their wives "even as Christ loved the church and handed himself over for her to sanctify her, cleansing her by the bath of water with the word, that he might present to himself the church in splendor, without spot or wrinkle or any such thing, that she might be holy and without blemish" (5:25–27). The Church is Christ's own Body, the Temple of the Holy Spirit, and

CATHOLICS MAKING A DIFFERENCE

Think about the men and women in your life and their chosen vocational states. The priest at your parish, the religious sister who works at the retirement center, the married couples you know. Each one of them went through a serious period of discernment before choosing their vocational state of life. They do not make these choices lightly. Discerning your own vocation involves prayer, guidance, a desire to live to the potential God created us with, and the help of the Holy Spirit. When you are ready to seek your calling, look to these men and women as your examples.

God's people, of which we are all members. Loving the Church does not mean excusing the sins of its members, but it does mean helping to heal the consequences of those sins. Loving the Church means loving its members, from the Pope in Rome to the parishioner in the next pew, and working to help the Church grow throughout the world to bring salvation to all people.

4. **Pray to the Holy Spirit to know God's will and to follow Christ.**
Our greatest prayer is the liturgy, in which we participate in Christ's own prayer to the Father in the Holy Spirit. Even when we pray in private, we are participating in the great prayer of Christ's Body, the Church. Whenever we take the opportunity to pray, we are praying "in the Spirit," for it is the Holy Spirit who prays within us: "In the same way, the Spirit too comes to the aid of our weakness; for we do not know how to pray as we ought, but the Spirit itself intercedes with inexpressible groanings" (Romans 8:26). We may not know what God's will is; we may not even know what to pray for. But the Holy Spirit knows, and he prays within us for all that we need, whether or not we know how to name our need.

© Monkey Business Images / Shutterstock.com

You can rely on the guidance of a parent, teacher, school counselor, priest, youth minister, or another trusted adult when making important decisions in your life.

The Body of Christ

As members of the Body of Christ, we have access to the counsel of others as we seek the right path. In addition to following the guiding principles just listed, it is always a good idea, when seeking God's will and making any important decision, to seek the advice of someone who, as a follower of Christ, also seeks to be faithful to the inspirations of the Holy Spirit. That person could be a parent, a teacher, a school counselor, a priest or religious, or a catechist.

As the Holy Spirit leads us, one step at a time, along our Christian journey, we are not alone. We travel as part of the Church, as members of the Body of Christ, each one sharing our gifts with one another, "living the truth in love" (Ephesians 4:15). Therefore, we can rely on the guidance of other faithful followers of Christ to help us to discern God's will for our lives, whether it is in the big questions in life, such as knowing what vocation God is calling us to, or the smaller but still important ones, such as whether to continue a particular relationship or which service project to take part in.

UNIT 2

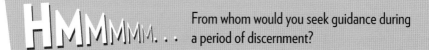

HMMMMMM. . . From whom would you seek guidance during a period of discernment?

1. Describe briefly what one of the prophets from the Old Testament prophesied about the Holy Spirit.

2. What were the signs of the presence of the Holy Spirit on Pentecost?

3. Name two differences in the Sacrament of Confirmation as administered in the Eastern Churches compared to the Western (Latin) Church.

4. What is Apostolic Succession?

5. Who is eligible for the Sacrament of Confirmation?

6. What is the meaning of the renewal of baptismal promises in Confirmation?

7. What are the essential elements of the Order of Confirmation?

8. What is the relationship between Baptism and Confirmation?

UNIT 2

ART STUDY

1. What symbols of the Holy Spirit do you see in this piece of artwork?

2. What feelings, questions, or impressions surface as you meditate on this art?

3. In what way is this portrayal of Pentecost similar to or different from other depictions you have seen?

UNIT 2 HIGHLIGHTS

CHAPTER 3   Baptism

Water and Baptism

The waters of Baptism remind us of these events that bring new life!

The Effects of Baptism

Die and Rise with Christ

Freed from Original and Personal Sin

Adopted Children of God

Member of the Church

Permanent Sacramental Character

Empowered for Discipleship

UNIT 2

CHAPTER 4   CONFIRMATION

The Sacraments of Initiation

Baptism   **Confirmation**   **Eucharist**

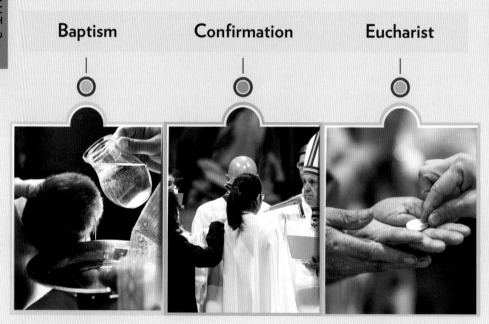

Stages of the RCIA

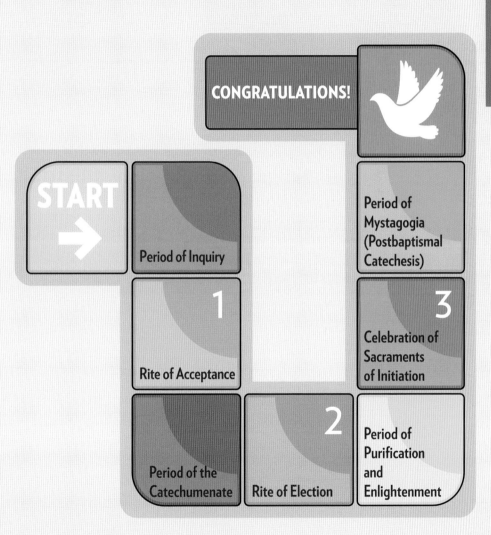

CONGRATULATIONS!

START →

Period of Inquiry

Period of Mystagogia (Postbaptismal Catechesis)

1

Rite of Acceptance

3

Celebration of Sacraments of Initiation

Period of the Catechumenate

2

Rite of Election

Period of Purification and Enlightenment

CHAPTER 5 Confirmation

The Holy Spirit = *Ruah*

Wind   Breath   Spirit

Images: Shutterstock.com

The Holy Spirit at Pentecost

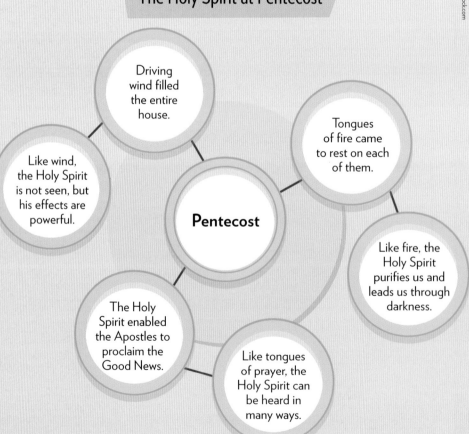

Driving wind filled the entire house.

Tongues of fire came to rest on each of them.

Like wind, the Holy Spirit is not seen, but his effects are powerful.

Pentecost

Like fire, the Holy Spirit purifies us and leads us through darkness.

The Holy Spirit enabled the Apostles to proclaim the Good News.

Like tongues of prayer, the Holy Spirit can be heard in many ways.

Confirmation: East and West

Confirmation in the East	Confirmation in the West
• Baptism, Confirmation, and Eucharist were never separated.	• Bishops could not be present for every infant Baptism. • Confirmation was delayed until the bishop could be present.
• The age of Confirmation can be as early as infancy. • Confirmation immediately follows Baptism and is administered by the priest. • Eucharist immediately follows, even for infants.	• The Church mandates that a candidate for Confirmation must have reached the age of reason (age seven).
• The Eastern Church emphasizes the unity of Baptism, Confirmation, and Eucharist.	• Confirmation by the bishop emphasizes that the sacrament strengthens the communion of the newly confirmed with the bishop.
• A priest or the bishop can preside over the sacrament.	• The ordinary minister of Confirmation is the bishop, but a priest can be given permission to administer the sacrament.

UNIT 2

Gifts of the Holy Spirit

Wisdom

Understanding

Right Judgment

Courage (Fortitude)

Knowledge

Reverence (Piety)

Wonder and Awe (Fear of the Lord)

Fruits of the Holy Spirit

Joy

Generosity

Peace

Charity

Modesty

Patience

Faithfulness

Self-Control

Chastity

Gentleness

Kindness

Goodness

UNIT 2
BRING IT HOME

WHY DO I NEED TO BE INITIATED INTO THE CHURCH?

FOCUS QUESTIONS

CHAPTER 3   Is Baptism really necessary?

CHAPTER 4   How do you join the Church as an adult?

CHAPTER 5   Will I feel different after I'm confirmed?

MIKE
Red Bank Catholic High School

After reading this unit, I think it's very important to be initiated into the Church. Through the three Sacraments of Initiation we receive many special graces. During the Sacrament of Baptism, we are adopted as God's sons and daughters. We are also freed from Original Sin. Through the Sacrament of Confirmation, we receive the special Gifts of the Holy Spirit. Additionally, we confirm the promises our parents and godparents made at our Baptism. Finally, through the Sacrament of Eucharist, we receive the Body and Blood of Christ. This connection with God is unique and tangible. I feel so strongly about being a part of my faith community that I hope everyone takes these steps to be in close union with God.

REFLECT

Take some time to read and reflect on the unit and chapter focus questions listed on the facing page.

- What question or section did you identify most closely with?

- What did you find within the unit that was comforting or challenging?

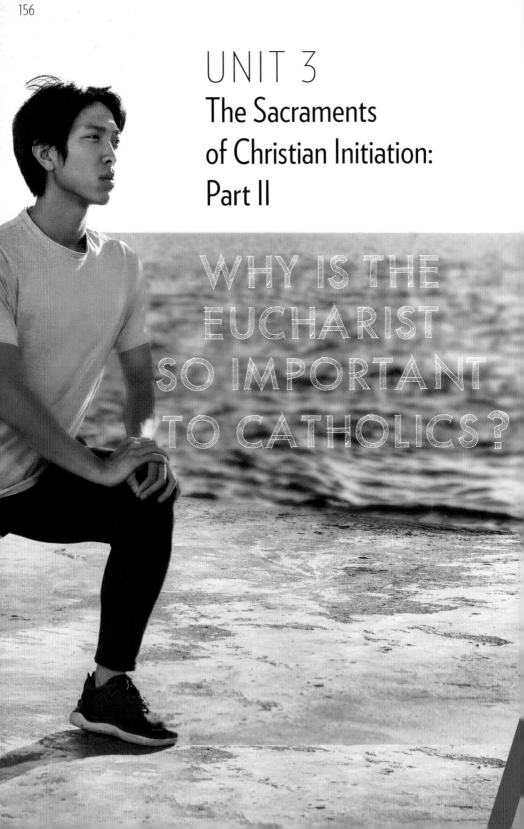

UNIT 3
The Sacraments of Christian Initiation: Part II

WHY IS THE EUCHARIST SO IMPORTANT TO CATHOLICS?

LOOKING AHEAD

UNIT 3

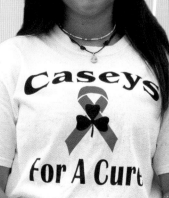

Many people look at the Eucharist as if it's just a circular piece of bread. In fact, it is so much more than that. The Eucharist is a symbol of God's covenant with us. The Eucharist is important to Catholics because it is our way of receiving Jesus' Body and Blood. It is a reminder that Jesus died for us and saved us from our sins. When I receive the Eucharist, I feel a stronger and closer bond to God.

VICTORIA
Red Bank Catholic High School

CHAPTER 6
The Eucharist: Culmination of Christian Initiation

WHAT IS THE EUCHARIST, AND WHERE DID IT COME FROM?

SNAPSHOT

Article 23

What Is the Eucharist?

The three Sacraments of Christian Initiation—Baptism, Confirmation, and **the Eucharist**—are in reality one movement, inserting us into the Paschal Mystery of Christ, into his **Passion**, death, Resurrection, and Ascension. Through the Sacraments of Christian Initiation, we begin the fullness of life in Christ.

The Eucharist is the culminating initiation sacrament, and the "source and summit"[1] (*Catechism of the Catholic Church [CCC]*, number 1324) of our life in Christ. In the Eucharist, Christ brings the Church and all of us, members of his Body, into his own sacrifice of thanksgiving and praise, offered to his Father once and for all on the cross. By this sacrifice (or offering), he pours out the graces of salvation upon his Body, the Church.

The Eucharist is the sign and cause of our union with Christ. As he did at the Last Supper, Christ gives us himself in the Eucharistic elements—his Body and Blood. As Christ becomes one with us, we become one with him. Our lives are caught up in the resurrected life of Christ.

UNIT 3

This icon of Christ is found in the dome of the Church of the Holy Sepulchre in Jerusalem, the church built on Calvary, the site of the Crucifixion.

Eucharist, the ➤ The celebration of the entire Mass. The term can also refer specifically to the consecrated bread and wine that have become the Body and Blood of Christ.

Passion ➤ The suffering of Jesus during his final days in this life: his agony in the garden at Gethsemane, his trial, and his Crucifixion.

TAKE IT TO GOD

God,
Thank you for this indescribable gift!
When I forget where I belong, Jesus is present in a tangible way.
When I am defeated, Jesus gives me reason to rejoice.
Today, I give thanks that through your mercy, Jesus became incarnate.
I am grateful that Jesus has redeemed me from sin and eternal death.
I count among my many blessings, the gift of participating in the
   Eucharist
where you are most clearly present to me.
Amen.

The Eucharist is the sacrament that makes present in the Mass the death and Resurrection of Christ. The Eucharist is "a sacrament of love, a sign of unity, a bond of charity, a Paschal banquet 'in which Christ is consumed, the mind is filled with grace, and a pledge of future glory is given to us'"[2] (*CCC*, number 1323). As food is essential for physical growth, the Eucharist is essential for spiritual growth and should be a central part of one's entire life as it strengthens the life of grace first received at Baptism. It nourishes Christ's life in us.

The Signs of Bread and Wine

At Mass, during the Preparation of the Gifts, we offer bread and wine. We give thanks to the Creator for these gifts, the fruits of the Earth as well as of human hands, not only because these gifts will soon become the Body and Blood of Christ but also because they are symbolic of all the gifts God has given to us.

Bread and wine have been significant throughout salvation history. In the Old Covenant, bread and wine were offered in thanksgiving to God as symbols of all his gifts. The offering of bread and wine of the priest Melchizedek (see Genesis 14:18) prefigures our own offering of bread and wine at the Eucharist (see *Roman Missal*, Eucharistic Prayer I). Bread, as a gift of God, took on a new meaning during the events of the Exodus. When fleeing from Egypt, the only bread the Jews could take with them was unleavened. Eating unleavened bread at the Passover became a symbol of God's faithfulness and the Jews' freedom. This was not the only time that bread sustained the Israelites. After they fled Egypt, when the people had nothing to eat in the desert, God sent bread from Heaven, called manna, to sustain them. Again, bread was a tangible sign of God's faithfulness and love (see Exodus, chapter 16).

Wine also had significant meaning in the Old Covenant. The drinking of wine, especially at "the cup of blessing," was a sharing of joyful anticipation of the coming of the Messiah in a New Jerusalem.

In the New Testament, Jesus' multiplication of the loaves and fish prefigures the Eucharist and recalls the manna of the desert. (You can compare the accounts in all four Gospels in the pre-read Scripture passages.) The people listening to Jesus were in a deserted place, with no markets nearby. Yet Jesus, the Son of God, gave his people bread—the miracle of loaves, like manna in the desert.

© Magdalena Kucova / Shutterstock.com

UNIT 3

The gifts of bread and wine are offered during the Preparation of the Gifts. Bread and wine have been significant throughout salvation history in the Old and New Testaments.

In the wedding at Cana, Jesus used the miracle of water turned to wine to announce his presence among his people (see John 2:1–12). In this sign, he announced his saving presence. The wedding at Cana is a sign of the heavenly wedding feast to come: Jesus himself is the Bridegroom, the Church is the Bride, and the members of the Church will drink new wine, the Blood of Christ.

In the synoptic Gospels, Jesus instituted the Last Supper at the **Passover** meal. In doing this, Jesus gave new meaning to the traditional Passover. He took on the role of the Paschal Lamb, sacrificing his life for us. He made the Passover bread and wine his own Body and Blood. Jesus made himself our Pasch, our Passover from the slavery of sin into the freedom of his risen life. When Jesus took up this cup, he looked forward to the Kingdom of God that he would initiate through his death and Resurrection.

Passover ➤ The night the Lord passed over the houses of the Israelites marked by the blood of the lamb, and spared the firstborn sons from death. It also is the feast that celebrates the deliverance of the Chosen People from bondage in Egypt and the Exodus from Egypt to the Promised Land.

In the Eucharist today, the bread and wine that become the Body and Blood of Christ (by the words of the priest and the invocation of the Holy Spirit) remain at the heart of the Eucharist.

The Institution of the Eucharist

Jesus' love is infinite. He showed that love throughout his earthly ministry, especially through the gift of himself so that we might be saved. In Eucharistic Prayer IV, the priest, addressing God the Father, speaks of the love of Jesus and this gift of himself to us:

> For when the hour had come
> for him to be glorified by you, Father most holy,
> having loved his own who were in the world,
> he loved them to the end.
> *(Roman Missal,* page 658)

Jesus' institution of the Eucharist is a sign of his love. Jesus, in his own Body and Blood, left to his chosen companions a pledge of his deep love. And he asked his Apostles to share in, and to celebrate, this memorial of his death and Resurrection until he would come again in glory.

Significantly, it was at Passover that Jesus chose to institute the Eucharist. By doing so, he connected this Old Testament sacrifice with his sacrifice, showing that his love was sacrificial. Just as the Passover lamb was killed and eaten to sustain the life of God's people, so Jesus would also suffer, die, and be buried. Jesus, the Lamb of God, would triumph eternally; his sacrifice would never need repeating. This resurrected Lamb would share his sustenance with his people, would share his Body and Blood, not as an empty remembrance but as a living reality.

This Passover of Jesus fulfilled the hopes of the Passover of the Old Covenant. The Eucharist is the new Passover. In it, we celebrate the passing

© Theorn / Shutterstock.com

Saint Paul made a parallel with the sacrifice offered by Christ with the Passover lamb. Christ is referred to as the Paschal Lamb in 1 Corinthians 5:7.

over of Jesus from death to Resurrection. In every Eucharist, we share in the Passover of Jesus and celebrate the hope of our own Passover from death to life in the glory of God's Kingdom. In the Body and Blood of Christ, we share even now in that glory.

"Do This in Memory of Me"

Jesus' words "Do this in memory of me" have a particular meaning for the Church. The memory the Church has of Jesus' words and actions at the Last Supper is not the kind of memory we might have of a special day or a special event. When we say, "I will remember this moment for the rest of my life," that moment stays in the past. The "memory," or memorial, of the Eucharist is different; it is a living memory. The Church not only remembers Jesus and all he did for the sake of our salvation but also makes it present. We call this kind of memory by the Greek term *anamnesis*.

In one sense, the Last Supper was really the "First Supper"—the first of many celebrations of the Eucharist that the Risen Jesus would share with his followers. After Jesus' return to his Father in Heaven, the memorial of the Last Supper continued through the work of the Apostles, who, like Jesus, took bread, broke it, blessed it, and gave it. Jesus' command to repeat these actions is not just about remembering Jesus and what he did. It is a memorial of Christ's life, death, Resurrection, and his intercession. Ever since the Last Supper, the Church has continually celebrated the memorial of the Eucharist in this same fundamental structure.

When we celebrate the Eucharist today, we share in and proclaim the Paschal Mystery of Jesus until he comes again, when we will all be brought together at the table of the Lord in the heavenly Kingdom. The Eucharist, as our making present of the Paschal Mystery of Christ, is both our strength for today's journey and our promise for the unending "tomorrows" of eternity.

Giving Thanks and Praise

The word *eucharist* itself comes from a Greek word meaning "thanksgiving." In the Eucharist, we thank God for all that is good, holy, beautiful, and just in our world and in our lives, and we thank him in a special way for the gift of his Son, Jesus. Not only did God create us, but he also redeemed us, sanctified us, and made us worthy to be called his children. For these reasons, in the Eucharist, we sing his glory through Christ.

anamnesis ▶ The Greek word for *memory*. In the Eucharist, this refers to the making present of the Paschal Mystery, Christ's work of salvation. The *anamnesis* refers also to a particular section of the Eucharistic Prayer after the words of institution in which the Church remembers Christ's saving deeds—his Passion, death, Resurrection, and glorious return.

I DIDN'T KNOW THAT!

Christ is wholly present in both the bread and the wine. Each of these individual elements conveys the grace of the Sacrament of the Eucharist. However, Catholics are encouraged to receive the Body and Blood of Christ in both "species" or forms. Receiving both the Body and the Blood of Christ is the most complete sign of communion because it recalls the Last Supper, when Jesus presented both the bread and wine as his Body and Blood.

In the Eucharist, Jesus Christ unites us to himself, to his praise of the Father and to his intercessions for us. Jesus, as our High Priest, approaches God the Father on our behalf. He "is always able to save those who approach God through him, since he lives forever to make intercession for them" (Hebrews 7:25). In every Eucharist, Jesus himself prays for you!

Sacrifice and Memorial of Christ

In every Eucharist, after the words of institution, we find a prayer called the memorial, or, in Greek, the *anamnesis* (meaning "memory"):

> Therefore, O Lord,
> as we celebrate the memorial of the blessed Passion,
> the Resurrection from the dead,
> and the glorious Ascension into heaven
> of Christ, your Son, our Lord . . .
> (*Roman Missal*, Eucharistic Prayer I, page 641)

But, like the word *memory* in the words of institution, this word *anamnesis* means more than just remembering Jesus or recalling a past event. In the Eucharist, when we remember Christ's Passion, death, Resurrection, and Ascension, we are remembering, yes, but we are primarily proclaiming the mighty works of God that are made present in our midst. For God and his works are not limited to the past; they are present now, and they will be present in the future: "We proclaim your Death, O Lord, and profess your Resurrection until you come again" (*Roman Missal*, Eucharistic Prayer III, page 652).

Christ died once and for all on the cross, but his sacrifice remains ever present to us in the Eucharist. Christ's Body, the body he gave up on the cross, and Christ's Blood, the blood he poured out for our salvation, is given to us. Every Eucharist is our participation in that one single sacrifice. In the Eucharist, we, as members of the Church, the Body of Christ, participate in Christ's sacrifice. Our prayers, our praise, our sufferings, and our work are united with him and are given priceless value.

The Cosmic Eucharist

Shortly before his death, Pope Saint John Paul II wrote "The Eucharistic Church" (*"Ecclesia de Eucharistia,"* 2003). In this encyclical, the Pope explains the Eucharist as bringing about a "oneness in time" between the Triduum (the three days of Christ's suffering, death, and Resurrection) and our own time. This is the "making present" of the Paschal Mystery in every Eucharist ("The Eucharistic Church," number 5). He also recounts his own experiences:

> I have been able to celebrate Holy Mass in chapels built along mountain paths, on lakeshores and seacoasts; I have celebrated it on altars built in stadiums and in city squares. . . . This varied scenario of celebrations of the Eucharist has given me a powerful experience of its universal and, so to speak, cosmic character. Yes, cosmic! Because even when it is celebrated on the humble altar of a country church, the Eucharist is always in some way celebrated on the altar of the world. It unites heaven and earth. It embraces and permeates all creation. . . . Truly this is the mysterium fidei [mystery of faith] which is accomplished in the Eucharist: the world which came forth from the hands of God the Creator now returns to him redeemed by Christ. (Number 8) ✱

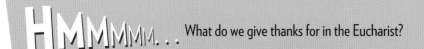

HMMMMM... What do we give thanks for in the Eucharist?

Article 24
The Eucharist in Scripture

The Manna and the Bread of Life

Remember the passage from Exodus that you read preparing for this chapter? After the Israelites escaped from Egypt, they were led into a vast desert. The land was barren, and they couldn't find food. They complained to Moses and Aaron, saying that they would rather have died in Egypt, where they had their fill of bread, but "you have led us into this wilderness to make this whole assembly die of famine!" (Exodus 16:3). To answer their complaint, the Lord told Moses, "I am going to rain down bread from heaven for you" (16:4). This was manna, which appeared as fine flakes on the ground. Such was the loving care God showered on his people.

Bread and wine are ordinary gifts, but at the Eucharist they are transformed into something extraordinary. What ordinary gifts do you have? Will you give them to God to transform into something extraordinary?

Saint Teresa of Ávila (1515–1582) once said, "God has no body now on earth but yours; no eyes but yours; no feet but yours; no hands but yours. Yours are the eyes through which the compassion of Christ must look out on the world. Yours are the feet with which he is to go about doing good. Yours are the hands with which he is to bless his people." This isn't just an affirmation of the good we can do. Rather, it is a challenge! Christ is present to us in the Eucharist. When we receive the Eucharist, Christ is truly present in us! Saint Teresa reminds us that we are the hands and feet of Christ for others. How will you do good? How will you bless God's people? How will you be the face of Christ for others?

UNIT 3

Centuries later, Jesus explained the deeper spiritual meaning of this manna, and of himself as the true Bread, in an incident recorded in the Gospel of John. One day Jesus was teaching in the synagogue at Capernaum. Jesus had just multiplied the loaves and fish for the people. Then he walked on water. Now, as he taught, he engaged the crowd in a discussion. The crowd asked him: "What sign can you do, that we may see and believe in you? What can you do? Our ancestors ate manna in the desert, as it is written: 'He gave them bread from heaven to eat'" (John 6:30–31).

Jesus eventually told them plainly: "I am the bread of life. Your ancestors ate the manna in the desert, but they died; this is the bread that comes down from heaven so that one may eat it and not die. I am the living bread that came down from heaven; whoever eats this bread will live forever; and the bread that I will give is my flesh for the life of the world" (John 6:48–51).

When God gave manna in the desert, it was to sustain life in this world; the bread that Jesus Christ, his Son, gave is a pledge of eternal life. We say that the manna from Heaven *prefigured* the Eucharist; it was a glimpse of the true Bread from Heaven, the life-giving Bread: Jesus himself.

Unleavened Bread

Think back to the pre-read Scripture passage for this article, Exodus 12:31–51. The Old Testament Passover event, when the Lord passed over the houses of the Israelites and spared the firstborn sons from death, prefigured the passing over of Jesus from death to life. In that Passover event, the Israelites ate unleavened bread because they did not have time to wait for bread with yeast in it to rise before leaving Egypt in haste. In fact, the Scripture passage refers specifically to the Israelites carrying the unleavened dough in kneading bowls, wrapped in their cloaks (see 12:34). And then again, baking the unleavened bread into loaves. They "could not wait. They did not even prepare food for the journey" (12:39). To this day, the Jewish people celebrate the Passover with unleavened bread. And, in the Western Church, our Eucharistic bread is also unleavened, just as was the Passover bread that Jesus took, blessed, broke, and gave to his disciples.

The Jewish Passover supper begins with the youngest child asking this question: "What makes this night different than all other nights?" Then the story of the Passover is told and celebrated.

Melchizedek

The first prefiguring of the Eucharist in the Old Testament was in the Book of Genesis (see 14:18–19), when the King of Salem and priest of God, Melchizedek, brought out bread and wine to greet Abram, later to be called Abraham, the father of the Jewish nation. In the Old Testament, Melchizedek offered the gifts of God's creation to Abraham; in the New Covenant, we offer our gifts of bread and wine to Christ, who makes them a perfect offering to the Father. Both Abraham and Melchizedek are named in Eucharistic Prayer I, in which, after the consecration, the priest prays to the Father to accept our offerings:

> . . . as once you were pleased to accept
> the gifts of your servant Abel the just,
> the sacrifice of Abraham, our father in faith,
> and the offering of your high priest Melchizedek,
> a holy sacrifice, a spotless victim.
>
> (*Roman Missal*, page 641)

UNIT 3

The Eucharist in the Synoptic Gospels

Now we turn to the New Testament, and the Gospel accounts that teach us about the Eucharist. Let's first consider the multiplication of the loaves and fish. This is also a prefiguring of the Eucharist, even though it is a New Testament event. As you know from the pre-read Scripture excerpts, the synoptic Gospels (Matthew, Mark, and Luke) all have fairly similar versions of the loaves and fish account. They all start with five loaves and two fish, and end with twelve wicker baskets full of fragments. Only in the Gospel of John do we find the detail of the young boy who offered to share his five loaves and two fish with the Apostles, who gave them to Jesus, who then gave them back in abundance to the crowd. You may want to go back to the Scripture listed at the beginning of the chapter to compare and contrast the accounts.

You will find that in all the accounts, the actions of Jesus remind us of his actions at the Last Supper: in Mark, for example, he "said the blessing, broke the loaves, and gave them to [his] disciples" (Mark 6:41) to share with the people. The language of Matthew and Luke is similar.

The Gospel accounts that have been most influential in our celebration of the Eucharist are, of course, the accounts of the Last Supper and their recording of the words and actions of Jesus when he broke the bread and gave it to his disciples, saying: "Take and eat; this is my body." Then he took the cup, gave thanks, and gave it to them, saying, "Drink from it, all of you, for this is my blood of the covenant" (Matthew 26:26–28). These synoptic Gospel

UNIT 3

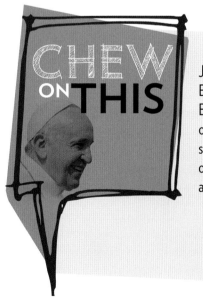

Jesus speaks in silence in the Mystery of the Eucharist. He reminds us every time [in the Eucharist] that following him means going out of ourselves and not making our life a possession of our own, but rather a gift to him and others. (Pope Francis, "Homily on Solemnity at Corpus Christi," May 30, 2013)

accounts are Matthew 26:26–29, Mark 14:22–25, and Luke 22:14–20. You may want to find these accounts yourself, just like you did with the accounts of the feeding of the five thousand, and note their similarities and differences. The words given in the Gospel of Matthew are the words we pray in our liturgy.

The Eucharist in the Gospel of John

The Gospel of John is quite different from the synoptic Gospels. Chief among those differences is that John includes more sacramental imagery and sacramental teaching, especially about the Eucharist. For example, the Gospel of John records the wedding at Cana and names it "the beginning" of Jesus' signs (2:11). The wine has run out, and Jesus reveals his power by changing water into wine. It is such good wine that the headwaiter tells the bridegroom, "You have kept the good wine until now" (2:10). This miracle prefigures the events of the Last Supper, when Jesus transforms the bread and wine into his Body and Blood, given up for our salvation.

A few chapters later, John's Gospel has an account of the multiplication of the loaves and fish (6:1–15) followed by a lengthy teaching that reveals Jesus as the "bread of life" (see 6:22–59). The teaching is called "The Bread of Life Discourse." In this discourse, Jesus reveals his true presence in the Eucharist and tells those who are listening: "Whoever eats my flesh and drinks my blood has eternal life, and I will raise him on the last day. For my flesh is true food, and my blood is true drink. Whoever eats my flesh and drinks my blood remains in me and I in him" (6:54–56). The miracle of the loaves had always been a sign of the Eucharist; in the Gospel of John, the meaning of the sign is deepened by the teachings of Jesus.

The Gospel of John does not include a Last Supper account of the words of institution. However, we have already seen that the Gospel of John teaches us about the true meaning of the Eucharist. In the Last Supper account in John, Jesus is again teaching, by his actions, when he washes the feet of his disciples; and by his words, when he assures his disciples that he will prepare a place for them, that the Holy Spirit will come to help them, and that his life-giving love will remain with them. Chapters 14 and 15 of John's Gospel open the heart of Jesus to us and are among the most beautiful in the New Testament. These teachings reveal to us the inner meaning of the Eucharist.

The Apostle Paul and the Eucharist

As we know, the Apostle Paul was not with Jesus and the other Apostles and disciples at the Last Supper. Among the Jews, he was called Saul, and he was not yet a follower of Christ. After the Resurrection, when the followers of

In John's account of the Last Supper, the focus is on Jesus humbling himself to wash the feet of his disciples, rather than the words of institution of the Eucharist that we read about in the other three Gospels.

Jesus were gathering in prayer and the breaking of the bread, Saul was actively persecuting them. He would have probably continued this indefinitely, had Jesus not intervened (see Acts of the Apostles 9:1–18). In time, Saul became known by his Gentile name, Paul, and he became one of the pillars, with Peter, of the Church that Jesus founded.

Paul was not present at the Last Supper, yet his is the earliest written account of the institution of the Lord's Supper in the New Testament. How did he know what Jesus said and did? He knew because Jesus told him. Paul wrote, "For I received from the Lord what I also handed on to you." (1 Corinthians 11:23). ✳

HMMMMM. . .   After reading the scriptural background for the Eucharist, does the celebration of the Eucharist hold more meaning for you? If so, how?

Article 25

The Eucharist: Then and Now

In every age, since the beginnings of the Church, the Eucharist has been "the source and summit of the Christian life"[3] (*CCC*, number 1324). Everything else the Church is and does—in all the other sacraments, in the various ministries of the Church, and in every apostolic work—finds its life-giving source in the Eucharist, for in the Eucharist we encounter Christ himself.

God acts to make us holy in the Eucharist. In cooperation with his grace, our action consists in the worship and praise of Christ, and through him, of the Father, in the unity of the Holy Spirit. The Eucharist takes up into this praise and thanksgiving our own lives now, as they are, and unites us to heavenly liturgy, the worship and praise of the angels and saints in Heaven. In the Eucharist, we also have a pledge of future glory, for the Body and Blood of Christ is a sign of "the new and everlasting covenant" that Christ initiated at the Last Supper. The Eucharist is thus "the sum and summary of our faith" (*CCC*, number 1327).

The Eucharist is the source and summit of Christian life.

The Names of the Eucharist

Throughout the centuries, the Eucharist has been called by many different names. Each name reveals something more of the rich depths of this sacrament and invites us to see it from another aspect. Let us consider some of these names.

Eucharist

As was mentioned earlier, the word *eucharist* comes from the Greek word *eucharistein*, meaning "thanksgiving." The Greek prefix *eu* means "good." The word *charistein* comes from the Greek word *charisma*, meaning "grace." Together they came to mean "thanksgiving," just as the "grace" we say at meals is a thanksgiving for our food.

The word *blessing* is also related to the Eucharist, for "Jesus took bread, said the blessing, broke it" (Matthew 26:26), and gave it to his disciples. This aspect of the Eucharist as blessing comes from the Jewish custom of the *be-rakah*, or prayer of blessing, which has overtones of thanks and praise, integral to the celebration of the Eucharist. As the Gospel expanded into the Greek world, so did the language of the liturgy. The Greek word *eulogein* means "good word" (*eu* combined with *logos*, meaning "word"). Thus, it came to mean "a blessing." In the early writings of the Church, it sometimes means the Eucharist itself, as in 1 Corinthians 10:16: "the cup of blessing."

The Lord's Supper

This recalls the meal that Jesus shared with his disciples before his Passion and is also an anticipation of the supper of the Lamb we will share with Jesus in the Kingdom of Heaven (see 1 Corinthians 11:20, Revelation 19:9).

The Breaking of the Bread

It was the duty of the host at a Jewish meal to break the bread and distribute it. We have seen Jesus do this at the feeding of the five thousand. At the Last Supper, it has special significance, for here Jesus distributes his Body to the Apostles and from them to the entire Church. In the account of Jesus' appearance to the two disciples on the road to Emmaus (Luke 24:13–35), we see the power of the "breaking of the bread." It was only when the two disciples broke bread with Jesus that they recognized him as the resurrected Christ (see Luke 24:31).

In the Emmaus account, we see what an affirming and eye-opening action the breaking of the bread is. Indeed, the two disciples didn't

This painting depicts the supper at Emmaus. Read Luke 24:13–35. How has the artist captured the mood of the account? Picture yourself at the table. What is your reaction to Jesus?

Logos ➤ Greek word meaning "Word." *Logos* is a title of Jesus Christ found in the Gospel of John that illuminates the relationship between the three Divine Persons of the Holy Trinity. (See John 1:1,14.)

recognize Jesus the entire time he walked with them, until they reached their destination and he broke bread to share a meal with them. It was only then that their eyes were opened. The breaking of the bread signifies that even though the Bread is broken to share with all, it is the one Christ that we share in his one Body (see 1 Corinthians 10:16–17).

The Eucharistic Assembly

The life of the early Christians in Jerusalem was centered around the Eucharist: "They devoted themselves to the teaching of the apostles and to the communal life, to the breaking of the bread and to the prayers" (Acts of the Apostles 2:42). Sunday, the day of Resurrection, was the day of assembly (see 20:7). As it was then, the Eucharist today is, and always will be, at the heart of the Church's life.

Because Sunday was the day on which Christ rose from the dead, it is the most significant day to celebrate the Eucharist. It is the day around which the entire Liturgical Year is built. Sunday is called "the Lord's Day" and should be a day of joy. The primary way we keep the Lord's Day holy is by worshipping God at Mass. We should also rest from work and spend time with family and friends. Those who must work on Sunday are urged to spend time in leisure at another time during the week (see *CCC*, number 2187).

How do you honor the Lord's Day?

© Lincoln Beddoe / Shutterstock.com

The Holy Sacrifice

Similar names for the Eucharist include the Holy Sacrifice of the Mass, the "sacrifice of praise," the spiritual sacrifice, the pure and holy sacrifice. All these refer to the Eucharist as the sacrifice of Christ made present to us in the liturgy. This sacrifice of Christ, as the sacrifice of the New Covenant, surpasses all the other sacrifices offered to God throughout the history of salvation.

The Holy and Divine Liturgy

The Eucharist is sometimes referred to as the holy and divine liturgy, a term that seems to refer to the Church's liturgy in general rather than one sacrament, because the Eucharist is the source and summit of the lives of Christians. For the same reason, this sacrament is sometimes called the Sacred Mysteries. Another name for the Eucharist, Most Blessed Sacrament, also captures the centrality of the Eucharist. "It is the Sacrament of sacraments" (*CCC*, number 1330).

Holy Communion and Holy Mass

In the Eucharist, we are united to Christ, and so we share with him and with the entire Church, as a single body, in a "holy communion." The Body and Blood of Christ are also called *holy things*, and, in the Eastern Churches, after the consecration, the Body and Blood of Christ are raised on high, and the priest sings out: "Holy things for the holy!" The Eucharist is also known as the bread of angels, bread from Heaven, medicine of immortality, and viaticum. The word *viaticum* means "with you on the way" and is the Eucharist given to the dying as they make their way toward eternal life. "Holy Mass" refers to the entire Eucharistic celebration but takes its name from *missa*, a Latin word for *dismissal*. The term *Mass* underlines the importance of the dismissal, which is a sending forth of the assembly to accomplish God's will in the world. ✳

UNIT 3

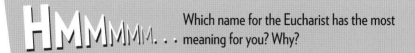

Which name for the Eucharist has the most meaning for you? Why?

1. What is the Paschal Mystery?

2. What does *anamnesis* mean in relation to the Eucharist?

3. How are the Passover, the Last Supper, and the Eucharist connected?

4. Name three Old Testament accounts that prefigure the Eucharist.

5. How do the words of Jesus in John 6:48–51 help us to understand the meaning of the Eucharist?

6. What is Saint Paul the Apostle's connection to the words and actions of Jesus at the Last Supper?

7. Name at least six significant names by which the Eucharist is known.

EUCHARIST STILL LIFE PHOTOGRAPH

1. What connection can you make between the Eucharist and bread and fish?
2. What religious meaning can be given to these domestic items of bread and fish?

UNIT 3

CHAPTER 7
The Celebration of the Eucharist

WHY IS IT IMPORTANT TO ATTEND MASS EVERY SUNDAY?

SNAPSHOT

Article 26
Gather Faithfully Together

Jules read to her stepsister every night on the weeks they were together. She liked spending time with Sarah. She had always wondered what it would be like to have a little sister. Now she had one! For the past month or so, she had been reading from the *Little House on the Prairie* series by Laura Ingalls Wilder. When she finished the chapter and closed the book, Sarah commented, "I don't know if I would have liked living in the late 1800s." Sarah thought about the little girls from the story living in the cabin their father had built. It was cozy, but it didn't have a bathroom inside. The family built their homestead in the open fields of the Midwest, and their closest neighbors were a few miles away! Sarah said, "It sounds like they had a lot of fun. But they didn't have TV or the internet. Even the little kids had a lot of jobs to do. When did they see their friends?"

"Well," said Jules, "most people went to church on Sunday. They didn't do any more work than they had to. They saw their friends and neighbors at church, and afterward they would have picnics or supper with the faith community. Sunday was a day to focus on God, and their lives revolved around this."

UNIT 3

TAKE IT TO GOD

Dear God,
As we gather in prayer,
thank you for reminding me that it matters that I am here.
I feel your presence, and I know I am not on my own.
When we pray together, I am reminded of how encouraging that is.
When we pray together, we are united, and I feel part of something
    bigger than me.
Praying together humbles me.
I am reminded that there are many other people who have needs,
and that I can help them simply by lifting them up in prayer.
Praying together makes me feel useful and closer to you.
Amen.

Sarah explains to Jules how Sundays are a day to focus on God.

Even though our lives might seem very different from those portrayed in the time of the early settlers, it is still true that Sunday is an important day for our faith, our church community, and our family. Sunday is the Lord's Day, the quintessential day for the celebration of the Eucharist. The Eucharist is celebrated on the other days of the week, but the Sunday Eucharist is the Eucharist at which the entire community gathers. The Eucharistic celebration follows the pattern of a family gathering with four main parts. First, we come together (Introductory Rite). Next, we listen to stories (Liturgy of the Word). Then, we share a meal (Liturgy of the Eucharist). And finally, we say our good-byes (Concluding Rite). This article takes a deeper look at the first of these parts, the Introductory Rites.

Overview: The Celebration of the Eucharist

As you continue to examine the Order of the Mass, use this chart as a reference for the different parts of the Eucharistic celebration.

The Eucharistic celebration is one single act of worship.	This act of worship includes: • the proclamation of the Word of God • thanksgiving to God for all his gifts—above all, the gift of his Son • the consecration of the bread and wine • our participation by receiving the Body and Blood of Christ
The Eucharistic celebration consists of two main parts.	• the Liturgy of the Word • the Liturgy of the Eucharist
The Eucharistic celebration begins with the Introductory Rites.	These rites include: • Gathering of the Assembly • Penitential Act • *Kyrie* (Lord, Have Mercy) • Gloria (Glory to God) • Collect (Opening Prayer)
The Liturgy of the Word follows the Introductory Rites.	The order of the Liturgy of the Word: • First Reading (usually from the Old Testament) • Responsorial Psalm (usually sung) • Second Reading (usually from the New Testament) • Gospel Acclamation (Alleluia) • Gospel Reading • Homily • Profession of Faith (Nicene Creed) • Prayer of the Faithful
The Liturgy of the Eucharist follows the Liturgy of the Word.	The order of the Liturgy of the Eucharist: • Presentation and Preparation of the Gifts • Eucharistic Prayer • Communion Rite
The Concluding Rites follow the Liturgy of the Eucharist.	These rites include: • Greeting, Solemn Blessing, or Prayer over the People • Dismissal (usually with a closing song)

UNIT 3

In second-century Syria, a bishop compiled a book of instructions for his fellow bishops. One of the topics was the Sunday assembly. The bishop wrote: "Exhort the people to be faithful to the assembly of the **Church**. Let them not fail to attend, but let them gather faithfully together. Let no one deprive the Church by staying away; if they do, they deprive the Body of Christ of one of its members!" (*Didascalia*, chapter 13).

Wouldn't Mass be the same whether you are there or not? Actually, it wouldn't. The Church isn't a building. We are the Church. As you read in the quote above, if we stay away, we deprive the whole Body of Christ of one of its members! Remember, it isn't just about warming a seat in the pew. We have to participate for our presence to be meaningful to us or to anyone else!

From the early days until now, Christians have assembled for worship and praise, particularly on Sunday. The first Christians were Jews, and when they assembled, they were following in the great Jewish tradition of coming together as a people to worship God. As believers in Jesus Christ, the Messiah, they continued to live and worship as Jews, adding "the breaking of the bread" to their usual worship, as Jesus had instructed them. In the Acts of the Apostles, we read that the first Christians did this every day: "They devoted themselves to the teaching of the apostles and to the communal life, to the breaking of the bread and to the prayers. . . . Every day they devoted themselves to meeting together in the temple area and to breaking bread in their homes" (2:42–46).

Enter the Gentiles

With the apostolic efforts of the Apostle Paul and others, more and more Gentiles from various places in the Roman Empire became Christian. They gathered, like the Jewish Christians, to read from the writings of the prophets and the letters of Paul and others, to pray together, and to celebrate the Eucharist together. The day chosen for this gathering was Sunday, the day of Christ's Resurrection. Not having synagogues or other special buildings available for worship, they gathered in private homes for the entire celebration.

Fortunately, many Middle Eastern and Roman homes were built around a central large room and could accommodate large groups. In the letters of Saint Paul, we find references to these gatherings: "Greet Prisca and Aquila, my

UNIT 3

Church ➤ The term Church has three inseparable meanings: (1) the entire People of God throughout the world; (2) the diocese, which is also known as the local Church; and (3) the assembly of believers gathered for the celebration of the liturgy, especially the Eucharist.

co-workers in Christ Jesus . . . greet also the church at their house" (Romans 16:3,5). A reference to "Chloe's people" in 1 Corinthians 1:11 means "the people who meet at Chloe's house." These "house churches" were dynamic, small Christian communities of love and service.

A home built around a central large room that could accommodate a gathering of groups of people.

UNIT 3

The Gathering of the Assembly

The **assembly** is the gathering of the baptized, and the head of this assembly is Christ himself. He is the invisible presider over every Eucharist. The bishop or priest represents him and acts *"in the person of Christ the head"* (*CCC*, number 1348) as he presides over the assembly, gives the Homily, accepts the offerings, and prays the Eucharistic Prayer. The assembly and other ministers (lectors, those who bring up offerings, and those who distribute Communion) have active roles as well.

Our participation in the liturgy is vital. If you recall, the literal meaning of the word *liturgy* is "the people's work." We can participate in a variety of ways, some of them more involved than others, but they are all important! Think about the responses of the assembly during the liturgy. They are usually very short: "Amen" is the most common. But they are important. They are the

assembly ➤ Also known as a congregation, a community of believers gathered for worship as the Body of Christ.

UNIT 3

Our participation in the liturgy is crucial. We can participate in many ways, including singing, reading as a lector, actively responding, taking up the collection, ushering, and praying.

ordinary means of our participation in the celebration of the Eucharist. Not everyone can sing in the choir, or read from Scripture as a lector, or take up the collection, or lead people to their places in the pews. But each one of us is a member of the one Body of Christ, and we are all called to participate in the celebration of the Eucharist by responding in prayer and raising our voices in song with the assembly.

We all know what it feels like to be part of an assembly in which many of the people seem willing to be "dead weight." They allow others to do their responding for them, and they stay silent during the singing of hymns. Charitably, we can say that they do not realize they are missed. Yes, the Mass will go on without their "Amen" and "Alleluia," but, just as it is rude to ignore a question or comment made by someone conversing with you, it is rude to ignore the invitations of the liturgy to affirm and to help carry out the action of Christ in our midst.

The solution? Saint John of the Cross (1542–1592) once wrote, "If you want love, put love, and you will find love." It is the same with the Eucharist: If you want enthusiasm (*enthusiasm* literally means "having God inside you"), then give enthusiasm, and you will find enthusiasm. As an assembly, we need the respectful and attentive enthusiasm of each person present.

Introductory Rites

The Introductory Rites of the Mass bring us together as a worshipping community and prepare us for listening to the Word of God and for the celebration of the Eucharist.

After the entrance chant or gathering song, the assembly makes the Sign of the Cross, the sign in which we begin all our prayers. The priest then greets the assembly by saying something like, "The grace of our Lord Jesus Christ, and the love of God, and the communion of the Holy Spirit be with you all," and the people answer, "And with your spirit" (*Roman Missal*, page 513). Next, the priest, deacon, or other minister may provide a brief introduction to the Mass.

Unless the rite for the blessing and sprinkling of water is done, the Penitential Act follows. The Penitential Act provides a moment for repentance of sin in silence. Ideally, we have come to Mass having already prepared ourselves by examining our conscience. In the Penitential Act, we recall Christ's role in salvation, and our venial sin is forgiven. We do not want lingering sin to interfere with the message of God to us or our becoming more closely united to Christ. We want to give the Holy Spirit an assembly of clean hearts in which to dwell.

UNIT 3

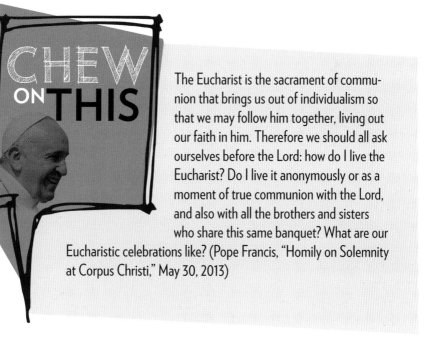

The Eucharist is the sacrament of communion that brings us out of individualism so that we may follow him together, living out our faith in him. Therefore we should all ask ourselves before the Lord: how do I live the Eucharist? Do I live it anonymously or as a moment of true communion with the Lord, and also with all the brothers and sisters who share this same banquet? What are our Eucharistic celebrations like? (Pope Francis, "Homily on Solemnity at Corpus Christi," May 30, 2013)

The Gloria follows—on Sundays (outside of Advent and Lent), on solemnities and feasts, and in solemn local celebrations. The Gloria expresses our joy in the Lord. It praises God for being who he is, and who he is to us: heavenly King, God, Father; Jesus Christ, Son of the Father, Lord God, Lamb of God, Holy One, Most High; "with the Holy Spirit, in the glory of God the Father. Amen" (*Roman Missal*, page 522).

At the invitation of the priest, "Let us pray," we share a short time of silence. Then the priest prays the Collect, or Opening Prayer. This prayer (pronounced COL-lect) sets our hearts and spirits "in sync" with the Church, with the readings of the day, and in anticipation of the celebration of the Eucharist to come. While praying the Collect, the priest extends his hands, as if gathering, or collecting, all our own unspoken yearnings. We respond, "Amen."

We have been welcomed. We have proclaimed God's goodness in Christ. We have expressed sorrow for sin and hope in the Lord's mercy. We have expressed joy in the living God. We, as members of the Body of Christ with the rest of the Universal Church, have responded to the Collect that helps us to speak our hopes and our needs. Now we are ready to listen to the Word of God. ✳

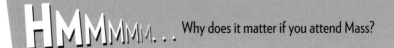

HMMMMM. . . Why does it matter if you attend Mass?

UNIT 3

Article 27

The Liturgy of the Word

When Jesus, the Son of God, was tempted by the Devil to use his power to turn stones into bread, Jesus' reply emphasized the power of the Word of God:

> It is written,
> "One does not live by bread alone,
>   but by every word that comes forth from the mouth of God."
>   (Matthew 4:4)

When Jesus says, "It is written," he is introducing a quote from the Book of Deuteronomy, the book of Jewish laws given to the people by Moses. That quotation refers to the manna God gave to his people.

Recall the manna God provided as sustenance for the Israelites in the desert. The Eucharist is the New Manna.

UNIT 3

The manna we eat in the Eucharist is the New Manna, the New Bread from Heaven. The Word we hear in the Liturgy of the Word is the new and living Word of God, directed to us, in our time, and in our lives. The Word of God is not confined to the pages of Holy Scripture. It is ever "living and effective, sharper than any two-edged sword, penetrating even between soul and spirit, joints and marrow, and able to discern reflections and thoughts of the heart" (Hebrews 4:12).

Through the work of the Holy Spirit, the Word proclaimed supports and sustains our entire celebration of the liturgy. If we are attentive to the Word, the Holy Spirit plants that Word deep in our hearts, so that what we hear influences us on the deepest level. The Word becomes the root and foundation not only of our participation in the Eucharist but of the whole of our lives. In the liturgy, the Spirit is also at work bringing us, as the Body of Christ, into greater unity and nurturing the development of our unique and diverse spiritual gifts (see *Lectionary for Mass*, introduction, number 9).

Elements of the Liturgy of the Word

The main part of the Liturgy of the Word consists of three readings from Sacred Scripture (on Sundays) as well as psalms, canticles, and other Scripture verses between the readings. Following these are the Homily, the Profession of Faith, and the Prayer of the Faithful.

Each Sunday Mass has three readings. The first is usually from the Old Testament, the second is from one of the Epistles, and the third is from one of the Gospels. This arrangement highlights the unity of the Old and New Testaments, for each one recounts a facet of the history of our salvation and looks to Christ and all he has done for us and our salvation as central to that history.

The First Reading

The First Reading draws us into the roots of our faith. The events of the Old Testament record the joys and sorrows, the tribulations and triumphs, of our brothers and sisters, those who have gone before us and have handed down their faith in God to us. They are the ancestors of Jesus, and their response to God prepared the world for the Messiah. The readings proclaimed at Sunday

The reader plays an important role during the Eucharist, because the Word of God must be heard by all in order to be received and acted upon.

UNIT 3

The Liturgy of the Word is an essential element in every sacrament. But did you know that the Liturgy of the Word can be celebrated on its own? Perhaps you have celebrated the Liturgy of the Word when gathered for a special prayer service. In this case, a blessing and a dismissal usually follow the general intercessions. A celebration of the Liturgy of the Word is a beautiful way to begin or end a youth-group session or a day of retreat. It is also a wonderful way to pray when gathered at times of special joy or crisis.

UNIT 3

Masses were selected because of their relationship to the chosen Gospel readings, and so the assembly would hear many of the most significant Old Testament passages (see *Lectionary for Mass*, introduction, number 106).

The Responsorial Psalm

The Responsorial Psalm is a response to the first reading. On Sundays, it is usually sung. This psalm gives us an opportunity to meditate on the Word of God. The custom of reading passages and singing psalms from the Old Testament reflects customs in Jewish worship that have been continued in the liturgy of the New Covenant.

The Second Reading

The Second Reading is usually from one of the letters of Saint Paul or from the writings of the other Apostles. In these letters, we can find many similarities to our life of faith today: the assemblies, the description of the Eucharist, the joy of sharing in a community of faith, the human problems involved in such a community—all are reflected in these letters from the founders of the earliest communities. But we do not read them because they are historical accounts; we read them because they are the Word of God and through them God speaks to our lives today.

The Gospel Acclamation

The proclamation of the Gospel is preceded by an acclamation, consisting of the Alleluia and a Scripture verse. In Lent, the Alleluia is omitted and is replaced by "Glory and praise to you, Lord Jesus Christ" (*Roman Missal*, page 34).

The Gospel Reading

The Gospels occupy a central place in the liturgy and in the life of the Church because they have Jesus Christ as their center. Because the proclamation of the Gospel is the high point of the Liturgy of the Word, it is often accompanied by special elements. For example, it is proclaimed by the priest or deacon, and the assembly stands while listening. Before the proclamation, the priest or deacon carries the Book of the Gospels to the ambo (the reading stand) and is sometimes accompanied by servers with candles and incense. Another special element is the threefold Sign of the Cross that in many churches everyone makes on their foreheads, lips, and chests before the proclamation of the Gospel. You may wonder what the meaning of the threefold Sign of the Cross is. We cross our forehead so the Word of God may always be in our thoughts and purify our minds. We cross our lips so our speech will be holy and we will share the Gospel with others. And we cross our hearts to invite God to always be in the intentions of our hearts.

Typically the priest proclaims the Gospel. The Homily, which follows the Gospel, helps us to discover the Word of God for us today.

UNIT 3

The Homily

In the Homily, we are helped to discover the meaning of the Word of God for us today. We have listened to the Word in two readings, a psalm, and an acclamation. Then we heard God's Word in the Gospel proclamation. What can we make of all this? What can we take with us to help shape our lives in the image of Christ? What can we do to respond to the Word of God that we hear? The Homily helps us to answer these questions: "By means of the homily the mysteries of the faith and the guiding principles of Christian life are expounded from the sacred text during the course of the liturgical year" (*Constitution on the Sacred Liturgy* [*Sacrosanctum Concilium*, December 4, 1963], number 52).

It may be frustrating to sometimes feel that the Homily isn't being directed toward you as a young person. Keep in mind that it is a challenge for the priest to bring the readings and the Gospel message to life for people of different ages, backgrounds, and experiences. But if we listen carefully, we can almost always hear at least one thing that can be helpful and lead us to reflection on how the readings have meaning for our lives.

Profession of Faith

When we say the Nicene Creed together, we respond with faith to the Word of God proclaimed in the readings and in the Homily. Proclaiming the Creed (our profession of faith) reminds us of the truths of our faith and so prepares us to celebrate the Eucharist.

The Prayer of the Faithful

The Prayer of the Faithful is also called the Universal Prayer. In this prayer, we pray for worldwide, national, and local needs; we pray for our government officials and our Church leaders; we pray for our parish, for neighbors and friends in need, and for those among us who have died. In his First Letter to Timothy, Saint Paul urges that "supplications, prayers, petitions, and thanksgivings be offered for everyone, for kings and for all in authority, that we may lead a quiet and tranquil life in all devotion and dignity. This is good and pleasing to God our savior, who wills everyone to be saved and to come to knowledge of the truth" (1 Timothy 2:1–4).

The Readings of the Liturgical Calendar

Catholic churches all over the world read the same readings every day of the year. These readings are organized by the Church according to a set order. The readings are arranged in two cycles, one for Sundays and one for weekdays.

UNIT 3

The Sunday and Weekday Cycles

The Sunday cycle is divided into three years: Year A, Year B, and Year C. In Year A, we read mostly from the Gospel of Matthew. In Year B, we read mostly from the Gospel of Mark. In Year C, we read mostly from the Gospel of Luke. We read from the Gospel of John during the Easter season of all three years. If you attended Mass every Sunday and every weekday, after three years you will have heard 14 percent of the Old Testament and 71 percent of the New Testament.

The weekday cycle is divided into two years: Year I and Year II. We read Year I in odd-numbered years (2021, 2023, 2025, and so on). We read Year II in even-numbered years. The Gospels are the same for both Year I and Year II. Each year begins with the Gospel of Mark, followed by Matthew, and then Luke. We read the Gospel of John during the Easter season. For the seasons of Advent, Christmas, Lent, and Easter, for Sundays and weekdays, we read selections appropriate to the season.

The United States Conference of Catholic Bishops' (USCCB) website provides the Mass readings for each day of the year. This can help you to prepare for the Sunday or weekday liturgy, or to pray and meditate on the Mass readings. ✳

UNIT 3

HMMMMM. . . Who has made the Mass and Gospel message most relatable for you?

Article 28
The Liturgy of the Eucharist

The Real Presence of Christ in the Eucharist

In the Liturgy of the Eucharist, the second main part of the Eucharistic cele-
bration, we enter into Christ's Paschal Mystery in the most direct way possible.
It is no wonder that the Eucharist is called "the Sacrament of sacraments"
(*CCC*, number 1211).

The bread that we offer becomes, through the words and actions of the
priest and the work of the Holy Spirit, the Body of Christ. The Bread of
Life is then broken and shared by all.

In this sacrament, Christ is present in many ways. He is present in the
priest. For it is Jesus Christ, our eternal High Priest, acting through the ministry of the priest, who offers the Eucharistic sacrifice. Only a validly ordained
priest, acting in the name of Christ, can preside at the Eucharist and conse-
crate the bread and wine so they become the Body and Blood of the Lord (see
CCC, number 1411).

Christ is also present in the proclamation of the Word of God, and in the
assembly, for he has assured us, "Where two or three are gathered together in
my name, there am I in the midst of them" (Matthew 18:20). Whenever we
gather in the Eucharistic assembly, we gather as the Body of Christ, and he is
present in us and with us. But Christ is most especially present in the Eucharist
in his Body and Blood.

The way Christ is present in the Eucharistic elements is unique. Christ is present in his Body and Blood in the fullest sense: "It is a *substantial* presence by which Christ, God and man, makes himself wholly and entirely present"[1] (*CCC*, number 1374). This presence is called the Real Presence of Christ.

In the Sacrament of the Eucharist, we become more closely united to Christ, and we are strengthened for our life as his disciples. As Saint Augustine, pointing to the Eucharist on the altar, said, "Be what you see; receive what you are" (Sermon 272). That is, be the Body of Christ and receive the Body of Christ. Christ becomes one with us so that we can become one with him, so that we can *become him*, as the Body of Christ in the world.

CATHOLICS MAKING A DIFFERENCE

Have you ever felt that it didn't matter if you went to Church or not? Are your friends, activities, and social media a higher priority in your life than your faith? At this stage of your life, you might relate to Clare Crockett when she was a teenager in Derry, Ireland. Clare dreamed of being a movie star. She was artistic, creative, beautiful, and had an amazing singing voice. But God had other plans for Clare. When she was seventeen, Clare was invited to go on a retreat for Holy Week in Spain. She admitted that she went because she was looking for a suntan and was curious about the boys in Spain, but she found herself with a group of people who were committed to their faith in a way that was deeply moving to her. Clare first tried to ignore what she experienced as a pull to commit herself to religious life. But when she was eighteen, Clare took vows and joined the Servant Sisters of the Home of the Mother. Can you imagine feeling so compelled to commit yourself to Christ that you would be willing to give up your life as it is today? As you encounter Jesus through the Eucharist at Mass and continue to grow in your faith, your life, too, can go in directions you may never have considered if you are open!

Presentation and Preparation of the Gifts

The celebration of the Eucharist begins with an altar cloth and possibly a crucifix (if there is not one placed near the altar) and two candles (if they are not on separate stands next to the altar). Other necessary items are brought to the altar while an offertory hymn is being sung. These include:

- **the corporal:** This is a square white linen cloth upon which all the sacred vessels are placed during the celebration of the Mass. The word *corporal* comes from the Latin word for *body*, which is related to Body of Christ *(Corpus Christi)*.
- **the purificator:** This is a small piece of white linen, folded in three layers, much like a napkin, marked with a cross in the center. The priest uses it to purify (clean) his fingers, the chalice, and the paten (the round dish used to hold the Host).
- **the chalice:** This is the vessel into which the wine will be poured.
- **the *Roman Missal*** (or *Sacramentary*)

The gifts of bread and wine are then brought to the altar, on Sundays usually by members of the assembly in procession. In every parish, money is collected for the support of the parish and for poor people. In some parishes, this collection is brought up with the gifts of bread and wine. Sometimes, parishes present food for poor people as well. Offerings for the support of the local parish and for the poor have been traditional in the Church from its very beginning.

In the offering of the gifts, you might remember the offering of the bread and the wine of the priest Melchizedek. In this offering, we are like Melchizedek, but we give our gifts of bread and wine into the hands of Christ, who will bring our gifts to perfection by changing them, by the words and actions of the priest and the work of the Holy Spirit, into his own Body and Blood.

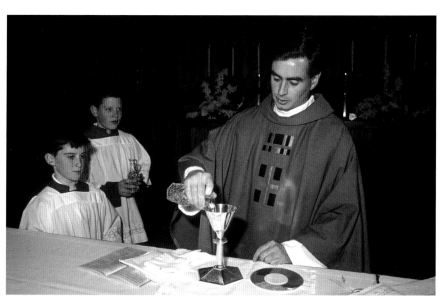

Two altar boys assist the priest in the Preparation of the Gifts.

UNIT 3

After the priest has accepted the gifts, he raises the Host slightly and thanks God for the gift of this bread, which will "become for us the bread of life." The assembly responds: "Blessed be God for ever" (*Roman Missal*, page 529). (If there is music or singing, the priest prays quietly, and the assembly does not respond.)

The priest then pours wine into the chalice. But before he says the blessing, he adds a little water to the wine. This gesture has great significance, as it reminds us of the whole reason for Christ's coming to us in the flesh, and of what will soon be taking place for us in the reception of Holy Communion. The priest says, "By the mystery of this water and wine may we come to share in the divinity of Christ who humbled himself to share in our humanity" (*Roman Missal*, page 529). The priest prays that we will become intermingled with Christ, as intermingled as the water is with the wine!

Then the priest raises the chalice slightly and thanks God for the gift of wine, which will "become our spiritual drink." The assembly responds, "Blessed be God for ever" (*Roman Missal*, page 529).

After washing his hands (see article 1, "What Is the Liturgy?"), the priest concludes the Preparation of the Gifts by facing the people, extending his hands, and praying:

> Pray, brethren (brothers and sisters),
> that my sacrifice and yours
> may be acceptable to God,
> the almighty Father.
> (*Roman Missal*, page 530)

Note that this is *our* sacrifice, not the priest's alone. The assembly concurs with the priest's prayer and says:

> May the Lord accept the sacrifice at your hands
> for the praise and glory of his name,
> for our good
> and the good of all his holy Church.
> (*Roman Missal*, page 530)

The priest then prays the Prayer over the Offerings, and the assembly affirms the prayer with "Amen."

In the offering of our gifts, which will be transformed into the Body and Blood of Christ, we also offer ourselves. In the Eucharist, through the Body and Blood of Christ, we ourselves will be transformed.

Criteria for Receiving the Eucharist

Saint Justin Martyr (ca. AD 100–165), an early Church apologist (someone who explains and defends the faith), offered these criteria for the reception of the Eucharist:

> Because this bread and wine have been made Eucharist ("eucharisted" according to an ancient expression), "we call this food *Eucharist*, and no one may take part in it unless he believes that what we teach is true, has received baptism for the forgiveness of sins and new birth, and lives in keeping with what Christ taught."[2] (*CCC*, number 1355)

In these criteria, we can easily see that receiving the Eucharist encompasses our entire lives of faith: membership in the Church, belief in the teachings of the Church, including the Real Presence of Christ in the Eucharist through **Transubstantiation**, and a life lived according to the teachings of Christ. This is a goal toward which we strive, making progress little by little. A recipient of the Eucharist must also be in the state of grace and thus free from grave sin. This means that the recipient must be absolved from mortal sin in the Sacrament of Penance and Reconciliation before approaching the Sacrament of the Eucharist.

In addition, we also prepare for the Eucharist by fasting. This is a bodily reminder that the Eucharist is not ordinary food and drink. It also reminds us that as we fast from food (for one hour in the Western Church, and usually from midnight in the Eastern Churches), we must also fast from thoughts and actions that would be unworthy of a follower of Christ, so soon to receive the Body and Blood of the Lord.

Our outward appearance and behavior should reflect our inward respect and seriousness. "Dressing up" for Sunday Mass is perhaps no longer the norm in many places, but we should be neat, clean, and modest in dress when attending the Mass.

How Often Do We Receive the Eucharist?

The Eucharist is our lifeline to Christ. Frequent reception of Holy Communion, especially when participating in the Eucharistic celebration, is highly recommended by the Church. This is the most perfect form of participation in the celebration of the Eucharist. In fact, every Catholic is obliged to receive the Eucharist at least during the Easter season.

Transubstantiation ➤ In the Sacrament of the Eucharist, this is the name given to the action of changing the bread and wine into the Body and Blood of Jesus Christ.

UNIT 3

UNIT 3

Receiving the Eucharist under the species of bread alone is sufficient to receive the full grace of the Eucharist. However, we are encouraged to receive under both species, bread and wine, whenever possible.

We participate in the Eucharistic celebration on Sundays and holy days of obligation. On those days, receiving the Body and Blood of Christ at the Eucharist is highly recommended. In addition, daily reception is encouraged. The petition of Jesus in the Lord's Prayer, "Give us this day our daily bread," refers not only to the bread we need for our sustenance but also the Holy Eucharist. In fact, we are permitted to receive the Eucharist twice in one day if special circumstances call for it. For example, suppose you receive the Eucharist at a weekday morning Mass. Later, you recall that in the evening your parish's fiftieth Jubilee Mass will be celebrated by the bishop. Can you receive Communion at the Jubilee Mass? Of course—as long as you participate in the entire Eucharistic celebration. ✳

HMMMMM. . .

How often do you think you should receive the Eucharist? Why?

Article 29
The Liturgy of the Eucharist: The Eucharistic Prayer and Communion Rite

The Liturgy of the Eucharist continues with the Eucharistic Prayer, the high point of the Mass. The Eucharistic Prayer includes the following elements:

- the Preface and Preface Acclamation (Holy, Holy, Holy)
- thanksgiving to the Father for all his benefits, especially the gift of his Son
- the *epiclesis*, the institution narrative, the *anamnesis*, the offering, the intercessions, the Concluding Doxology and Amen

The Preface and Acclamation

In the Eucharistic Prayer, which is the prayer of thanksgiving and consecration, we offer the bread and wine to be transformed into the Body and Blood of Christ. The Eucharistic Prayer begins with the Preface Dialogue between the priest and the assembly. The priest greets the people with "The Lord be with you," and the people respond, "And with your spirit." The priest continues, "Lift up your hearts." The people offer their hearts to the Lord by responding, "We lift them up to the Lord" (*Roman Missal*, page 635).

The priest then introduces the theme of the entire Eucharistic Prayer: "Let us give thanks to the Lord our God." The people speak their agreement and say, "It is right and just" (*Roman Missal*, page 635).

UNIT 3

© wideonet / Shutterstock.com

At the Preface Dialogue, the priest invites us to join with him in the Eucharistic Prayer.

The Preface follows immediately. "In the *preface*, the Church gives thanks to the Father, through Christ, in the Holy Spirit, for all his works: creation, redemption, and sanctification" (*CCC*, number 1352). The Preface of the Eucharistic Prayer introduces us to the meaning of the Eucharist for us on this particular day. There are many prefaces, and they are quite beautiful. For example, in Preface I of the Nativity of the Lord, we hear:

> So that, as we recognize in him [Christ] God made visible,
> we may be caught up through him in love of things invisible.
> *(Roman Missal,* page 538)

At the end of the Preface, as usual, the priest invites us to join with all the angels and saints in a hymn of praise, sometimes called the Preface Acclamation: "Holy, holy, holy . . ." We are never alone at the Eucharist. We are one with the entire Church on Earth and in Heaven, and are surrounded by a cloud of heavenly witnesses.

TAKE IT TO GOD

Anima Christi (Soul of Christ)

This prayer is an appropriate one to pray before or after receiving Holy Communion. You may want to choose a few favorite lines to pray.

> Soul of Christ, sanctify me.
> Body of Christ, heal me . . .
> Passion of Christ, strengthen me.
>
> Good Jesus, hear me.
>
> In your wounds shelter me.
> From turning away keep me.
> From the evil one protect me.
> At the hour of my death call me.
> Into your presence lead me,
> to praise you with all your saints
> for ever and ever.
>
> Amen.

Epiclesis

As we thank the Father for all his gifts, especially the gift of his Son, we include prayers for the living and the dead. We realize that we are in union with the entire Church.

At the *epiclesis*, the priest stretches both his hands over the offering, invoking the Holy Spirit to come upon these gifts, to make them holy, that they might become the Body and Blood of Christ.

UNIT 3

Then the priest stretches both hands out over the offerings. This is the traditional gesture signifying the invocation of the Holy Spirit. In this prayer, called the *epiclesis* (meaning "invocation" in Greek), the priest asks the Father to send the Holy Spirit upon these offerings:

> Make holy, therefore, these gifts, we pray,
> by sending down your Spirit upon them like the dewfall,
> so that they may become for us
> the Body and ✝ Blood of our Lord Jesus Christ.
> (*Roman Missal,* Eucharistic Prayer II, page 646)

The Institution Narrative and Consecration

At this point in the Eucharistic Prayer, we approach the consecration of the essential elements of the Sacrament of the Eucharist, the bread and wine. The Eucharistic bread is unleavened (without yeast) and made of wheat. The wine is made from grapes. The bread and wine must be consecrated together, not separately, and they both must be consecrated in the Eucharistic celebration.

The Holy Spirit has been invoked upon these gifts, and so the priest pronounces the words of the Lord that he gave to his Church at the Last Supper: "This is my Body, which will be given up for you. . . . This is the chalice of my Blood" (*Roman Missal*, page 639).

This part of the Eucharistic Prayer is called the institution narrative, as it records the institution of the Holy Eucharist by Jesus. By these words, the action of Christ, and the power of the Holy Spirit, the Body and Blood of Christ is made sacramentally present, together with the sacrifice of Christ offered for all on the cross. By this consecration, the Transubstantiation of the bread and wine is brought about. The word *transubstantiation* means "a change of substance." The physical attributes of bread and wine remain the same, but the substance (what the bread and wine essentially *are*) has been changed.

The Eucharist is not merely a symbol of Christ's presence; rather, Christ himself, living and glorious, is truly present in his Body and Blood, under the appearance of bread and wine. He is present as the whole Christ—Body, Blood, soul, and divinity. How long does this Real Presence of Christ last? It begins at the moment of consecration and lasts as long as the Eucharistic species is present. It is important to note that when the Host is broken into parts, Christ himself is not divided into parts. Christ remains whole and entire in each part.

The *Anamnesis*, Offering, and Intercessions

The *anamnesis* ("remembering" and making present) begins with the Mystery of Faith (or Memorial Acclamation), in which we proclaim the Paschal Mystery of Christ and what it means to us. This is one example:

> Save us, Savior of the world,
> for by your Cross and Resurrection
> you have set us free.
> (*Roman Missal*, page 640)

We then recall all that Christ has done for us, and we offer his sacrifice to the Father:

> Therefore, as we celebrate
> the memorial of his Death and Resurrection,
> we offer you, Lord,
> the Bread of life and the Chalice of salvation.
> (*Roman Missal*, Eucharistic Prayer II, page 648)

UNIT 3

This is followed by another *epiclesis*, still addressing the Father and calling on the Holy Spirit to make us one in Christ:

> Humbly we pray
> that, partaking of the Body and Blood of Christ,
> we may be gathered into one by the Holy Spirit.
> (*Roman Missal*, Eucharistic Prayer II, page 648)

Intercessions for the entire Church follow, signifying that this Eucharist is celebrated in communion with the whole Church, the living and the dead, and with the pastors of the Church—the Pope, the local bishop, his priests, and all the bishops of the entire world.

The Amen

The Eucharistic Prayer ends with a Concluding Doxology, literally "words of praise," beginning with "Through him, and with him, and in him" (*Roman Missal*, page 649). In Christ's Body and Blood, we have been made one. To the Doxology, in the unity of the Holy Spirit, the assembly responds with "Amen." This amen assents to the greatest prayer, the prayer in which we become one with Christ in his Paschal Mystery.

The Communion Rite

The Liturgy of the Eucharist concludes with the Communion Rite. This part of the Mass begins with the praying of the Lord's Prayer, the Our Father. In this prayer, we pray as one Body of Christ, asking for forgiveness of our trespasses "as we forgive those who trespass against us" (*Roman Missal*, page 663).

UNIT 3

© robertharding / Alamy Stock Photo

The Communion Rite begins with the Lord's Prayer.

The priest extends this prayer by continuing, "Deliver us, Lord, we pray, from every evil." We pray for freedom from sin and anxiety "as we await the blessed hope and the coming of our Savior, Jesus Christ" (*Roman Missal*, pages 664–665). Although we hope for his coming at the end of time, we also joyfully prepare ourselves for his coming to us personally in this very Eucharist.

The assembly ends this prayer with the acclamation: "For the kingdom, the power and the glory are yours now and for ever" (*Roman Missal*, page 665).

The priest or deacon invites us to share a sign of Christ's peace with one another. In the Eucharist, Christ gives us his peace. We share a sign not only of our own goodwill but of the very gift of peace that Christ has given us.

While the priest prepares the Eucharist for the people by breaking the large Host into pieces (this part of the Communion Rite is called the Breaking of Bread or the Fraction), the "Lamb of God" is said or sung. The priest takes a small piece of the Host and places it into the chalice, saying quietly, "May this mingling of the Body and Blood of our Lord Jesus Christ bring eternal life to us who receive it" (*Roman Missal*, page 667).

Before Holy Communion is offered, the priest takes the Host, raises it slightly over the paten, and says, "Behold the Lamb of God" (*Roman Missal*, page 669). This is our invitation to "the supper of the Lamb." Together with the priest, the entire assembly prays:

> Lord, I am not worthy
> that you should enter under my roof,
> but only say the word
> and my soul shall be healed.
> (*Roman Missal*, page 669)

This is a reference to the centurion who asked Jesus to heal his servant. He had such faith that he would not allow Jesus to make the journey to his home: "Only say the word and my servant will be healed" (Matthew 8:8). With this kind of faith in Jesus, we approach the reception of the Eucharist, the Bread of Heaven and the Cup of Salvation, the Body and Blood of Christ.

After Holy Communion, a short period of silence is observed, in which we offer a prayer of thanksgiving for the gift we have just received, or a song of praise may be sung. Then all stand for the Prayer after Communion. This prayer asks that the Sacrament of the Eucharist may take effect in our lives. The assembly responds "Amen." Yes! It is true! ✻

HMMMMM... What does "Lord, I am not worthy that you should enter under my roof" mean to you?

Article 30
Ministries at Mass

When you started high school, it's likely that many things were different from your middle school experience. When Chris started attending Sacred Heart High School, he felt overwhelmed and out of place. It was much bigger than his middle school, and he got lost a few times. Every night, Chris would sit at the dinner table in silence. He was too exhausted to talk about his day. His mom kept asking questions, but Chris didn't really know what to say. Finally, she suggested: "If you want to feel like you fit in, maybe you should try getting involved in something. Then you would have a group of people to talk to." Chris saw the bulletin boards with posters for joining clubs, and he heard the announcements about trying out for sports. But he just wasn't in to sports, and walking into a club meeting was the last thing he wanted to do.

On the day of the first school Mass, Chris noticed the campus minister and his religion teacher looking through the crowd of students. "I can't believe that we don't have any returning altar servers!" Chris turned around. He didn't even mean to say it, but it just kind of came out of his mouth. "I'm an altar server. I serve at my parish every other week." They looked so relieved; Chris didn't even have time to say he was nervous! They introduced him to the priest. He put on an alb, and that was how it started. Chris served at the school Masses all four years. He joined campus ministry. He participated in retreats. He made friends that introduced him to their friends, and pretty soon he knew a ton of people. Chris found a way to serve and to be part of his community. Let's look at more ministries involved in the celebration of the Eucharist.

The word *ministry* means "service." Those who help with the celebration of the Eucharist are often referred to as ministers. Various roles of service are carried out by both ordained and lay ministers in the celebration of the Eucharist. Before we begin discussing these, we must point out that the greatest minister of all, the greatest "servant of all," as he described himself (see Mark 9:35), is Jesus Christ.

The Role of the Ordained

In every Eucharist, we are united with the entire Church. The liturgy is God's work, in which the whole People of God participate. Every liturgy affects the entire Church, as well as the individual members of the Church. In the liturgy, each member has a role, in accordance with that member's particular vocation,

UNIT 3

office, ministry, or participation in the Eucharist. The liturgy is ordered so that each person can carry out to the full their own role, without taking on the role of another.

The Pope and Bishops

In every Eucharist, we are particularly united with the Pope as a sign of unity. We offer every Eucharist for the entire Church, and we pray for the Pope and for our local bishop by name. We name the bishop because he is responsible for the celebration of the Eucharist in our diocese, even if a priest offers that Eucharist. Even though the bishop is not physically present at every Eucharist in his diocese, he is present in spirit, for every Eucharist is the celebration of a local church gathered around its bishop. As Saint Ignatius of Antioch (ca. 35–107) wrote in the early centuries of the Church: "Let only that Eucharist be regarded as legitimate, which is celebrated under [the presidency of] the

MAKE IT SO

Be Part of the Miracle

One well-known Jesuit retreat director and writer on spirituality once commented as follows on Matthew 14:19, the miracle of the loaves:

> Christ breaks the loaves and works the miracle, but he distributes it through [us]. Normally Christ's miracles will reach [all people] only in this way. The light of God's lamp burns with the oil of our lives. This is the aspect of apostolic activity which raises it immediately into the realm of prayer. God needs us just as he needs the grain of wheat for the Eucharist. We too are to be broken, to be distributed, to be eaten. In this way we become part of the miracle; it is worked through us—but then, we have to be broken and distributed. (Peter G. van Breemen, *Called by Name*, page 168)

How will you share your time and talents with your school or parish? How will you be broken and distributed among those who need your help? How will you be part of the miracle of the Eucharist?

bishop or him to whom he has entrusted it"³ (*CCC,* number 1369). Bishops, priests, and deacons are ordained ministers of the Church. They have all received the Sacrament of Holy Orders in varying degrees. (For more information, see chapter 11, "The Sacrament of Holy Orders.")

Priests

In the Eucharist, the priest follows the command of Jesus and makes present the offering of Jesus to the Father. He, in the person of Christ, thus unites us, the Body of Christ, to our Head, Christ himself, in the very Body and Blood of the Lord. His entire ministry, to preach the Good News of Christ, draws its strength from the Eucharist. In the liturgy, the priest stands at the head of the people, presides over their prayer, proclaims to them the Word of God, includes them with him in the offering of the Body and Blood of Christ to the Father in the Holy Spirit, and gives them the Bread of Life and the Cup of Salvation.

Deacons

The deacons of the Church assist the bishop and the priests in the celebration of the sacraments, especially the Eucharist. In their role of service at the liturgy, deacons, because of their ordination, are given first place. In the Eucharist, they may proclaim the Gospel, preach the Homily, announce the Prayer of the Faithful, direct the people as needed, pour the water into the chalice of wine at the Preparation of the Gifts, announce the Sign of Peace, assist in the distribution of Holy Communion, prepare the people for the Solemn Blessing ("Bow down . . ."), and dismiss the assembly.

The liturgy is ordered in a way that each person should carry out their role to the fullest. Deacons assist the priest during the liturgy in many ways.

The Role of the Assembly

The assembly as a whole has a role in the liturgy. Through the priest, who is acting in the person of Christ, our sacrificial offerings are united with the sacrifice of Christ. As children of the Father, we are to make every effort to be a sign of unity to one another as brothers and sisters, and should not allow any individual preference, however devout, to detract from this unity. Whatever we do in the liturgy, we do as one body, whether that be listening to the Word

UNIT 3

of God, joining in the prayers, singing, or receiving Holy Communion. There is a beauty in the unity of liturgical gestures and postures (standing, sitting, or kneeling as appropriate), which is a sign of the beautiful unity of the Body of Christ (see *General Instruction on the Roman Missal*, page 41).

Particular Ministries for Laity

At the Eucharist, the ordained ministers of the Church are, as needed, assisted by lay ministers. You may be familiar with the following lay ministries: altar server, lector, and extraordinary minister of Holy Communion.

Being an altar server is a privilege. Although most altar servers are young, many adults serve in this role as well. Altar servers must always be alert to the needs of the priest and deacon at the altar, and must assist in the liturgy in a dignified way.

The role of lector, or reader, is another ministry that can be filled by laypeople. Being a lector requires preparation and even some training. In order to read Scripture with meaning, the lector must first understand the assigned Scripture passage. Lectors are encouraged to practice their reading several times aloud at home, and even a few times in church, before reading it to the assembly. Everything in the liturgy deserves our best effort, and that certainly includes the readings, by which the Holy Spirit guides our lives.

© Godong / Alamy Stock Photo

Altar servers perform an important role as lay ministers. They assist the priest and deacon at the altar during Mass.

UNIT 3

The extraordinary ministers of Holy Communion assist at the Eucharistic celebration by distributing the Body and Blood of Christ. They also are privileged to take Holy Communion to those who are sick or homebound and unable to participate in the Mass. This ministry is an ancient one in the Church. Those who are vulnerable due to illness or advanced age require sensitive and reliable ministers. Thus, this ministry requires preparation and prayerful dedication.

Several other ministries are ordinarily filled by laypeople. The psalmist (the singer of the responsorial psalm), the choir, and the cantor or choir director are laypeople. Musicians are also vital to the celebration. Other ministries fulfilled by laypeople help with the Eucharistic celebration: the sacristan (who arranges the liturgical books, vestments, and other things necessary for the celebration), the commentator (who may introduce the celebration and occasionally, with brief remarks, help the assembly understand the liturgical action better), and greeters and ushers (who greet the worshippers at the doors of the church, offer songbooks, help worshippers find seats, take up the collection, and sometimes direct processions). In larger churches and cathedrals, often a master of ceremonies is needed to help plan and carry out the liturgy with proper order and devotion.

You may already have taken on one or more of these ministries in your parish church or at your school. If so, you may have found that taking an active part in the liturgy gives you a unique perspective on "the work of God" in your parish. Ministers at the Eucharist are ordinary people, our neighbors and friends, who assist with something extraordinary: the great gift to us of the Body and Blood of Christ. ✳

UNIT 3

HMMMMMM. . . What ministries of the laity are most appealing to you to participate in more fully in the Mass?

1. Describe the worship of the first Christians. What common elements does it share with our worship today?

2. In the Eucharist, what is the purpose of the Introductory Rites?

3. What is the purpose of the Penitential Act in the Eucharist?

4. In what ways is Christ present in the celebration of the Eucharist?

5. How is the Holy Spirit at work in the celebration of the Eucharist?

6. In what ways does the Liturgy of the Word prepare us to celebrate the Liturgy of the Eucharist?

7. What is the Eucharistic Prayer, and why is it the high point of the Eucharist?

8. How is Christ's Paschal Mystery proclaimed and made present in the Eucharist?

9. Describe the role of the assembly in the celebration of the Eucharist.

10. From where do priests draw their strength to preach the Good News and minister to their faith communities?

UNIT 3

1. What is the first thing you notice about this artwork?

2. What are some traditional elements you can see in this modern painting?

3. How does this artwork connect Christ's sacrifice to the Mass?

CHAPTER 8
The Eucharist in Daily Life

HOW DOES RECEIVING THE EUCHARIST MAKE A DIFFERENCE IN MY LIFE?

SNAPSHOT

Article 31

The Concluding Rites: To Love and Serve

In his poem "East Coker," T. S. Eliot wrote, "In my end is my beginning." This is certainly true of the ending of the Eucharistic celebration. The Concluding Rites, as we will discuss in this chapter, both end the Mass and strengthen us to continue our Christian discipleship in prayer and action. The particular elements of the Concluding Rites unfold in the following order: the greeting, the Final Blessing, and the Dismissal.

The Greeting

The Concluding Rites begin with the greeting by the priest, "The Lord be with you," and the assembly's response, "And with your spirit" (*Roman Missal*, page 671). This particular greeting functions as a goodbye. In fact, our English word *goodbye* is a shortened form of the phrase "God be with you." The priest—the president of our assembly, our presider, and our minister of the Eucharist—has brought us to Christ and Christ to us, and our last greeting to him is a greeting of goodbye, and also of thanks.

UNIT 3

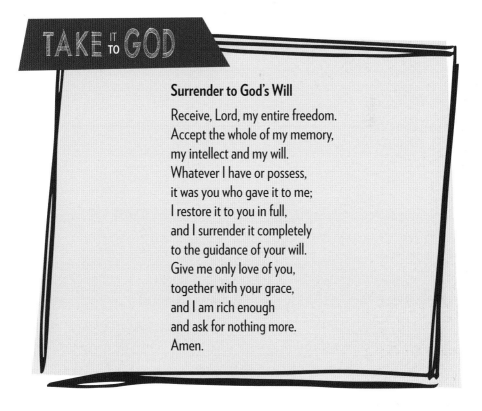

TAKE IT TO GOD

Surrender to God's Will

Receive, Lord, my entire freedom.
Accept the whole of my memory,
my intellect and my will.
Whatever I have or possess,
it was you who gave it to me;
I restore it to you in full,
and I surrender it completely
to the guidance of your will.
Give me only love of you,
together with your grace,
and I am rich enough
and ask for nothing more.
Amen.

The Blessing

Following the greeting, the priest blesses the assembly. He may choose the Simple Blessing, the Solemn Blessing, or the Prayer over the People.

Blessing Options	
Option 1: **The Simple Blessing**	This blessing follows the greeting and is often this simple form: May almighty God bless you, The Father, and the Son, ✝ and the Holy Spirit. The assembly responds: Amen. (*Roman Missal*, page 671)
Option 2: **The Solemn Blessing**	Some days in the Liturgical Year call for a solemn blessing. The priest addresses the assembly: "Bow down for the blessing" (*Roman Missal*, page 674). The solemn blessing consists of three petitions to which the assembly responds each time: "Amen." The blessing concludes with: "And may the blessing of almighty God, the Father, and the Son, ✝ and the Holy Spirit, come down on you and remain with you for ever." (*Roman Missal*, page 674)
Option 3: **The Prayer over the People**	This third option begins with an invitation to bow for the blessing. The priest extends his hands over the people while he says or sings the prayer. The prayer has only one petition, and ends with the priest saying, "Through Christ our Lord," or a similar phrase, with the people responding, "Amen." After the prayer, the priest then adds the ending formula of the solemn blessing (see *Roman Missal*, page 685).

The Dismissal

Next, the priest or deacon dismisses the assembly. He uses one of the following four options:

"Go in peace, glorifying the Lord by your life" (*Roman Missal*, page 673).
The message here is that now that you have received Christ, remain in him and remain in his peace. Let this Eucharist be the rock and the stronghold of

UNIT 3

your life. Remember the words of the Risen Christ to his disciples: "Peace be with you" (John 20:19). The implication is that if you are steady in the peace of Christ, you will be able to offer that peace to others, bringing glory to God.

The final blessing sends us forth to glorify the Lord with our lives and to bring Christ's Good News and peace to all. We are the disciples of Jesus in the world today.

"Go forth, the Mass is ended" (*Roman Missal,* page 673).

This option reflects the traditional Latin dismissal, *"Ite Missa est,"* or "Go, the Mass is ended." In this phrase, the word *Missa* has given us the very word we use often for the celebration of the Eucharist: Mass. In another sense, it is related to the Latin word *missio,* meaning "mission." So the sense of this dismissal is, "Go, you are sent on a mission for Christ." This dismissal reminds us that we are sent into the world by Christ to do his work and to follow his way.

"Go and announce the Gospel of the Lord" (*Roman Missal,* page 673).

In Jesus' Parable of the Judgment of the Nations, the king said, "Whatever you did for one of these least brothers of mine, you did for me" (Matthew 25:40). This is what Jesus, the King, expected of his disciples, and this is what he expects of us. He expects us to be Good News and to bring Good News to

MAKE IT SO

We do not have to go far to find brothers and sisters to love—our family and friends, our relatives, our neighbors, and the people we meet in school and stores, along the street, on public transportation, and at special events. The kind of love we offer each person is appropriate to that person. Showing love does not mean hugging everyone in sight, but it does mean respecting each person we meet as a unique human being, made in the image of God. We do that with small acts of kindness, such as saying "please" and "thank you"; greeting friends or anyone else we meet with pleasant hellos and goodbyes; and extending a cheerful smile, even amid a trying situation. Showing Christ's love certainly means we do not treat people (a clerk in a store, a librarian, an usher in a theater) as if they are machines dispensing services, to whom we can act with an "attitude" if all does not go exactly as we want.

others, especially to those who need us the most. The Good News is the Good News of God's love, and as the beloved disciple Saint John the Apostle wrote to his assembly, his local church, so long ago: "The way we came to know love was that [Christ] laid down his life for us; so we ought to lay down our lives for our brothers. . . . Children, let us love not in word or speech but in deed and truth" (1 John 3:16,18).

"Go in peace" (*Roman Missal,* page 673).
We have responded to Christ's invitation to come to him in the Sacrament of the Eucharist. He has given us his gift of peace. We go now to share that peace with a world that badly needs it.

Every dismissal formula encourages us to walk with the Lord as we leave the assembly and reminds us to follow God's will in every event of our daily lives.

The people's response to the dismissal is "Thanks be to God." Our thanksgiving for the entire Eucharistic celebration is wrapped up in this one phrase. We have so much to be thankful for: the Mass itself and all the gifts of God—especially the gift of his Son, Jesus Christ, given to us in his own Body and Blood in the Eucharist. Our thanksgiving is also a thanksgiving for what is to come after we leave this Eucharist, for God's gifts are never finished.

Before he leaves the altar, the priest, bowing, reverences it with a kiss. Then he bows with the other ministers and leaves. On Sundays, there is usually a recessional—a procession from the altar to the back of the church—and a closing hymn.

Often, we repeat the familiar words and begin to gather up our belongings. It is unfortunate that in doing so, we are missing out on an important focus of the Mass. Each of the different dismissal options includes a common directive "Go forth!" Whether we are going in peace, announcing the Gospel, or glorifying the Lord in life; we are to go forth and share the Good News with others. When you are in meditative silence after Communion, perhaps you could think of what this means for you. How can you share the Good News? Can you share Christ with others through your kind and helpful actions? Are you a person who creates a peaceful environment and helps others reconcile their differences? Have you ever offered to pray with a friend in need? Have you ever invited anyone to come to Mass with you? The dismissal reminds us that it isn't only participating in Mass that is important. What we do when we leave Mass is equally as important. What good is our attendance at Mass if we keep our faith to ourselves, tucked away in a box only to be opened on Sunday. The dismissal reminds us to go forth and spread the Good News! ✳

UNIT 3

HMMMMMM. . . What does it mean to you to "go and announce the Gospel of the Lord?"

Article 32

The Power of the Eucharist

The eating and drinking of the Body and Blood of Christ have certain effects within us, in our own hearts and lives, and within the Body of Christ, of which we are a part. The Eucharist changes us. In this article, we discuss five powerful effects the Eucharist has on those who receive it and on the entire Church.

The Eucharist Strengthens Our Union with Christ

This is the principal effect of receiving Holy Communion: the strengthening of our personal and intimate union with Jesus Christ. This primary effect reflects the words of the Lord himself: "I have called you friends" (John 15:15), and "Whoever eats my flesh and drinks my blood remains in me and I in him" (John 6:56).

When you spend some time unpacking chapter 15 of the Gospel of John, it explores how Christ describes our relationship with him as the life-giving connection between a vine and its branches. If a branch separates from the vine, it withers. In the Eucharist, we are connected to Christ as branches to the vine. Just as we need material food for growth and strength, so we need the spiritual food of the Eucharist to grow into the fullness of Christ during our entire lifetime.

In the Gospel of John, the vine and the branches are symbols of our life in Christ. In fact, the union of vine and branch is so close that we usually cannot tell them apart. How can this be true of you and Christ?

The Eucharist Strengthens Our Union with the Church

"The Eucharist makes the Church" (*CCC*, number 1396). Through our participation in the Eucharist, we are united more closely to Christ, and therefore our incorporation into the Church, which began at Baptism, is renewed and deepened. In Baptism, we are called to form one body with the Church. The

Eucharist fulfills this baptismal call. Saint Augustine explained the union of Christ and his Body, the Church, in this way:

> If you are the body and members of Christ, then it is your sacrament that is placed on the table of the Lord; it is your sacrament that you receive. To that which you are you respond "Amen" ("yes, it is true") and by responding to it you assent to it. For you hear the words, "the Body of Christ," and respond "Amen." Be then a member of the Body of Christ that your *Amen* may be true.[1] (*CCC*, number 1396)

The Eucharist Encourages Our Prayer for the Unity of All Christians

Unfortunately, all who are baptized in the name of the Father, and of the Son, and of the Holy Spirit do not share a common table of the Lord in the Eucharist. We are called to pray for the full unity of all those who believe in Christ and have been baptized in him. Because we are not fully united, Eucharistic intercommunion is not permitted. This means the reception of Holy Communion in the Catholic Church by non-Catholics is not allowed. Neither are Catholics permitted to receive Communion in non-Catholic congregations. Eucharistic intercommunion is not allowed with those faith communities that have not preserved Apostolic Succession through the Sacrament of Holy Orders. These include the faith communities usually described as Protestant.

UNIT 3

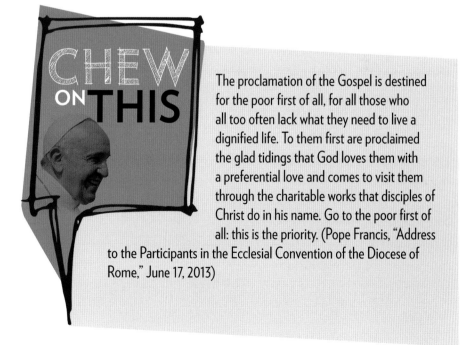

CHEW ON THIS

The proclamation of the Gospel is destined for the poor first of all, for all those who all too often lack what they need to live a dignified life. To them first are proclaimed the glad tidings that God loves them with a preferential love and comes to visit them through the charitable works that disciples of Christ do in his name. Go to the poor first of all: this is the priority. (Pope Francis, "Address to the Participants in the Ecclesial Convention of the Diocese of Rome," June 17, 2013)

However, in the Eastern Orthodox Churches (the Eastern Churches not in full communion with the Catholic Church), the line of Apostolic Succession has never been broken. The Eastern Orthodox Churches possess true sacraments, especially in the priesthood and in the Eucharist. Therefore, in certain circumstances, and with the approval of Church authority, the receiving of Communion in the Catholic Church by members of the Orthodox Churches is permitted.

We pray for unity with all these Churches and faith communities, especially during the Week of Prayer for Christian Unity. During this week, parishes are urged to pray each day for a particular ecumenical intention. In some places, the Week of Prayer for Christian

Priests in the Eastern Orthodox Churches remain in the line of Apostolic Succession.

Unity is celebrated by an ecumenical prayer service, hosted each year by a different Catholic parish, Orthodox church, or Protestant community.

The Eucharist Separates Us from Sin

Because the Body of Christ was "given up for us" and the Blood of Christ was "shed for the forgiveness of sins," the Eucharist cleanses us from past sin and preserves us from future sin, with our freedom and cooperation. Saint Ambrose (ca. 340–397) called the Body and Blood of Christ the remedy for sin (see *CCC*, number 1393). We do not come to the Eucharist because we are perfect; we come because we need the nourishment of Christ and the forgiveness of our sins. When we come to the Eucharist, we come to Christ, the Divine Physician, who said, "Those who are well do not need a physician, but the sick do. . . . I did not come to call the righteous but sinners" (Matthew 9:12–13). Thus, as the Eucharist renews our charity and love, this very charity wipes away our venial sins.

The Eucharist, because it unites us more closely with Christ, also protects us from mortal sin. It does not forgive mortal sin; for this we need the Sacrament of Penance and Reconciliation. However, as we share more in the life of Christ and grow in our friendship with him, committing a mortal sin becomes more and more unthinkable—because it would separate us from the One who loves us.

The Eucharist Commits Us to the Poor

Saint Paul found it necessary to correct the Corinthian church for its excesses. In First Corinthians, Saint Paul addresses a situation in which people began bringing their own food to eat at a community meal—with some having plenty while others had little. Saint Paul scolded them for it, writing: "In eating, each one goes ahead with his own supper, and one goes hungry while another gets drunk. Do you not have houses in which you can eat and drink? Or do you show contempt for the church of God and make those who have nothing feel ashamed?" (1 Corinthians 11:21–22).

Note that Saint Paul wrote that the selfishness and lack of sharing on the part of the Corinthians shows "contempt for the church of God," which is the Body of Christ. Saint Paul solved the immediate problem by telling everyone to eat at home! However, the root problem, lack of charity and love—for God, for our neighbors, and for our brothers and sisters in Christ—can be solved only by sharing our time, talents, and treasure with one another and with those in need. ✳

How can you share your time, talent, or treasure with others?

UNIT 3

HMMMMMM. . .

Which of the five effects of the Eucharist are you most grateful for? Why?

Article 33
Living the Eucharist

In the previous article, we discussed some effects of the Sacrament of the Eucharist, among them a stronger and deeper union with Jesus and the Church, and a commitment to those who are poor and in need. In this article, we begin by discussing the importance of gathering for the Sunday Eucharist, and then we explore two of the many ways to live out our union with Christ and the Church: worship of the Eucharist and a commitment to poor people.

The Sunday Eucharist

Celebrating the Resurrection of Christ at the Sunday Eucharist is "the foundation and confirmation of all Christian practice" (*CCC*, number 2181). Because attending the Mass on Sundays and holy days of obligation is so important, every Catholic is obliged to do so unless excused for a serious reason or dispensed by the pastor. Deliberately failing to do so is a grave sin. This obligation is the first precept, or rule, of the Church.

Resting from unnecessary work on Sundays, so that time may be set aside for worship and relaxation, is also a matter of obligation. Sunday is a day to spend time with family, to participate in social and cultural activities, and to spend time in quiet prayer and reflection. We must also avoid asking others to do any unnecessary work that would hinder their observance of Sunday worship and rest. However, the Church recognizes that some people must work on Sundays. In that case, the Church urges those people to take advantage of another day of rest during the week.

Sunday is a time for worship and relaxation—time to spend with family. How do your activities honor Sunday religious obligations?

CATHOLICS **MAKING** A DIFFERENCE

Catholic Relief Services (CRS) is the official international humanitarian agency of the Catholic Church in the United States. It operates under the auspices of the United States Conference of Catholic Bishops (USCCB), and its mission is to assist the poor and vulnerable in other lands. Contributing to CRS is one way Catholics in the United States can live out our Eucharistic commitment to those who are poor or in need around the world.

As chair of the board of directors of Catholic Relief Services, Timothy Dolan, Archbishop of New York, wrote in a CRS brochure:

> For Catholic Relief Services, who we are and who we serve are even more important than what we do. . . . We are committed Christians. We serve the poor, in whom we see the reflection and the face of Jesus Christ. That is more important, and that gives rise to what we do. CRS serves people because of need, not creed. We don't help people because they're Catholic; we do it because we are.

How does this fit in with your lifestyle? Do you participate in sports, theater, band, gaming, or other activities that have scheduled events on Sundays? Likely, your parents or grandparents didn't have to choose to attend Mass and spend time with family by skipping a tournament or performance when they were young. However, scheduled activities on Sundays are a common occurrence in today's world. How can you participate in your activities as well as honor your commitment to keep holy the Sabbath? If your activities are scheduled on Sundays and participation is necessary, you could attend Mass on Saturday evenings. You could also consider asking your coach or moderator to schedule practices or activities in such a way that there is time for you to attend Mass. You might be surprised; many people are open to supporting a request to honor faith obligations.

Why is participating in the Eucharist on Sunday so important? Because it is a sign of faithfulness to Christ and a way of thanking Christ for his total faithfulness to us. Gathering with others for the Mass on Sunday (or Saturday evening) also gives witness to our union with Christ and with one another in the solidarity of faith and love that is shared by the members of the Church. At the Eucharist, in word and action, we show that we are united in faith and love. Together, the community gratefully acknowledges the holiness of God and his saving love for his people. By our very presence, we show that we trust in him for our salvation. In coming together to worship and to share the Bread of Life, we, as followers of Jesus, strengthen one another, and, with the guidance of the Holy Spirit, deepen our union with Christ as sons and daughters of the Father.

This union with Christ does not end when the Mass ends. We can live out this union with Christ in many ways, ways that flow directly from our active and reverent participation in the Eucharist. Two significant ways are the worship of the Eucharist and commitment to those who are poor and in need.

Worship of the Eucharist

Eucharistic worship flows from the Real Presence of Christ, in his Body and Blood, in the Eucharist. Eucharistic worship is expressed in three important ways: reverence at the Mass and toward the Sacrament of the Eucharist, respect shown toward the tabernacle, and adoration of the Eucharist.

I DIDN'T KNOW THAT!

For most of Church history, Catholics were required to attend Mass on Sunday to fulfill their obligation to keep the Sabbath holy. However, after the Second Vatical Council, a decision was made to permit Masses celebrated on Saturday evenings to fulfill this obligation. Why the shift? It was motivated by changes in the world. Many governments and cultural changes no longer protected Sunday as a day free from work. The Saturday evening Mass provides an opportunity for those who must work on Sundays. It also cements a strong bond with our Jewish brothers and sisters, who observe their Sabbath from sundown Friday evening to sundown on Saturday.

Reverence

Within the Eucharistic celebration, we show our reverence for the Body and Blood of Christ by certain gestures, among them, genuflecting or bowing deeply when approaching the altar (where the Body and Blood of Christ is consecrated) or the tabernacle. Reverence for the Eucharist means we must prepare ourselves well and prayerfully to receive the Body and Blood of Christ, realizing that we are in the presence of this great and holy Mystery of our faith. Such reverence extends to the way we treat the consecrated Hosts within and outside the Mass. Our reverence for the Eucharist extends to those times when the Host is exposed to solemn veneration (as at a service of Benediction) and when it is carried in procession (as on the Feast of the Body and Blood of Christ).

The Tabernacle

Every church has a tabernacle set aside for the reservation of the Eucharist. The tabernacle contains the consecrated Hosts that are taken to those who are sick or dying. A light is kept burning before the tabernacle at all times. This is a symbol of the presence of Christ, who is always with us in the Eucharist. Quiet prayer before the tabernacle, in the presence of Christ in the Eucharist, has become an important tradition in the Church. These times of quiet prayer are often called visits to the Blessed Sacrament. In his encyclical "Mystery of Faith" ("*Mysterium Fidei*," 1965), Pope Venerable Paul VI (1897–1978) described such a visit as "a proof of gratitude, an expression of love, and a duty of adoration toward Christ our Lord" (*CCC*, number 1418). The Church recommends that a special place for the tabernacle be reserved in every church.

Adoration

It is entirely appropriate that Christ, present in the Eucharist, be honored with our worship and adoration. In this way, we express our gratitude and love for him who loved us so much and loved us "to the end" (John 13:1).

Many parishes today have obtained the privilege of having special times and days of **Eucharistic adoration**. The Host, placed in a sacred vessel called a **monstrance**, is set on the altar so it can be seen, for as little as an hour a day or for several hours at a time. In some places, parishioners are urged to commit a certain hour of the day to spend in prayer before the Blessed Sacrament.

UNIT 3

Eucharistic adoration ➤ The practice of praying in front of the Blessed Sacrament, which is exposed in a monstrance or ciborium on an altar or in a church or chapel.

monstrance ➤ A sacred vessel, usually in the form of a cross, used for the exposition of the Blessed Sacrament for adoration and benediction.

UNIT 3

The practice of Eucharistic adoration emerged in the Middle Ages, when reception of the Eucharist was more rare than it is today. During adoration, the people could see, honor, and adore the Body of Christ.

Many find that in this way they answer the request Jesus made of his disciples during his agony in the garden at Gethsemane: "Could you not keep watch for one hour?" (Mark 14:37).

Our lives are full of socializing and media distractions. We also might not be used to or comfortable with silence. But the disciplined practice of Eucharistic adoration can help us to shut out distractions, focus on Christ, and find some peace we might not have even known we craved and needed. The urge to fidget, nod off, or even abandon the effort altogether can be very strong at first, so it can be helpful to start with only fifteen minutes and slowly increase this over time. By spending time in prayer before the Blessed Sacrament every so often—in quiet adoration and prayer for ourselves, for our families and friends, and for the world—we will, in our deepening connection with Christ, be all the more ready to share the love of Christ with those who so desperately need it.

No Longer for Ourselves

The Eucharist commits us to live for Christ and his people, and therefore to serve those who are poor. Poverty is not only an absence of money. It can be that, and such poverty is devastating to human life. But someone can be in need—of a friend, companionship, a helping hand or a kind word—without being economically poor. How can you carry the love of Christ, the love you find in the Eucharist, to those in need around you, perhaps among your own family and friends?

And what, then, does the Eucharist have to do with those who suffer from poverty and grave injustices that threaten their welfare and even their existence? Everything, because when we reach out with love and care for those in need, we are serving and showing love for the Christ who comes to us and gives us his life in the Eucharist, and who identifies with "the least" among us (see Matthew 25:40).

Pope Paul VI, in his encyclical "On the Progress of Peoples" (*"Populorum Progressio,"* 1967), made this connection between the Eucharist and those in need. He alluded to the miracle of the loaves and fish (you may recall that this is an anticipation of the Eucharist) when he wrote: "No one is permitted to disregard the plight of his brothers living in dire poverty, enmeshed in ignorance and tormented by insecurity. The Christian, moved by this sad state of affairs, should echo the words of Christ: 'I have compassion on the crowd'" (number 74, Mark 8:2).

Union with Christ in prayer and sharing the compassion of Christ in action are intimately related. The more we discover the real meaning of the Eucharist in our prayer and reflection, the more we will discover opportunities to share with others the dying and rising of Christ, his self-giving love, and his compassion. ✳

UNIT 3

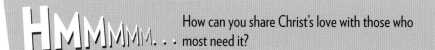

HMMMMMM. . . How can you share Christ's love with those who most need it?

1. Name and describe the three elements of the Concluding Rites.

2. What is the message of the priest or deacon's exhortation to the assembly at the end of the Mass to "go in peace, glorifying the Lord by your life"?

3. Name the principal effect of receiving Holy Communion, and explain what this means.

4. How does the Eucharist strengthen our union with the Church?

5. Another effect of the Eucharist is that it commits us to those who are poor. Describe what this means in your life.

6. What is the relationship between Apostolic Succession and the prohibition of intercommunion between the Catholic Church and Protestant faith communities?

7. What is the goal of the Week of Prayer for Christian Unity?

8. Describe three aspects of Eucharistic worship.

9. How are union with Christ in prayer and sharing the compassion of Christ in action intimately related?

ART STUDY

1. How does this icon represent Christ as "life-giving"?

2. What details in the icon spark your interest or curiosity?

3. In what way does the lighting and color that the artist uses give us a clue about the relationship between the vine and the branches?

UNIT 3 HIGHLIGHTS

CHAPTER 6   The Eucharist:
Culmination of Christian Initiation

The Sacraments of Initiation

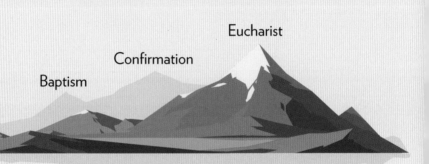

Eucharist

Confirmation

Baptism

The Eucharist is the culminating initiation sacrament, the source and summit of our life in Christ.

Scripture That Points to Jesus as the Bread of Life

God gave the Israelites manna to sustain them in the desert.

The Israelites took unleavened bread with them when they fled Egypt.

Jesus is the Bread of Life; the Living Bread come down from Heaven. Whoever eats this Bread will live forever.

The Feeding of the Five Thousand with five loaves and two fish

The Last Supper: Jesus broke the bread and gave it to his disciples.

Names for the Eucharist

Eucharist	• *Eucharist* means "thanksgiving." • Comes from the Jewish custom of a prayer of blessing that has overtones of thanks and praise. • Central to the celebration of the Eucharist.
Lord's Supper	• Recalls the meal that Jesus shared with his disciples before his Passion. • An anticipation of "the supper of the Lamb" we will share with Jesus in the Kingdom of Heaven.
Breaking of the Bread	• The common name by which the Eucharist was known. • Signifies that even though the Bread is broken to share with all, it is the one Christ that we share in his one Body.
The Eucharistic Assembly	• The life of the early Christians was centered around the Eucharist. • Sunday, the day of Resurrection, was the day of assembly. • The Eucharist was then, and is today, the heart of the Church's life.
The Holy Sacrifice	• Refers to the Eucharist as the sacrifice Christ made present to us in the liturgy. • The sacrifice of Christ surpasses all the other sacrifices offered to God throughout salvation history.
The Holy and Divine Liturgy	• Refers to the Church's liturgy in general rather than one sacrament. • Emphasizes the Eucharist as the source and summit of the lives of Christians.
Holy Communion and Holy Mass	• In the Eucharist, we are united to Christ. • We share with him and with the entire Church, as a single body, in Holy Communion.

CHAPTER 7   The Celebration of the Eucharist

Introductory Rites

UNIT 3

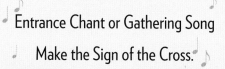

Entrance Chant or Gathering Song
Make the Sign of the Cross.

Penitential Act:
Provides a moment
for repentance of sin
in silence

The Gloria:
Expresses our joy in the Lord

The Liturgy of the Word Part I

The First Reading

- Draws us into the roots of our faith.
- Selected from the Old Testament for its relationship to the chosen Gospel.

Responsorial Psalm

- A response to the first reading.
- On Sundays, it is usually sung.
- Gives us an opportunity to meditate on the Word of God.

The Second Reading

- Usually from one of the letters of Saint Paul or the other Apostles.
- In these, we find many similarities to our life of faith today.

The Gospel Acclamation

- Consists of the Alleluia and a Scripture verse.
- The assembly stands for this acclamation, showing their readiness to hear God's Word.

Gospel Reading

- The proclamation of the Gospel by the priest or deacon, the assembly stands while listening.

The Liturgy of the Word Part II

Homily

- Helps us to discover the meaning of the Word of God.
- Must lead the assembly to active participation in the Liturgy of the Eucharist.

Profession of Faith

- We say the Nicene Creed together.
- The creed prepares us to celebrate the Eucharist.

Prayer of the Faithful

- We pray together for worldwide, national, and local needs.

Presentation of the Gifts

bread and wine

offering

Preparation of the Gifts

the *Roman Missal*

the chalice

the purificator

the corporal

The Eucharistic Prayer

the Preface and Preface Acclamation (Holy, Holy, Holy)

thanksgiving to the Father

epiclesis

the institution narrative and consecration

anamnesis

offering

intercessions

Concluding Doxology

Amen

The Communion Rite

Concluding Doxology and Amen

Lord's Prayer

Sign of Peace

Lamb of God

Communion

Prayer after Communion

CHAPTER 8 The Eucharist in Daily Life

The Concluding Rites

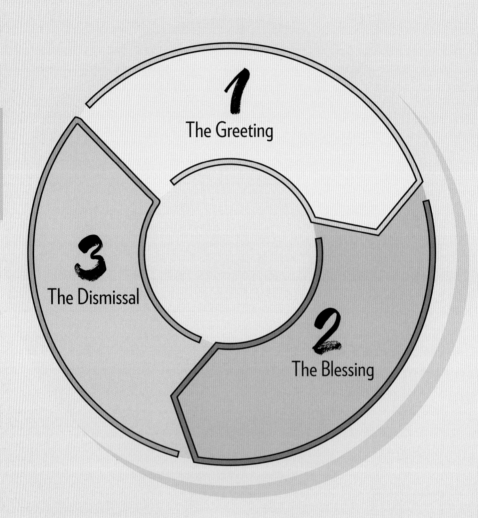

1 The Greeting

2 The Blessing

3 The Dismissal

The Effects of the Eucharist

strengthens our
union with Christ
and the Church

encourages our
prayer for the unity
of all Christians

separates us
from sin

commits us to
those who are poor

UNIT 3

Images: Shutterstock.com

UNIT 3
BRING IT HOME

WHY IS THE EUCHARIST SO IMPORTANT TO CATHOLICS?

FOCUS QUESTIONS

CHAPTER 6   What is the Eucharist, and where did it come from?

CHAPTER 7   Why is it important to attend Mass every Sunday?

CHAPTER 8   How does receiving the Eucharist make a difference in my life?

VICTORIA
Red Bank Catholic High School

UNIT 3

The Eucharist is important to Catholics in many ways. When we receive the Eucharist, we are receiving Christ himself. The bread and wine, which become the Body and Blood of Christ during the Mass, bring us closer to God. Jesus is most clearly present to us in the Eucharist. Because of Christ's presence in our lives, he helps guide us away from sin. All Catholics are called to participate in the Eucharistic celebration. So we are connected to the whole Church when we receive the Eucharist. And when we receive the Eucharist, we are strengthened to become the Body of Christ in the world.

REFLECT

Take some time to read and reflect on the unit and chapter focus questions listed on the facing page.

- What question or section did you identify most closely with?

- What did you find within the unit that was comforting or challenging?

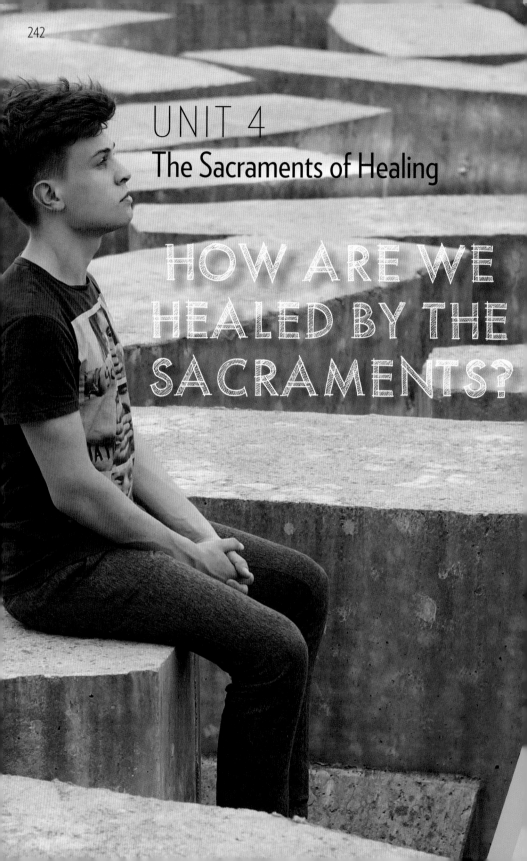

UNIT 4
The Sacraments of Healing

HOW ARE WE HEALED BY THE SACRAMENTS?

LOOKING AHEAD

UNIT 4

I believe that we are healed by the sacraments through the grace they impart to us
from God. For example, the healing power of
the Sacrament of Reconciliation strengthens
us to be more Christlike despite our sins.
I know we receive grace through the
sacraments, but I wonder where that
grace comes from—Christ or the Holy
Spirit? I also know that sanctifying
grace and actual grace are different,
but I'm not sure of the difference
between them.

DEMETRIOS
Our Lady of the Hills College
Preparatory School

CHAPTER 9
The Sacrament of Penance and Reconciliation

WHY ISN'T IT ENOUGH TO JUST TELL GOD I'M SORRY FOR MY SINS?

SNAPSHOT

Article 34
The Sacrament of Pardon and Peace

Even at first glance, it seems easy to see why both the **Sacrament of Penance and Reconciliation** and the Sacrament of Anointing of the Sick are called the Sacraments of Healing: one is the sacrament for the forgiveness of sins and the other is the sacrament for the strengthening of those who are seriously ill as well as for the forgiveness of sins. Because most people will receive it more often in their life, we discuss the Sacrament of Penance and Reconciliation first. It is a wonderful sacrament but, admittedly, can be a difficult one for many people. Even in this era of psychological sophistication, with a wide availability of counseling and therapies for almost every human need, we, individually

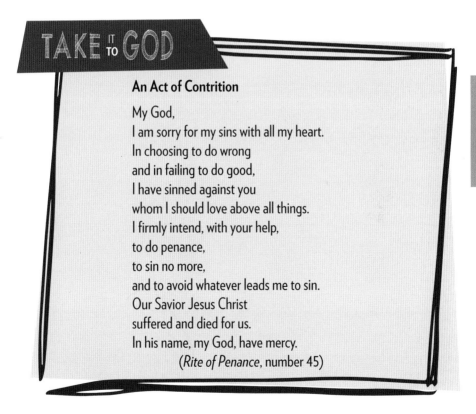

TAKE IT TO GOD

An Act of Contrition

My God,
I am sorry for my sins with all my heart.
In choosing to do wrong
and in failing to do good,
I have sinned against you
whom I should love above all things.
I firmly intend, with your help,
to do penance,
to sin no more,
and to avoid whatever leads me to sin.
Our Savior Jesus Christ
suffered and died for us.
In his name, my God, have mercy.
(Rite of Penance, number 45)

UNIT 4

Penance and Reconciliation, Sacrament of ➤ One of the Seven Sacraments of the Church, the liturgical celebration of God's forgiveness of sin, through which the sinner is reconciled with both God and the Church.

and as a culture, still seem averse to the kind of soul-searching and admitting of fault that this sacrament requires. However, by the end of this chapter, you may find that with a deeper understanding of this sacrament, you will be more eager to ask God for the forgiveness that only he can give.

The Sacrament of Penance and Reconciliation is the sacrament through which sins committed after Baptism can be forgiven, and we are reconciled with God and community. In this sacrament, we are pardoned and reconciled with the Church through God's mercy. Because we are members of the Body of Christ, everything we do—for good or ill—affects the rest of the Body. In the Sacrament of Penance and Reconciliation, our sins, which have brought harm to ourselves and others, are forgiven.

This sacrament has many names because it is a sacrament rich in meaning. It can be called the Sacrament of Conversion. The Greek word for *conversion* is *metanoia*. This word means "a turning around." When we realize that we have been going in the wrong direction, we turn around and take another path that will get us to where God wants us to be. This is what this Sacrament of Conversion does for us.

This sacrament is also called the Sacrament of Confession, as the confession of sins is an integral part of the sacrament. In confessing our sins, we must name them. And, to paraphrase a familiar slogan, "You name it, you own it." Therefore, confession is a way of taking responsibility, a necessary step for the penitent. Our confession is also an acknowledgment of God's holiness and mercy.

© Vigen M / Shutterstock.com

The philosopher Socrates once said, "The unexamined life is not worth living." Does this apply to your life today?

UNIT 4

Another name for this sacrament is the Sacrament of Forgiveness, for in this sacrament, through the priest's absolution, we receive pardon for our sins and the gift of God's peace. It is called the Sacrament of Penance because the action of penance (in prayer or in deed) on the part of the **penitent**—the recipient of God's forgiveness—is necessary for the completion of the sacrament. This sacrament is also called the Sacrament of Reconciliation, because by it, in God's love, we are reconciled to him and our brothers and sisters in Christ.

The Sacrament: A Dialogue in Wholeness

Ethan did not like participating in the Sacrament of Penance and Reconciliation. He didn't like thinking about the things he had done wrong, much less telling them to a priest. He also was nervous that he wouldn't remember everything he was supposed to say or do. When Ethan and his parents were on their way to confession at the beginning of Lent, Ethan told his parents how he felt.

Ethan's father offered some thoughts, "I used to think that I could just tell my sins to God. Why would I tell a priest when I could pray in my own room? But when I met your mom, we talked about how important communication is in a relationship. Something in my mind just clicked. Words are really important. When I tell your mom I'm sorry and she says, 'I forgive you,' I feel a huge sense of relief! So having a dialogue with God, through the priest, is meaningful!" Ethan leaned back in the seat and thought about what his dad said.

Ethan's mother added, "If you ever wonder why you confess your sins to a priest, keep this in mind. Jesus specifically gave the power of forgiveness to the Apostles and their successors. They are not offering forgiveness themselves; rather, they are offering forgiveness in God's name. You know how your dad said hearing me say the words 'I forgive you' is powerful? The same is true when the priest says, "You're forgiven." These words make the Sacrament of Penance and Reconciliation incredibly powerful and healing."

The Sacrament of Penance and Reconciliation is structured as a dialogue between the priest, who is the minister of the sacrament, and the penitent. It consists of four actions: three made by the penitent and then the absolution of the priest. The actions of the penitent are repentance, confession (admission of sins to the priest), and the intention to do what is possible to repair the harm caused by sin. This last action on the part of the penitent is often called a penance.

UNIT 4

penitent ➤ Refers to the person who repents of wrongdoing and seeks forgiveness through the Sacrament of Penance and Reconciliation.

Sin

To understand the Sacrament of Penance and Reconciliation and its power of forgiveness, we must understand what sin is. **Sin** is "an utterance, a deed, or a desire contrary to the eternal law"[1] (*Catechism of the Catholic Church [CCC]*, number 1849). It is a conscious and free choice to violate God's Law; a failure in genuine love for God and neighbor; and a fault against reason, truth, and right conscience. Sin wounds human nature and injures human solidarity.

In our culture, the attitude of "no harm, no foul" is common. This attitude can sometimes be an excuse for thinking that because the harm is not immediate or obvious, it does not exist. A sin that is temporarily hidden is still a sin; and making a habit of even less serious sins can lead to serious consequences that are suddenly not so hidden after all. Sometimes we can be lulled into thinking that if others are doing it, it can't be so bad. In fact, it is worse—because the sin is multiplied. A "group" does not have a conscience; only individuals do. And each individual is responsible for their own actions.

An individual's sin harms the Church because her members are intimately linked. We are one Body in Christ. Through the sacraments, we are united, and we influence one another in a deep and spiritual way. When sins are committed, this communion is damaged.

Sin is divided into two categories: mortal sin and venial sin. To commit a **mortal sin** is to deliberately, knowingly, and willingly choose to commit a serious violation of God's Law, and it is contrary to the final goal of a human being: happiness with God forever in **Heaven**. Mortal sin is called mortal, or deadly, because it destroys charity, or love, within us. When we commit mortal sin, Heaven is closed to us, because Heaven is all love. An unrepented mortal sin leads to eternal separation from God.

Mortal sin is a choice. Three conditions make a sin a mortal sin: (1) it concerns a serious and grave matter, (2) it is committed with full knowledge that the action is sinful and in opposition to God's Law, and (3) it is committed freely and deliberately.

---

sin ➤ Any deliberate offense, in thought, word, or deed, against the will of God. Sin wounds human nature and injures human solidarity.

mortal sin ➤ An action so contrary to the will of God that it results in a complete separation from God and his grace. As a consequence of that separation, the person is condemned to eternal death. For a sin to be a mortal sin, three conditions must be met: the act must involve a grave matter, the person must have full knowledge of the evil of the act, and the person must give full consent in committing the act.

Heaven ➤ A state of eternal life and union with God in which one experiences full happiness and the satisfaction of the deepest human longings.

Venial sin is a sin committed in a less serious matter. Venial sin "constitutes a moral disorder" (*CCC*, number 1875), but it does not destroy our relationship with God or his love within us. It does weaken our relationship with him and with the Church community, and it weakens our ability to resist mortal sin. The repetition of sins, even venial ones, leads us to develop vices, which are sinful habits. Vices are often linked with the seven capital sins: pride, avarice, lust, wrath, gluttony, envy, and sloth.

Forgiveness

God gives us a way to ask for and receive forgiveness and to heal our spiritual weaknesses. Jesus, the Son of God, has the authority to forgive sins, and he passed this authority to the Apostles, the first leaders of the Church. Through Apostolic Succession that authority has been passed down to the bishops and through them to priests, and it is administered in the Sacrament of Penance and Reconciliation.

Jesus forgave sins and reconciled sinners not only with God but also with the People of God. One sign of this reconciliation is Jesus' sharing of meals with sinners. Reconciliation with God meant reconciliation with the community as well. Similarly, in the Sacrament of Penance and Reconciliation, sinners are reconciled not only with God but with the Church. In fact, "*Reconciliation with the Church is inseparable from reconciliation with God*" (*CCC*, number 1445).

Jesus gave Peter the symbolic keys to the kingdom. The Church today has the same authority Jesus gave to Peter: to forgive sins.

UNIT 4

© Joravo / iStockphoto.com

---

venial sin ➤ A less serious offense against the will of God that diminishes one's personal character and weakens but does not rupture one's relationship with God.

In handing over the authority to forgive sins and to reconcile the sinner, Jesus said to Peter: "I will give you the keys to the kingdom of heaven. Whatever you bind on earth shall be bound in heaven; and whatever you loose on earth shall be loosed in heaven" (Matthew 16:19–20). And, in the Gospel of John, Jesus said to all the Apostles: "Receive the holy Spirit. Whose sins you forgive are forgiven them, and whose sins you retain are retained" (20:22–23). This forgiveness and reconciliation are extended to us today. The Church today has the same authority, given by Jesus, to forgive sins and to welcome back the sinner.

Only God can forgive, and he has given that same power to bishops and priests, not so they can "lord it over" us, but so, as servants of God, they can assure us that if we are forgiven on Earth in the Sacrament of Penance and Reconciliation, we are forgiven by God as well.

The Minister of the Sacrament

The ministry of the forgiveness of sin is exercised today by the bishops and by their coworkers, the priests. This ministry is given to them through the Sacrament of Holy Orders. Bishops regulate this ministry in which the priests collaborate. To exercise the ministry of the Sacrament of Penance and Reconciliation, a priest must receive a commission from his bishop, his religious superior, or the Pope. Only priests who have received this commission from the authority of the Church can exercise this ministry. However, if someone is in danger of death, any priest can absolve the person's sins, even without an official commission.

A priest must be available for this sacrament each time a Christian asks for it, as long as the requests are reasonable. As a confessor, a priest must have respect and sensitivity toward those who confess to him. He must have good knowledge of human behavior with experience and understanding of ordinary human life. He must be faithful to the Magisterium of the Church. It is his responsibility to encourage the penitent toward mature and responsible living of the Gospel and to help the penitent discover the healing love of Christ. The priest is also expected to pray and do penance for those who come to see him in this sacrament, and to entrust them to the mercy of God (see *CCC*, number 1466).

A priest may never reveal to anyone what he hears in the Sacrament of Penance and Reconciliation. This is called "the sacramental seal" or "the seal of the confessional." A confessor is bound to secrecy even when a serious crime, like murder has been confessed. In smaller matters, if the priest wishes to discuss a particular confession with someone else, for advice or guidance, he must first ask permission of the penitent. If a priest violates the seal of the confessional, he is automatically excommunicated. Those who inadvertently overhear a confession are also bound to secrecy by the seal of the confessional. An interpreter who may be needed to help someone make a confession is also bound by the sacramental seal. ✳

HMMMMMM. . . What keeps people from receiving the Sacrament of Penance and Reconciliation?

UNIT 4

Article 35
Scriptural and Historical Background

It is important to understand Jesus' institution of the Sacrament of Penance and Reconciliation in the context of his mission on Earth. In his earthly ministry, Jesus, the Son of God, continually urged **conversion** (turning toward God), and also frequently taught about the importance of giving and receiving forgiveness. In Jesus' teaching on conversion and forgiveness, and in giving authority to the Apostles to forgive sins, the Sacrament of Penance and Reconciliation finds its roots.

We have already discussed the important Scripture passage in which Jesus gives Peter the power to forgive sins. This power has been passed on through the Sacrament of Holy Orders, to our present-day bishops and priests (see Matthew 16:19). This gift of Jesus to his Apostles, the power to forgive sins, is also recorded in John's Gospel. On the evening of the first day of the week after Jesus' death, when his followers were locked in the Upper Room out of fear, Jesus came and stood among them, and said, "Peace be with you" (John 20:19). He showed them the wounds in his hands and his side. He said to them again: "Peace be with you. As the Father has sent me, so I send you" (verse 21). And then he gave them the means to pass on his gift of peace and reconciliation to the entire Church and so to the world: "And when he had said this, he breathed on them and said to them, 'Receive the Holy Spirit. Whose sins you forgive are forgiven them, and whose sins you retain are retained'" (verses 22–23). Note that the gift of this power to forgive sins, to offer peace and reconciliation to the followers of Jesus from that time forward, comes with the reception of the gift of the Holy Spirit. Only God—the Father, the Son, and the Holy Spirit—can forgive sins, and this power of forgiveness, given to the Apostles and their successors, is exercised in the name of the Holy Trinity.

Forgiveness of the Paralytic

All through his public ministry, Jesus forgave sins and taught about God's loving mercy toward sinners. Let us look at one example in the Gospel of Mark. Mark records that Jesus was "at home" in Capernaum (2:1). So many people gathered to hear him preach that there was no room in the house, or even around the doorway. This posed a problem for the friends of a paralytic. They wanted to ask Jesus to heal their friend, but they could not get near Jesus. Then someone had an idea: Get him to Jesus through the roof!

conversion ➤ A profound change of heart, turning away from sin and toward God.

This is a depiction of the paralyzed man being lowered by his friends through the roof to bring him to Jesus. How do you bring your friends to Jesus?

UNIT 4

So the friends broke through the roof above Jesus and lowered their paralytic companion down. "When Jesus saw their faith, he said to the paralytic, 'Child, your sins are forgiven'" (Mark 2:5). The scribes criticized Jesus in their hearts: "He is blaspheming. Who but God alone can forgive sins?" (verse 7). Jesus knew what they were thinking and went on to prove that he had the authority to forgive sins by telling the paralytic, "I say to you, rise, pick up your mat, and go home" (verse 11). The paralytic rose, picked up his mat "at once," and went home (verse 12). In this way, Jesus proved his words ("Your sins are forgiven") by this action of healing.

When we hear in the Sacrament of Penance and Reconciliation "I absolve you from your sins" (*Rite of Penance*, number 46), we should remember this incident, for when the priest forgives our sins in this sacrament, it is truly Jesus saying to us, "Child, your sins are forgiven."

Conversion after Baptism

You may remember from other studies that the first followers of Jesus expected his return to be soon after the Ascension. They believed in Jesus, were baptized, and then did their best to live by his teachings until he would come again. The early Christians had "put on Christ," but they found that following Jesus' teachings and avoiding sin was not easy. As the Apostle John wrote, "If we say, 'We are without sin,' we deceive ourselves" (1 John 1:8). Christian initiation did not abolish human nature, nor what is called **concupiscence**, the human tendency toward sin resulting from Original Sin. The life of the early Christians was a life of ongoing conversion—that is, a continual turning toward God, even after Baptism. Baptism is, of course, the time and place for a person's first and fundamental conversion. In Baptism, as you remember, we renounce sin. All our sins are forgiven, and we are given new life in Christ.

Yet, because we continue to struggle with sin after Baptism, we are called to conversion over and over again. This post-baptismal conversion is sometimes called a second conversion or an ongoing conversion. If by grace we are drawn to respond to God's merciful love, we can turn around again and, with contrite hearts, repent and believe again in the newness of life.

UNIT 4

© Benjavisa Ruangvaree Art / Shutterstock.com

Conversion involves the mind, heart, and soul.

---

concupiscence ➤ The tendency of all human beings toward sin, as a result of Original Sin.

I DIDN'T KNOW THAT!

In some places in the very early years of the Church, reconciliation with the Church was only granted once after Baptism. This meant that often people wouldn't receive reconciliation until they were on their deathbed. The practice of receiving a penance, however, gained traction, and in the late 300s, confession and penance were public if mortal sins were confessed. The thinking behind this was that sin not only affects our relationship with God but with our neighbors and community as well. Eventually, the practice of private confessions became more popular. The Fourth Lateran Council, in 1215, stated that Catholics should confess any sins at least once a year. Most parishes have a regularly scheduled time for private confessions before most weekend Masses, and communal celebrations during Advent and Lent.

UNIT 4

For an example of a second conversion, we can look to Saint Peter. (His first conversion was his answering of Jesus' invitation to follow him. See Mark 1:17–18.) After Jesus' arrest, Peter denied his relationship with Jesus three times. After the third denial, Jesus turned and looked at Peter. Peter was filled with remorse and wept bitterly. Later, after the Resurrection, Peter declared three times to Jesus, "You know that I love you" (John 21:15). Jesus also commanded Peter, "Feed my sheep" (verse 17), which meant to care for the Church. Saint Peter's conversion restored him to right relationship with Jesus and with the followers of Jesus, the Church (see Luke 22:61, John 21:15–17).

You may wonder how the Bible, written so long ago, can have relevance to your life today. But accounts such as Peter's second conversion are encouraging to us. Even though we try very hard to live in a way that is pleasing to God, we will still sin. We can be swayed to make poor choices that lead us away from a healthy relationship with God. But we have the Sacrament of Penance and Reconciliation available to us. Through this sacrament, we are strengthened and renewed— just like Peter. When we truly desire forgiveness and commit to turning our lives around, we are not alone. And Peter is there to remind us of how loving and forgiving Christ will always be.

Historical Notes

The way of celebrating the Sacrament of Penance and Reconciliation has varied through the centuries. In the early centuries, those who had sinned gravely and wanted to return to the Church underwent a rigorous program of public penance, which often lasted for years. This was for grave sins only and was called the Order of Penitents. Admittance into the Order of Penitents was rare and could happen only once in a person's lifetime.

In the seventh century, the Irish missionary monks had some contact with monks of the Eastern Churches. The monks in the Eastern Churches practiced a more private form of penance. They confessed their sins privately to a spiritual father and did a private penance. Through the Irish monks, this custom gradually spread throughout the entire Church. This practice also had the advantage of being repeatable. It was not a once-in-a-lifetime conversion, but rather a sacramental support to ongoing conversion in Christ. In this way, both mortal sins and venial sins could be forgiven in one celebration. The Church's practice of the Sacrament of Penance and Reconciliation has followed this basic form ever since. Despite the variations over time, the fundamental structure of the sacrament has remained the same throughout the centuries. ✳

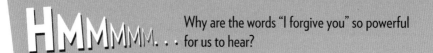

HMMMMM. . . Why are the words "I forgive you" so powerful for us to hear?

Article 36
The Rite of Penance and Reconciliation

As mentioned in the previous article, the Sacrament of Penance and Reconciliation is a single entity made up of four actions: three actions of the penitent and one action of the priest.

The Acts of the Penitent

Repentance or Contrition

Repentance, or contrition, is sorrow for one's sin and a hatred for sin, combined with the intention to avoid sin in the future. This is the primary act of the penitent. All contrition is based on faith in God's love for us. Contrition that springs purely from our love for God is called "perfect contrition." Contrition for other good reasons (the ugliness of sin, the fear of Hell, or earthly consequences) is called "imperfect." Both are gifts of God.

Confession of Sins

Honest conversations—though difficult—in which we take responsibility for our actions and seek to make things right again are an important part of human life. If you have admitted wrongdoing and asked for someone's forgiveness, if you have ever had a misunderstanding with a friend and then helped restore that friendship, you have some idea of what this kind of honesty can mean.

UNIT 4

In the Sacrament of Penance and Reconciliation, we go a step further along this path, and, by confessing our sins to the priest, we confess them to God. Thus, confession is an essential part of the sacrament. It is absolutely necessary after an examination of conscience to confess all mortal sins that are remembered so that they can be forgiven and the penitent can be reconciled with God and the Church. The Church also highly recommends the confession of venial sins. By confessing venial sins, we help form and strengthen our conscience, nip evil tendencies in the bud, open our hearts to the healing of Christ, and make progress in the life of the Spirit. In receiving the Father's mercy, we are encouraged to be merciful to others as well.

---

repentance (contrition) ➤ An attitude of sorrow for a sin committed and a resolution not to sin again. It is a response to God's gracious love and forgiveness.

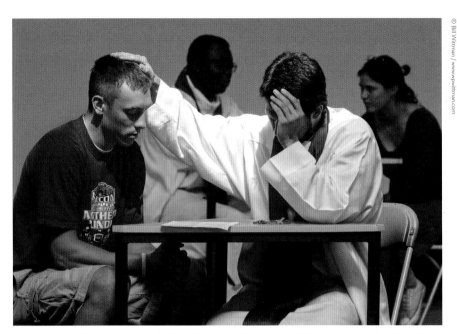

When we celebrate the Sacrament of Penance and Reconciliation, the Holy Spirit is with us, helping us to be sorry for our sins and to listen to the advice of the priest. It is helpful to get to know a priest to whom you can confess regularly.

Intention to Make Reparation

Within the sacrament, penitents have the opportunity to accept a penance, which is a prayer or action that repairs the harm caused by sin, from the priest. Sometimes this is a matter of justice: To repair the wrong we have done, we must return something stolen or pay for something we deliberately broke in anger. However, this is not the full reason for the act of **reparation**. "Absolution takes away sin, but it does not remedy all the disorders sin has caused" [2] (*CCC*, number 1459). For example, if we had been stealing and smashing things, **absolution** takes away our sin, but there is still chaos within us that must be dealt with. The penance we are given, which will often include prayer or an action, such as an act of mercy, is aimed toward our spiritual health and well-being, to help us deal with the chaos or disorder within ourselves that led us to sin. The penance, or "satisfaction," helps us to "reset" our hearts in the right direction and live, with reestablished good habits, as disciples of Christ.

---

reparation ➤ The act of making amends for something one did wrong that caused physical, emotional, or material harm to another person.

absolution ➤ An essential part of the Sacrament of Penance and Reconciliation in which the priest pardons the sins of the person confessing, in the name of God and the Church.

© Fresnel / Shutterstock.com

The Act of the Priest

Absolution is an essential part of the Sacrament of Penance and Reconciliation, in which the priest pardons the sins of the person confessing, in the name of God and of the Church. This is possible through the power Christ has given to the Church. In this absolution, Christ, the Good Shepherd, finds his lost sheep, and Christ, the Good Samaritan, binds up the wounds of the injured. In the forgiveness of sins, God, our Father, welcomes back his prodigal sons and daughters. In this absolution, we are given the gift of pardon and peace.

In the Sacrament of Penance and Reconciliation, the priest absolves you from your sins, not in his own name, but in God's name. It is God who forgives you. What does this mean to you?

UNIT 4

Celebration of the Sacrament

The Sacrament of Penance and Reconciliation is a liturgical action composed of these elements when celebrated by individual penitents:

Preparation of priest and penitent: The priest prays for enlightenment from the Holy Spirit; the penitent makes an **examination of conscience** and asks God for forgiveness.

Welcoming the penitent: The priest greets the penitent graciously.

Reading of the Word of God (optional): This reading may be a verse the priest recites from memory, or it may be a reading the priest and penitent choose together.

---

examination of conscience ➤ Prayerful reflection on, and assessment of, one's words, attitudes, and actions in light of the Gospel of Jesus; more specifically, the conscious moral evaluation of one's life in preparation for reception of the Sacrament of Penance and Reconciliation.

The first thing you should do before receiving the Sacrament of Penance and Reconciliation is to examine your conscience. This is a prayerful reflection on, and assessment of, our words, attitudes, and actions in light of the Word of God. Consider these questions based on the Ten Commandments as a starting point before your next confession:

- Have I made money, pleasure, or possessions more important than God?
- Have I ever used God's name out of anger, as a curse?
- Have I deliberately missed Mass?
- Have I disobeyed or disrespected my parents?
- Have I refused to forgive another, held a grudge, or cursed anyone?
- Have I ever given in to sexual temptation?
- Have I ever stolen or cheated on a test?
- Am I a liar? Do I gossip about others?
- Am I envious of others? Am I resentful? Do I put others down?

Penitent's confession and acceptance of the penance: The penitent may first say a general prayer ("I confess to Almighty God"), and then make a confession of sins. The priest may offer help and counsel as needed. He then proposes a penance, and the penitent agrees to do the penance.

Penitent's prayer and priest's absolution: After the penitent prays an Act of Contrition, the priest extends his hands, or his right hand, over the head of the penitent and pronounces the words of absolution:

> God, the Father of mercies,
> through the death and resurrection of his Son
> has reconciled the world to himself
> and sent the Holy Spirit among us
> for the forgiveness of sins;
> through the ministry of the Church

may God give you pardon and peace,
and I absolve you from your sins
in the name of the Father, and of the Son, ✝
and of the Holy Spirit.
The penitent answers: Amen.
> (*Rite of Penance,* number 46)

When the priest says the phrase beginning with "I absolve you," the essential words of absolution, he makes the Sign of the Cross over the penitent. The entire formula expresses the work of the Trinity in the Sacrament of Penance and Reconciliation: God the Father is the source of all mercy and forgiveness. Through the Paschal Mystery of his Son, Jesus Christ, the Father reconciled the entire world, including sinners, to himself. Through his gift of the Holy Spirit, the Father made forgiveness of sins possible. Through the work of the Church, forgiveness and reconciliation are offered today, in the name of the Trinity.

Proclamation of praise and dismissal of the penitent: The priest says, "Give thanks to the Lord, for he is good." The penitent completes this psalm verse with, "His mercy endures for ever" (*Rite of Penance*, number 47). The priest then dismisses the penitent with the words, "The Lord has freed you from your sins. Go in peace," or another similar option (number 47).

UNIT 4

God forgives every [person] in his sovereign mercy, but he himself willed that those who belong to Christ and to the Church receive forgiveness by means of the ministers of the community. Through the apostolic ministry the mercy of God reaches me, my faults are forgiven and joy is bestowed on me. In this way Jesus calls us to live out reconciliation in the ecclesial, the community, dimension as well. (Pope Francis, "General Audience," November 20, 2013)

The Communal Celebration

Most often, the Sacrament of Penance and Reconciliation is administered to individuals in private. However, this sacrament can also take place within a communal celebration. In this form, the assembly celebrates the Liturgy of the Word and then participates in an examination of conscience together. This is followed by a communal prayer asking God for forgiveness, and then the Lord's Prayer. After a short prayer, the assembly is invited to approach the priests who are designated for individual confession and absolution.

When all have finished individual confession, a psalm or hymn of thanksgiving may be sung. The presiding priest offers a concluding prayer of thanksgiving. The Concluding Rites follow, and then there is a blessing and dismissal.

This communal rite reminds us that we are members of the Church, the Body of Christ, and that what we do affects the entire Body. Of course, every liturgical action, including the Sacrament of Penance and Reconciliation, is an action of the entire Body of Christ, whether it is celebrated for one individual or communally.

Another form of this sacrament, called Communal Celebration of Reconciliation with General Confession and General Absolution, is used only in cases of dire emergency. Such an emergency might arise if there is danger of death in the immediate future and there is no time for one priest to hear each individual confession, or if there are not enough priests to hear confessions in a reasonable length of time. The diocesan bishop decides whether this is the case in a particular situation.

How to Make a Good Confession

The Sacrament of Penance and Reconciliation is a good way to take a closer look at your life and make a fresh start, at least once a year. Many parishes offer communal Penance and Reconciliation services during Advent and Lent, and private Penance and Reconciliation is usually available at some time every week. Before you go to confession, ask God for help in remembering your sins, specific actions, and general patterns of behavior. This is an outline of what you can expect in confession. The priest will also be happy to help you.

- *Go to the priest.* You can kneel behind a screen or sit and face the priest. He will welcome you and tell you to make the Sign of the Cross. He will pray for you and may read a Scripture passage.
- *Confess your sins.* The priest will then discuss your sins with you and give you spiritual advice.

UNIT 4

- *Receive a penance.* The priest will talk to you about doing something as a sign of your desire to change. It may be saying some prayers or doing a good action.
- *Tell God you are sorry.* You can use your own words or an Act of Contrition that you have memorized.
- *Receive absolution.* The priest proclaims the words of absolution, and God forgives your sins.
- *Conclude.* The priest says, "Give thanks to the Lord, for he is good," and you respond, "His mercy endures for ever" (*Rite of Penance*, number 47). The priest then dismisses you, and you can respond, "Thank you" or "Amen." ✳

How can understanding the Sacrament of Penance and Reconciliation be tied to how a person feels about this sacrament?

UNIT 4

Article 37
Penance and Reconciliation in Our Lives

What difference does the Sacrament of Penance and Reconciliation make in our lives? Although it is a sacrament that is celebrated quietly, it can have dramatic effects. For many people, this sacrament has been a major turning point in their lives, because, by the grace of God given in this sacrament, they are able to face themselves, be truly sorry, take responsibility for their sins, and be forgiven. They are able to carry their guilt, place it in God's hands, and move forward in hope. By the grace of this sacrament, they turn from being burdened by the sins of the past to being open to God's promise of a different future.

Friends are gifts from God. How can the Sacrament of Penance and Reconciliation help you to value your friendships and extend God's love to others?

Let us take a look at some of the effects of God's powerful action in this sacrament, and how we can take them to heart in our everyday lives:

The forgiveness of all sin: The Son of God shed his blood so that sin might be forgiven. Because bishops and priests have been given the authority to forgive sins in Christ's name, our sins can be forgiven in this sacrament.

UNIT 4

Reconciliation with God: This is the purpose of the sacrament. To those who are dead in sin, the Sacrament of Reconciliation brings a "spiritual resurrection" (*CCC*, number 1468) and new life as a son or daughter of God.

Reconciliation with the Church: If we are reconciled with God, we are also reconciled with the Church, the Body of Christ. The Sacrament of Reconciliation restores our relationship with all the members of Christ's Body, whether we know them personally or not. Sin harms or fractures our union, but the Sacrament of Penance and Reconciliation restores and repairs the broken places and, like bones in a human body, they grow stronger.

Remission of punishment for sin: Someone who dies with unrepented mortal sin has chosen to live without God for all eternity. This state of eternal separation from God, in whom alone we can have the happiness for which we were created, is called **Hell**. However, God's forgiveness and grace received in the Sacrament of Penance and Reconciliation remits eternal punishment for mortal sins committed after Baptism.

Even though the eternal punishment for sin can be removed through sacramental confession, there are also temporal consequences of our sin that can remain because sin causes disorder within us and our relationships that still requires healing. We can also attain remission of these temporal consequences of sin while we are still alive, through prayer, penance, and loving actions, especially the works of mercy. These works include actions that address the physical or spiritual needs of others. Physical, or corporal, works include feeding the hungry, clothing the naked, visiting the sick and those in prison, providing shelter for the homeless, and burying the dead. Spiritual works include forgiving those who hurt you, comforting those who suffer, being patient with others, sharing knowledge and advice with those who need it, and praying for others.

Another way remission of temporal punishment for sins can be obtained is through indulgences, either for ourselves or for those in **Purgatory**. One common way to gain indulgences is to participate in certain devotional practices, such as making a Holy Hour or praying the Rosary. An indulgence may be partial, meaning it removes some temporal punishment for sin, or plenary, meaning it takes away all temporal punishment for sin.

UNIT 4

Hell ❯ Refers to the state of definitive separation from God and the saints, and so is a state of eternal punishment.

Purgatory ❯ A state of final purification or cleansing, which one may need to enter following death and before entering Heaven.

CATHOLICS **MAKING** A DIFFERENCE

You might think that priests live such holy lives that they would not have anything to confess. But listen to how Pope Benedict XVI answered when a little girl asked him, "Do I have to go to confession every time I receive Communion, even when I have committed the same sins? Because I realize that they are always the same."

Even if, as I said, it is not necessary to go to confession before each Communion, it is very helpful to confess with a certain regularity. It is true: our sins are always the same, but we clean our homes, our rooms, at least once a week, even if the dirt is always the same; in order to live in cleanliness, in order to start again. Otherwise, the dirt might not be seen but it builds up. Something similar can be said about the soul, for me myself: if I never go to confession, my soul is neglected and in the end I am always pleased with myself and no longer understand that I must always work hard to improve, that I must make progress. And this cleansing of the soul which Jesus gives us in the Sacrament of Confession helps us to make our consciences more alert, more open, and hence, it also helps us to mature spiritually and as human persons. ("Catechetical Meeting of the Holy Father with Children Who Had Received Their First Communion During the Year," October 15, 2005)

UNIT 4

Peace and serenity of conscience, and spiritual consolation: Peace is a gift from God. It is not something we can manufacture for ourselves. If we are not at peace, it may be that something in ourselves is interfering with God's gift. One of the greatest effects of the Sacrament of Penance and Reconciliation is the restoration of peace and serenity to the heart and soul.

An increase of spiritual strength for the Christian battle: We like to think of life as satisfying, fun, filled with love, and peaceful. And much of the time it is. But sometimes it is also a battle. Anyone who has dealt with temptation, peer pressure, bullying, or betrayal or rejection by a friend knows that this is true. But even when you experience such challenges, you are not alone. The angels and saints and the entire Church are there for you, and the grace of the Sacrament of Penance and Reconciliation will help you to choose to stay on the right path in any difficulty.

Football players wear protective gear to guard against injuries. What spiritual "protective gear" does the Sacrament of Penance and Reconciliation give to you? Why do we call this sacrament a Sacrament of Healing?

A Life of Ongoing Conversion

The Sacrament of Penance and Reconciliation, with the individual and complete confession of grave sins, followed by absolution, is the only ordinary means of reconciliation with God and the Church. However, the sacrament was never meant to be a revolving door of free passes: sin, confess, be forgiven, commit the same sins, confess, be forgiven, over and over again without trying to reform our life. True sorrow requires a firm resolve not to sin again. Yes, we fail, but there is a difference between failing and not even trying. There is a difference between floating through life aimlessly, letting random thoughts and feelings carry you to one dead end after another, and choosing to live the Gospel life. The Sacrament of Penance and Reconciliation helps us to carry out our baptismal commitment to follow Jesus in love and service.

On the other hand, if you do find yourself confessing the same sins over and over again, do not let this discourage you. Continue to ask God for the grace to change, and continue participating in the Sacrament of Penance and Reconciliation. You may find other spiritual practices helpful too, such as retreats, prayer services, attentive listening to Scripture and the Homily at Sunday Mass, and reading Scripture or a spiritual book on your own. You may also want to seek a professional counselor, spiritual director, or support group. If you keep your heart (and your eyes and ears) open, the Holy Spirit will help you. ✳

UNIT 4

HMMMMMM. . . What are the most effective ways to repair the damage your sins have caused?

1. Explain how the authority to forgive sins and reconcile sinners was given by Jesus to Peter and the Apostles and extends to the Church today.

2. Give three other names for the Sacrament of Penance and Reconciliation, and explain how each describes an essential element of the sacrament.

3. Name and explain the three actions of the penitent in the Sacrament of Penance and Reconciliation.

4. Name and explain the action of the priest in the Sacrament of Penance and Reconciliation.

5. Explain the three conditions that must exist for a sin to be mortal, and the consequences of mortal sin.

6. Describe two Scripture accounts in which Jesus forgives sinners, and explain how these foretell the mercy God extends to us in the Sacrament of Penance and Reconciliation.

7. Name the six effects of the Sacrament of Penance and Reconciliation. Choose two and explain their meaning.

The Gift of Forgiveness

UNIT 4

Images: Shutterstock.com / © Adam Jan Figel / Shutterstock.com / iStock.com

UNIT 4

CHAPTER 10
The Sacrament of Anointing of the Sick

DO YOU HAVE TO BE DYING TO RECEIVE THE SACRAMENT OF ANOINTING OF THE SICK?

SNAPSHOT

Article 38

The Sacrament of Healing and Strength

Thinking about the possibility of serious illness or the reality of death is likely not at the top of your priority list. You have games to watch or play, movies to see, books to read, places to travel, friends to make, and a future to look forward to. But none of us can escape the reality of sickness and death. At some point in our lives, we will face suffering, sickness, and death.

Kyla never thought she would be going to her friend's funeral when she was a junior in high school. But there she was, sitting in the church, looking at Joe's casket in front of the altar. Kyla thought about how unfair it was that Joe was gone. He had been healthy and looking forward to the future at the end of last school year. But then he got leukemia. In just eight short months, he was gone. Kyla wondered why this had to happen.

Joe's family, friends, teammates, classmates, and camp buddies were all at the funeral. The church was full of teenagers. Father Mika reminded everyone gathered that teenagers often don't have to directly deal with suffering, sickness, or death. These are things that many teens often don't think can happen to them.

UNIT 4

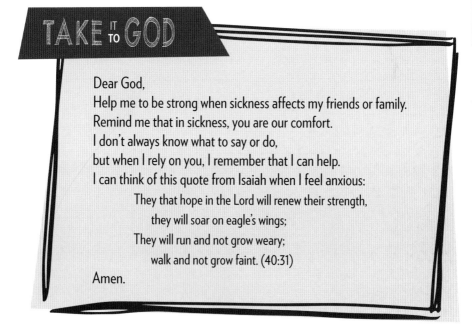

TAKE IT TO GOD

Dear God,
Help me to be strong when sickness affects my friends or family.
Remind me that in sickness, you are our comfort.
I don't always know what to say or do,
but when I rely on you, I remember that I can help.
I can think of this quote from Isaiah when I feel anxious:

> They that hope in the Lord will renew their strength,
> they will soar on eagle's wings;
> They will run and not grow weary;
> walk and not grow faint. (40:31)

Amen.

Father Mika walked in front of the altar and put his hand on Joe's casket. He told those gathered that they should know how they had helped Joe. Their cards, their visits, their posts, their videos of care—all these things helped Joe to accept his illness and prepare for the next life. Father Mika recalled some of his visits with Joe and his family. Kyla listened carefully when Father Mika said that when Joe received the Sacrament of Anointing of the Sick, he was comforted. Joe held his parents' hands and told them he loved them and he was tired. He expressed that he was ready to be with Jesus. Kyla blinked away tears, crying because she would miss Joe. Yet she knew that he was now with God.

The **Sacrament of Anointing of the Sick** is God's gift for those who are suffering from serious illness or old age and those who are dying. It gives spiritual healing and strength to a person who is seriously ill, and sometimes physical recovery is granted as well. When death is near, it prepares us so that when our time on Earth is over, we will look forward to meeting God, and to hearing from him, "Well done, my good and faithful servant. . . . Come, share your master's joy" (Matthew 25:23).

In this sacrament, in our weakest moments, we encounter Christ, the Good Shepherd. In the words of the prophet Ezekiel, whose prophecy of a true shepherd for God's people was fulfilled in Jesus Christ, we hear the voice of God saying: "I myself will pasture my sheep. . . . The lost I will search out, the strays I will bring back, the injured I will bind up, and the sick I will heal. . . . I will shepherd them in judgment" (Ezekiel 34:15–16).

The Meaning of Illness

Illness and injury disrupt our lives and throw us into turmoil. It is painful to watch someone we love and care about become extremely weak physically, mentally, and emotionally. In these desperate times, sick and injured people are vulnerable to fear, anguish, self-preoccupation, and sometimes even despair and revolt against God.

On the other hand, sometimes a serious illness can be a wake-up call, alerting us to the essentials of life. Take Lin's dad for example: He had a heart attack at just forty-two years old! He survived, but he was changed. He took his new diet and exercise plan seriously. But it wasn't just about losing weight or being more "heart healthy." He told Lin, "This heart attack made me stop in my tracks and evaluate what is really important in my life. But more than

---

Anointing of the Sick, Sacrament of ➤ One of the Seven Sacraments, in which a gravely ill, aging, or dying person is anointed by the priest and prayed over by him and attending believers. One need not be dying to receive the sacrament.

© Lopolo / Shutterstock.com

Lin's dad experienced a sharp reminder of his mortality when he had a heart attack. When our bodies fail us, it can serve as a reminder of how much we depend on God.

that, I realize how I was just doing the same thing every day. I had lost an appreciation for what is valuable to me. It's not how much I have or how hard I work, but it's my family. If I had nothing left but my faith and my family, I'd be a rich man."

Often illness can bring about a *metanoia* in the heart, a conversion toward God and a greater appreciation of his gifts in our lives. Thus, illness can be a turning point. But God sends healing, either physical or spiritual, because illness and death have been conquered through his Son, Jesus Christ. The Sacrament of Anointing of the Sick is the doorway to this healing.

Christ the Physician

Jesus Christ, the Son of God, came among us as a healer of body and soul. For some people who asked for physical healing, he both forgave their sins and sent them away physically whole. In these instances, his healing of bodily afflictions was a sign of the deeper healing of sin. He never turned away from those who asked him for healing, not even from the most "untouchable" of his day, those who suffered from leprosy.

In the Gospels, leprosy became a symbol for both physical and spiritual healing. When you read the accounts of Jesus curing the leper in each of the four Gospels, the scene is set so the reader understands that those who suffered from this disease were forced to live in isolation. Those suffering from leprosy were told to leave their homes and live in perpetual quarantine on the outskirts of town. Leprosy became a symbol of the worst of diseases and

UNIT 4

the worst of consequences: physical isolation, ostracism, and banishment. For that reason, it became a symbol of separation from God and the community—a symbol of sin. This is why Jesus' healing of the lepers is so significant. Jesus' healings are signs that even the worst separation from God and isolation from the community can be overcome and healed, that even the worst sin can be forgiven, and that the sinner can be restored to fullness of life. In the Sacrament of Anointing of the Sick, we meet Christ the Physician, who heals our sin, our isolation, and, if it is in God's providence, our physical ailments as well.

© Travel Stock / Shutterstock.com

The physical illness of leprosy became a symbol of separation from God and the community—a symbol of sin. What symbols of sin do you recognize today?

Faith and Healing

When Jules was sick, all she wanted was to lay in her mom's bed. More than any medicine, or chicken soup, Jules wanted her mom to lay down next to her and rub her hair or hold her hand. She wanted some assurance that she would get better. When Earl found out he had cancer, he wanted a cure. He had a future planned. When you are sick and suffering, it is sometimes hard to believe that relief will come and that you will ever feel better.

What did Jesus ask of the sick whom he met along his way, the sick who asked him for healing? Only faith. Sometimes Jesus healed by his word alone, even from a distance (see the pre-read verses from Luke, chapter 7). Sometimes Jesus offered his healing touch, and at other times he used spittle and the laying on of hands (see the pre-read verses from the Gospel of Mark) or mud and washing (see the pre-read verses from the Gospel of John). (See also *Catechism of the Catholic Church [CCC]*, number 1504.) Those who were sick tried to touch Jesus, even the tassel of his cloak, to be healed (see Luke 8:44).

Sharing in Christ's Suffering

The prophets foretold that the Messiah would heal not only by his word and his touch but also by actually taking on the sufferings of God's people (see Isaiah 53:4).

While he was among us, Jesus did not heal every sick person. But through his individual healings, Jesus announced a message for all: that the Kingdom of God was coming and indeed was here. By his death and Resurrection, his message was made even more clear: "He himself bore our sins in his body upon the cross, so that, free from sin, we might live for righteousness. By his wounds you have been healed" (1 Peter 2:24). Through his Paschal Mystery, Christ conquered the consequences of Original Sin: sin and death, sickness and suffering. Because of Christ, these are only temporary. Through them, we can become closer to Christ, we can align ourselves and our suffering to his on the cross, and we can be more closely united to him and to his Passion. In some small way, our suffering becomes a participation in Jesus' redemptive (saving) suffering.

Jesus invites each one of us to take up our particular cross, whatever it might be, to follow him as his disciples (see Matthew 10:38). Certainly, illness is a heavy cross, but what can those of us who are healthy do to share in this ministry of Jesus? What can we do if people are sick or suffering? How can we help if we aren't a doctor or haven't even graduated from high school yet? One important thing we can do to share in Jesus' ministry toward the sick is to offer our prayers and sacrifices for those who suffer illness, whether physical or mental. We can do more than just signing a card or ending a phone call with "I'll pray for you." We can truly lift up in prayer those who are sick and suffering. Setting aside time each day to hold them in prayer is a concrete way to minister to others.

The gift of healing is a gift of the Holy Spirit to some members of the Church to build up the Body of Christ. Yet, even intense prayer does not always bring about healing of illness. Saint Paul the Apostle begged to be healed from what he called "a thorn in the flesh" (2 Corinthians 12:7), but his prayer was not granted. The answer he received was, "My grace is sufficient for you, for power is made perfect in weakness" (verse 9). In enduring suffering with patience, we, like Saint Paul, are "filling up what is lacking in the afflictions of Christ on behalf of his body, which is the church" (Colossians 1:24). We can share one another's sufferings, we can bear one another's burdens, for we all belong to the one Body of Christ, the Church. ✳

HMMMMM. . . How are faith and healing connected?

Article 39

Scriptural and Historical Roots

The Sacrament of Anointing of the Sick was instituted by Christ, and we find the scriptural foundation for this sacrament in the Gospel of Mark (see 6:13) and the Letter of James (see 5:14–15). This sacrament also has roots in the earliest period of the Church. In this article, we look at both the scriptural and historical roots of this sacrament, including the meaning and use of oil, anointing in the early Church, and a short history of the sacrament.

The Meaning and Use of Oil

The Sacrament of Anointing of the Sick includes an anointing with a holy oil called the **Oil of the Sick**. It is pressed from olives and is blessed by the bishop. The oil is a sign of healing, strengthening, and the presence of the Holy Spirit.

© Renata Sedmakova / Shutterstock.com

How does Jesus answer the question, "Who is my neighbor?" What can you do to make enemies into neighbors in your life? (See Luke 10:36–37.)

UNIT 4

Oil of the Sick ➤ Blessed olive oil used in the Sacrament of Anointing of the Sick to anoint the forehead and hands of people who are seriously ill or near death.

The use of oil as a healing agent was familiar to the people of ancient times. It was a common remedy for wounds. In Jesus' Parable of the Good Samaritan, the Samaritan used it to help a man who had fallen into the hands of robbers: "He approached the victim, poured oil and wine over his wounds and bandaged them" (Luke 10:34). The wine, with its alcohol content, was a disinfectant; the oil eased the pain and soothed the skin.

Anointing in the Early Church

Scriptural accounts of the healing ministry of Jesus are numerous. In one scriptural account, in the Gospel of Mark, Jesus invites his Apostles to share in his healing ministry, using anointing with oil. Jesus sends them, two by two, to preach and to drive out demons. The account ends: "So they went off and preached repentance. They drove out many demons, and they anointed with oil many who were sick and cured them" (Mark 6:12–13).

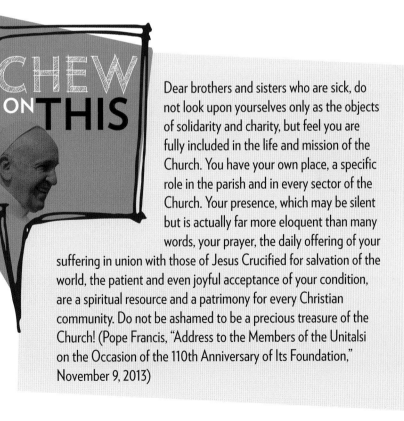

Dear brothers and sisters who are sick, do not look upon yourselves only as the objects of solidarity and charity, but feel you are fully included in the life and mission of the Church. You have your own place, a specific role in the parish and in every sector of the Church. Your presence, which may be silent but is actually far more eloquent than many words, your prayer, the daily offering of your suffering in union with those of Jesus Crucified for salvation of the world, the patient and even joyful acceptance of your condition, are a spiritual resource and a patrimony for every Christian community. Do not be ashamed to be a precious treasure of the Church! (Pope Francis, "Address to the Members of the Unitalsi on the Occasion of the 110th Anniversary of Its Foundation," November 9, 2013)

UNIT 4

In the early Church, the anointing of those who were sick is attested to by the Letter of Saint James the Apostle. In his letter, he wrote:

> Are there any who are sick among you? Let them send for the priests of the Church, and let the priests pray over them, anointing them with oil in the name of the Lord; and the prayer of faith will save the sick persons, and the Lord will raise them up; and if they have committed any sins, their sins will be forgiven them. (James 5:14–16, *Anointing of the Sick*, number 117)

Tradition has recognized in this account the Sacrament of Anointing of the Sick. This is essentially the same rite used today: the anointing with oil by the priest and prayer for the sick person, with the laying on of hands.

A Short History of the Sacrament

Since her beginning, the Church has celebrated sacramental anointing of those suffering from illness. Gradually, over the centuries, these anointings were used only to prepare people for death. Because of this, the sacrament became known as Extreme (or Last) Unction (or Anointing). However, the sacrament itself, in its liturgy, always asked for healing if it would be helpful to the person's salvation.

© Kristina Ismulyani / Shutterstock.com

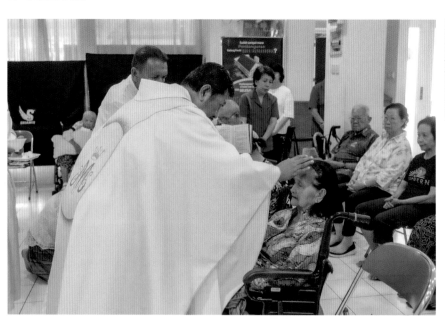

Parishes often offer a communal celebration of the Sacrament of Anointing of the Sick for those who are elderly or seriously ill. Why would you think a celebration with others in the parish church would be helpful to them?

UNIT 4

The Second Vatican Council restored the original purpose of this sacrament: to be a strengthening and healing grace for those who are seriously ill or in the frailty of old age. It is no longer necessary or advisable to wait until one is at the point of death before asking for this sacrament.

Although every sacrament is a liturgical and communal celebration of the entire Church, no matter how many people are participating, the Sacrament of Anointing of the Sick (in the form of Extreme Unction) had previously been celebrated with only the dying person and perhaps the immediate family present. Today, it is often celebrated within the Mass.

The Minister of the Sacrament

The ministers of the Sacrament of the Anointing of the Sick are bishops or priests. They use oil blessed by the bishop. If necessary, the oil can be blessed by the priest celebrating the sacraments. Pastors and priests must teach their people about the importance of this sacrament and its good effects, and should encourage them to call for a priest when they need it. The local parish should also be encouraged to pray for those who are ill (see *CCC*, number 1516). Many parishes publish prayer lists or use email or telephone chains to do this. Parishioners also visit those who are ill or who find it difficult to come to Mass. They pray with the sick person, share the Word of God, and make sure the sick and infirmed are scheduled to receive the Eucharist regularly. If parishioners have been trained and commissioned to do so, they may bring the Eucharist to those who are ill.

UNIT 4

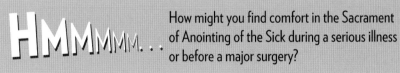

How might you find comfort in the Sacrament of Anointing of the Sick during a serious illness or before a major surgery?

Article 40
The Rite of Anointing of the Sick

All through the centuries, the Church has cared for sick people, especially when others hesitated to do so for fear of contagion or even death. In the Early Middle Ages, monastic guest houses became the first hospitals. Out of concern for the needs of the sick, religious orders of brothers and sisters were founded. Saint Damien of Molokai (1840–1889) served the men and women suffering from leprosy on the island of Molokai, in what is now Hawaii, until he succumbed to the disease. More recently, Saint Mother Teresa of Kolkata (1910–1997) began her society's work in India by taking in those who were literally dying in the streets and caring for them as for Christ himself.

Saint Damien of Molokai cared for people with leprosy in what is now Hawaii.

However, the Church's greatest gift to the sick is the Sacrament of Anointing of the Sick. In this sacrament, the Church offers the grace of God for strength and healing. This sacrament may be celebrated in various places with various groups of people: in the home, in a hospital or assisted-care center, or in church. It can take place outside the Mass or within the Mass. It may be offered to one person individually or to a group of people. It is often preceded by the Sacrament of Penance and Reconciliation and followed by reception of the Sacrament of the Eucharist.

Three Aspects of the Sacrament

The Sacrament of Anointing of the Sick has three integral aspects: the prayer of faith, the laying on of hands, and the anointing with the Oil of the Sick.

The Prayer of Faith

In the prayers of the sacrament, the entire community asks God's help for the sick, in a spirit of trust and in response to God's Word. If possible, those who are sick join in these prayers.

The Laying On of Hands

This is a sign of blessing and, as you may recall, a gesture signifying the coming of the Holy Spirit. The laying on of hands by the minister of the sacrament (a priest or bishop) is in direct imitation of Jesus, who often laid his hands on those who asked him for healing: "All who had people sick with various diseases brought them to him. He laid his hands on each of them and cured them" (Luke 4:40).

The Anointing with Blessed Oil

The anointing with oil is a sign of the presence of the Holy Spirit. Through God's power and grace, the sick person receives

Three important aspects of the Sacrament of Anointing of the Sick are the prayer of faith, the laying on of hands, and the anointing with oil.

UNIT 4

strength to face serious illness, especially the physical and spiritual deterioration that can wear down every defense. The celebrating priest prays that the Lord will help the sick person with the grace of the Holy Spirit.

Though the laying on of hands is important to the rite, the essential elements of the sacrament are "the anointing of the forehead and hands of the sick person (in the Roman Rite) or of other parts of the body (in the Eastern rite), the anointing being accompanied by the liturgical prayer of the celebrant asking for the special grace of this sacrament" (*CCC*, number 1531).

One of the worst consequences of serious illness or old age is isolation from family and friends. People in long-term care centers are vulnerable to isolation, not just for a few days, but for long stretches of time. Some have no families, and some have families that cannot visit as often as they would like. Think about what you can do to bring the joy of Christ to those who are sick, either in your parish or in a long-term care facility. Can you make cards? Can you provide some entertainment on a set evening or weekend? Can you "adopt a grandparent" and visit regularly? Find ways to share your gifts with those who are ill and isolated. You will be sharing Christ's love with those who will appreciate it the most. And, in caring for those who are sick, you will be fulfilling one of the Corporal Works of Mercy.

The Celebration of the Sacrament

The Sacrament of Anointing of the Sick can be conferred within the Mass or outside the Mass. Celebrating this sacrament within the Mass emphasizes the union of those who are sick with the self-giving of Christ in the Eucharist. Because the sacrament is celebrated amid the community, it also emphasizes the prayerful concern of the local church community for the sick persons in its midst.

If the Sacrament of Anointing of the Sick is celebrated during Mass, it begins after the Liturgy of the Word, and the litany for the Sacrament of Anointing of the Sick is prayed instead of the Prayer of the Faithful. The Homily follows, and the Liturgy of Anointing begins, followed by the Liturgy of the Eucharist. The Preface, the Eucharistic Prayer, and the other prayers of the Mass are adapted to include prayers and petitions for those who need healing.

Who May Receive the Sacrament?

Any baptized Catholic above the age of reason (age seven) who is suffering from serious illness may receive the sacrament, as well as those about to undergo serious surgery. People suffering from alcoholism or other addictions may receive the sacrament, as well as those suffering from mental illness.

UNIT 4

The Sacrament of Anointing of the Sick may be received more than once. In fact, if a person should recover from a grave illness and then be confronted with the return of that illness or another grave illness, the sacrament may and should be received again. If the person's condition becomes more serious in that same illness, the sacrament may be repeated. The Church especially encourages those who, because of illness or old age, are facing the near possibility of death to receive the strengthening grace of this sacrament.

Celebration Outside Mass

Whether celebrated within the Mass or outside it, the rite of the sacrament is essentially the same.

Greeting

If the Sacrament of Anointing of the Sick is celebrated outside the Mass, the priest begins by greeting the sick person and those present with, "The peace of the Lord be with you always," or a similar blessing.

Sprinkling with Holy Water and Instruction

The priest may sprinkle holy water on the sick person and those present, as a reminder of Baptism and the death and Resurrection of Christ. He then gives a short instruction on the meaning of this sacrament, ending with, "Let us therefore commend our sick brother/sister N. to the grace and power of Christ, that he may save him/her and raise him/her up" (*Rite of Anointing of the Sick Outside Mass*, number 117). If the Sacrament of Penance and Reconciliation is to be received, it is celebrated at this time.

Penitential Act and Liturgy of the Word

The Penitential Act follows, similar to the Penitential Act in the Eucharist, but is directed toward the needs of those who are ill. (It is omitted if the Sacrament of Penance and Reconciliation has been celebrated.) This is followed by the Liturgy of the Word. A Gospel Reading is usually proclaimed, followed by a period of silence. The priest then gives a short Homily addressed to the sick person, the family, and caregivers.

The Liturgy of Anointing

The Liturgy of Anointing begins with a litany of prayers for the sick person, for relief of sufferings, and for all who care for the sick. Then the laying on of hands takes place in silence. The priest lays both hands on the head of the sick person.

UNIT 4

CATHOLICS **MAKING** A DIFFERENCE

Many Catholics feel called to serve others in special ministries. Some have a specific calling to serve people who are sick and dying. Saint Juliana Falconieri (1270–1341) and Saint Aloysius Gonzaga (1568–1591) are two people whose lives were committed to serving sick, suffering, and dying people. Saint Juliana Falconieri lived in thirteenth-century Italy. Inspired by her devout uncle who was a priest, Juliana performed daily works of charity. She went out into the streets of Florence to help the sick, the helpless, and the abandoned. Because of her own struggle with illness, she became the patron of people suffering from any type of chronic illness. Saint Aloysius Gonzaga was the oldest son and heir of a wealthy family in sixteenth-century Spain. When he was just fifteen years old, he renounced his inheritance and set off to serve others. At first, he struggled to work in the city's hospitals, but when a terrible epidemic struck Rome, Aloysius went out to collect those who were sick and dying. He found beds for them, washed them, fed, them, comforted them, and prayed with them.

If the Oil of the Sick has already been blessed, the priest prays a prayer of thanksgiving to God. If it has not been blessed, the priest blesses it with a prayer. The priest then anoints the sick person on the forehead with the blessed oil, saying:

"Through this holy anointing
may the Lord in his love and mercy help you
with the grace of the Holy Spirit."
All respond: Amen.
The priest then anoints the hands and says:
"May the Lord who frees you from sin
save you and raise you up."
All respond: Amen.

(Anointing of the Sick, number 124)

The priest may also, if he chooses, anoint the particular area of pain or injury in the body, but he does not repeat the prayer.

This is followed by a prayer after anointing. The rite provides prayer options especially suited for people in particular circumstances, including those who may be close to death, in advanced age, preparing for serious surgery, or for a child or young person with a serious illness. Then the priest leads all present in praying the Lord's Prayer.

Reception of Communion and Concluding Rite

The reception of Communion may follow. If not, the blessing of the sick person concludes the rite.

Viaticum

If someone is in danger of death, that person can, in addition to receiving the Sacrament of Anointing of the Sick, receive the Sacrament of the Eucharist as viaticum. This Latin word means "with you on the journey." In the Eucharist, Christ is with the dying person who is ready to make the journey from this life to eternal life.

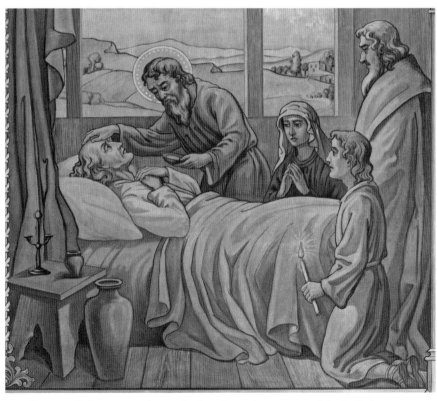

This neo-Gothic painting depicts the Apostles at the reception of the Eucharist as viaticum, preparing the dying person for the final transition to eternal life.

Christ himself is with the dying son or daughter of God, to lead him or her to the Father. The Sacrament of the Eucharist is the sacrament of the death and Resurrection of Christ, and so it is the sacrament of passing over from death to life, and the pledge of life with God forever.

You may remember that the Sacraments of Baptism, Confirmation, and the Eucharist together are called the Sacraments of Christian Initiation. At the end of life, the Sacraments of Penance and Reconciliation and Anointing of the Sick, along with the Eucharist as viaticum, are the sacraments through which we complete our journey here on Earth. They are the sacraments that prepare us for our final transition, with Christ, into eternal life. ✳

What significance do you think the laying on of hands and the anointing with oil have during the Sacrament of Anointing of the Sick?

Article 41

Christ's Healing Power

In this article, we consider the healing power of Christ in the Sacrament of Anointing of the Sick and its effect on the sick person receiving it.

The Effects of the Sacrament of Anointing of the Sick

First of all, does this sacrament really work? Yes, it does, just as all the sacraments really work, through the power and in the name of God—the Father, the Son, and the Holy Spirit. The effects, or gifts, of the Sacrament of Anointing of the Sick are many, including the following:

Effects of the Sacrament of Anointing of the Sick	
Union of the sick person to Christ in his Passion	• Those who suffer are not useless; their sufferings, united to Christ's, can participate in his saving work. • Suffering no longer is simply a consequence of Original Sin. It becomes redemptive.
Strength, peace, and courage to endure the sufferings of illness or old age	• The grace of this sacrament renews trust and faith in God and gives strength to accept death peacefully. • This is in itself a grace of healing.
Forgiveness of sins	• If someone is contrite and was not able to receive absolution in the Sacrament of Penance and Reconciliation, they can receive forgiveness for their sins now.
Possible restoration of health	• The person's health will be restored if God wills it.
Ecclesial grace of union with the Body of Christ	• Through this sacrament, the sick person benefits from the intercession of the saints. • The person contributes to the holiness of the entire Church and, through union with Christ, to the good of the entire world.

UNIT 4

Effects of the Sacrament of Anointing of the Sick, continued	
Preparation for passing over to eternal life	• The sacrament is rightly given to those who are close to death and even at the point of departing from this life. • In that case, the sacrament is "also called *sacramentum exeuntium* (the sacrament of those departing)"[1] (*CCC*, number 1523). • Baptism begins our journey in Christ, in his death and Resurrection, and the Sacrament of Anointing of the Sick completes that journey on Earth. It completes the anointings, which have marked us as Christ's own during our lifetime. • "This last anointing fortifies the end of our earthly life like a solid rampart for the final struggles before entering the Father's house"[2] (*CCC*, number 1523).

Christ's Healing Power in Our Lives

Jesus Christ is alive and risen and with us today, especially in his sacraments. The Sacrament of Anointing of the Sick teaches us that Christ's healing power is at work in the world, and that he is with us in all things, especially when we are weak and in need. This sacrament helps us to understand more fully the last words of Jesus, just before his Ascension, in the Gospel of Matthew: "And behold, I am with you always, until the end of the age" (Matthew 28:20).

I DIDN'T KNOW THAT!

The oil used in the Anointing of the Sick is no ordinary kitchen oil. The oil is olive oil that has been blessed at the Chrism Mass, which is celebrated on Holy Thursday. In the Roman Rite, the priest anoints the sick person's forehead and hands with oil (usually in the form of a cross). Oils have been used in anointing (for a variety of reasons) for centuries. The Old Testament describes myrrh, cinnamon, kaneh-bosm, and cassia oils as being used in holy anointing.

UNIT 4

This sacrament reminds us to reflect often on the healing power of Christ. Every time we receive the Eucharist, we pray to him, "But only say the word and my soul shall be healed" (*Roman Missal*, page 669). The healing power of Christ is at work in us, in body and in spirit, as he shares his risen life with us.

This sacrament encourages us to offer up our suffering for the good of the entire Body of Christ, the Church, and for the good of the entire world. It encourages us to bring the healing and compassion of Christ to those who suffer. It encourages us to accept pain, suffering, and death as the consequences of Original Sin—but it also encourages us to trust that we will be raised up with Jesus. Suffering and death are temporary. This sacrament helps us to live with the hope that one day we will live in perfect and eternal union with God—Father, Son, and Holy Spirit. ✳

Some healings are physical and some are spiritual. How have you experienced Christ's healing power in your life?

UNIT 4

HMMMMM. . .

If you were in a position of grave illness, in what ways do you think the Sacrament of Anointing of the Sick would be comforting to you?

1. What is the purpose of the Sacrament of Anointing of the Sick, and who may receive it?

2. How can illness be a turning point in human life?

3. What are the scriptural roots of using the Oil of the Sick?

4. The oil used in the Sacrament of Anointing of the Sick is a sign of what?

5. Where and with whom may the Sacrament of Anointing of the Sick be celebrated?

6. What are the three integral aspects of the Sacrament of Anointing of the Sick?

7. How can physical suffering be a way for us to take up our cross with Jesus and, in our own small way, participate in his redemptive suffering?

8. Among all Jesus' miracles of healing, why are his healings of lepers so significant in our understanding of the Sacraments of Healing?

9. What three sacraments prepare us for our journey into eternal life, and what is the work of each in our transition to eternal life?

10. In what ways has the Church, from the earliest days of Christianity, provided for the care of those who are ill?

ART STUDY

1. What do you notice about the figures of Jesus healing the blind man? Take into consideration the lighting, the facial expressions, and the way they are positioned in the painting.

2. Who do you think the group of men are off to the right? What can you infer from the expressions on their faces?

3. What is the overall tone or feeling you get when you examine this artwork?

UNIT 4 HIGHLIGHTS

UNIT 4

CHAPTER 9   The Sacraments of Penance and Reconciliation

The Four Actions of the Sacrament of Penance and Reconciliation

Teen

Repentance

Confession

Penance

Priest

Absolution

Mortal and Venial Sin

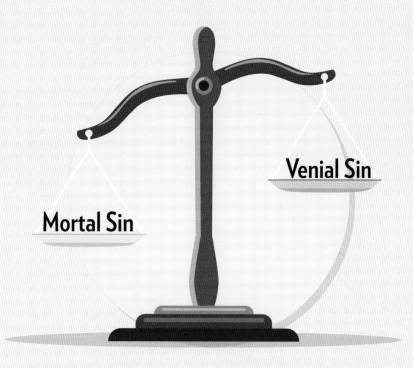

Mortal Sin

Venial Sin

Contrary to the final goal of happiness with God in Heaven.	Sin whose action is a less serious matter.
Has three conditions: 1. concerns serious and grave matter 2. committed with full knowledge that the action is sinful and opposes God's Law 3. committed freely and deliberately	Weakens but does not destroy our relationship with God
	Weakens our relationship with the Church community and weakens our ability to resist mortal sin

Scriptural and Historical Roots of Penance and Reconciliation

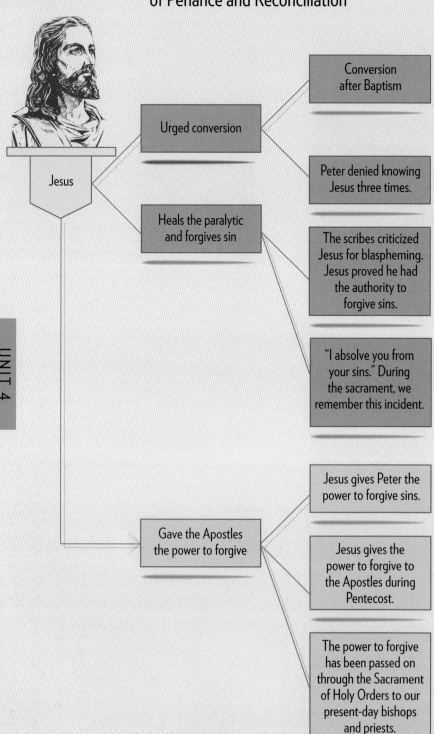

Jesus

Urged conversion
- Conversion after Baptism
- Peter denied knowing Jesus three times.

Heals the paralytic and forgives sin
- The scribes criticized Jesus for blaspheming. Jesus proved he had the authority to forgive sins.
- "I absolve you from your sins." During the sacrament, we remember this incident.

Gave the Apostles the power to forgive
- Jesus gives Peter the power to forgive sins.
- Jesus gives the power to forgive to the Apostles during Pentecost.
- The power to forgive has been passed on through the Sacrament of Holy Orders to our present-day bishops and priests.

UNIT 4

Steps of Celebrating the Sacrament

Proclamation of praise and dismissal of the penitent

Penitent's prayer and priest's absolution

Penitent's confession and acceptance of the penance

Reading the Word of God (optional)

Welcoming the penitent

Preparation of priest and penitent

The Effects of the Sacrament of Penance and Reconciliation

Reconciliation with the Church

The forgiveness of all sin

Reconciliation with God

Peace and serenity of conscience, and spiritual consolation

Increase of spiritual strength for the Christian battle

Remission of punishment for sin

UNIT 4

The Sacrament of Anointing of the Sick

What are Some Aspects of the Meaning of the Sacrament of Anointing of the Sick?

- Illness can be physical, mental, or emotional.

- Christ the Physician heals body and soul.

- Jesus only asked for faith from those who asked for healing.

- Christ healed not only by word and touch but also by taking on the suffering of God's people.

- We can share the cross with those who suffer with prayers and sacrifices.

- The gift of healing is a gift of the Holy Spirit that some members of the Church are given to build up the Body of Christ.

- Christ himself institutes the Sacrament of Anointing of the Sick.

Celebrating the Sacrament of Anointing of the Sick

Celebration within the Mass

- Introductory Rites

- Liturgy of the Word

- Liturgy of Anointing
  > litany of prayers for the sick person
  > laying on of hands
  > anointing with oil
  > prayer after anointing

- Liturgy of the Eucharist

- Concluding Rites

Celebration outside Mass

- Greeting

- sprinkling with holy water and instruction

- Penitential Act and Liturgy of the Word

- Liturgy of Anointing
  > litany of prayers for the sick person
  > laying on of hands
  > anointing with oil
  > prayer after anointing
  > Lord's Prayer
  > reception of Communion and blessing of the sick person

UNIT 4
BRING IT HOME

HOW ARE WE HEALED BY THE SACRAMENTS?

FOCUS QUESTIONS

CHAPTER 9   Why isn't it enough to just tell God I'm sorry for my sins?

CHAPTER 10   Do you have to be dying to receive the Sacrament of Anointing of the Sick?

DEMETRIOS
Our Lady of the Hills College
Preparatory School

Everyone experiences suffering or failure in life, and we can find healing in the sacraments. We are healed by the sacraments in many astounding ways, especially through the Sacraments of Reconciliation and Anointing of the Sick. In the Sacrament of Reconciliation, we are healed partly by our own admission of guilt and sin. The realization that we are fallen and the ability to choose to amend our ways is the first part of our journey of healing. In the Sacrament of the Anointing of the Sick, the effects also heal us by forgiving our sins, uniting our suffering to Christ, and helping us to understand that we are united to the whole Church in times of suffering. We may even receive physical healing if it is God's will.

REFLECT

Take some time to read and reflect on the unit and chapter focus questions listed on the facing page.

- What question or section did you identify most closely with?

- What did you find within the unit that was comforting or challenging?

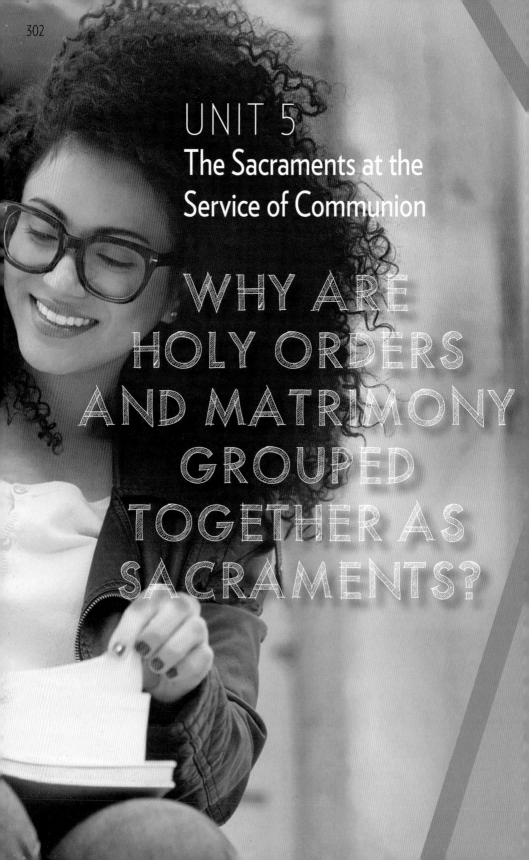

UNIT 5
The Sacraments at the
Service of Communion

WHY ARE
HOLY ORDERS
AND MATRIMONY
GROUPED
TOGETHER AS
SACRAMENTS?

LOOKING AHEAD

Holy Orders and Marriage are grouped together as the Sacraments at the Service of Communion. God has called us to serve him in our lives in a way that is unique to each one of us. Whatever plan God has in store for us will determine which of these sacraments we may participate in, but they are both concerned with our committed vocation in life. These two sacraments are our call to live in accordance with his plan for us.

MATTIAS
Seton Catholic Preparatory School

UNIT 5

CHAPTER 11
The Sacrament of Holy Orders

WHY CAN ONLY MEN BE ORDAINED?

SNAPSHOT

Article 42
Consecrated to God's People

Have you ever wondered if God is calling you to a special vocation? Of course, he is! Through Baptism, God calls everyone to ministry, to holiness, to Christian witness. But how can you figure out what vocation God is calling you to? Consider the following:

- *Trust that God wants you to discover your vocation.* God has planted his call within your heart, and you simply need to be faithful in discovering it. Be honest about your deepest feelings, and do not be afraid of the vocation to which you are attracted.

- *Look for clues.* Do you enjoy being part of a community of people that is dedicated to God? Are you drawn to the idea of a life of prayer and service to others in community? You should take a good look at the ordained or consecrated life. Or perhaps you have given serious thought to the joys and sacrifices involved in a lifetime commitment to another person. Perhaps you love to be with children and cannot imagine not having children of your own. If so, marriage is probably your vocation.

- *Serve God in any way you can.* Try out different ministries in the Church: liturgical ministries, catechetical (teaching) ministries, and ministries of charity and social action. These will help you to discover your gifts and interests.

- *Spend time with people you admire.* Learn from them what the joys and challenges of their vocation are.

- *Seek out a spiritual director who can guide you through a prayerful process of discovering God's will for you.* A spiritual director can help you follow God's path in truth and freedom.

We begin our life in the Church as followers of Christ through the Sacraments of Christian Initiation—Baptism, Confirmation, and the Eucharist. These sacraments are in themselves a call, a vocation, to personal holiness and to participation in the spread of the Good News of Jesus Christ to all the world. Two other sacraments—the Sacraments at the Service of Communion—give the grace and strength to serve others through specific vocations. These two sacraments are the Sacrament of Holy Orders and the Sacrament of Matrimony. In this chapter, we focus on the Sacrament of Holy Orders.

UNIT 5

TAKE IT TO GOD

The Church will always need generous men and women to give of themselves in service. We can support our bishops, priests, deacons, religious, and lay ministers in their efforts to serve us by praying that God will send more workers into the vineyard of the Church!

Loving and Generous God,
it is You who call us by name
and ask us to follow You.
Help us to grow in the Love
and Service of our Church
as we experience it today.

Give us the energy and courage
of Your Spirit
to shape its future.

Grant us faith-filled leaders
who will embrace Christ's Mission
of love and justice.

Bless the Church of _____ (name your diocese)
by raising up dedicated and generous leaders
from our families and friends
who will serve Your people as Sisters,
Priests, Brothers, Deacons, and Lay Ministers.

Inspire us to know You better
and open our hearts
to hear Your call.

We ask this through our Lord.
Amen.

(USCCB, "Prayer #3 for Vocations")

Called to Servant Leadership

The People of God is a priestly people who participate in the one priesthood of Christ. We all share, through Baptism, in "the common priesthood of the faithful" (*Catechism of the Catholic Church [CCC]*, number 1591). Yet springing from this baptismal call is another participation in Christ's priesthood, the ministerial priesthood of priests and bishops. The ministerial priesthood gives a sacred power through the Sacrament of Holy Orders to serve the Church, helping all of us to fulfill our baptismal call. This ministry serves the People of God in the name of Christ and represents Christ within the community of the Body of Christ.

Those ordained to the ministerial priesthood (priests and bishops, who are also priests) are called to be "servant leaders": to serve and to lead the Church by teaching the Word of God, by offering divine worship in the liturgy, and by governing the Church as representatives of Christ, who is the Head of the Church. In this way, they carry out the mission of Christ in the world today. Deacons are also ordained for service in the Church through the Sacrament of Holy Orders, but they do not participate in the ministerial priesthood. Because of their important work, they are mentioned throughout this chapter.

In this article, we consider the origins of the term *ordination* and the priesthood of the Old Covenant. We also begin to explore the fulfillment of the Old Covenant priesthood by Christ and his institution of the priesthood of the New Covenant.

© Bill Wittman / www.wpwittman.com

UNIT 5

Many young men explore the idea of a priestly vocation during high school and college. Your diocesan vocation office may have materials and other helps to acquaint you with the work of priests in your area.

The Meaning of *Ordination*

The **Sacrament of Holy Orders** is the sacrament by which baptized men are ordained for permanent ministry in the Church as bishops, priests, or deacons. In ancient Rome, the word *order* referred to an established grouping that ordered Roman society. The Church uses this word to describe the state of life of various groups of people. Therefore, the liturgy names the order of bishops, the order of priests, and the order of deacons. Today, we reserve the term *ordination* for the Sacrament of Holy Orders, through which men are integrated into one of three Holy Orders: bishop, priest, or deacon.

The Priesthood of the Old Covenant

As you may remember from the pre-read Scripture passage from the Book of Exodus, God chose the entire nation of Israel to be a holy and priestly people of his own. Aaron, the brother of Moses, was the first high priest. God then chose one of the Twelve Tribes of Israel, the tribe of Levi, to be priests and to carry out liturgical sacrifice and worship. The Levites alone had charge of the Dwelling Place of God, a special tent that held the stone tablets of the Ten Commandments and journeyed with the people wherever they went. Through Moses, God gave the Twelve Tribes of Israel a certain section of land as their inheritance: "But Moses gave no heritage to the tribe of Levi: the Lord, the God of Israel, is their heritage, as he had promised them" (Joshua 13:33).

In the pre-read selection from the Book of Leviticus, we see the Lord giving Moses instructions for the Israelites about offerings. If fact, the first seven chapters of Leviticus are specific instructions about what type of sacrifices are to be offered, who should offer them, how sacrifices should be offered, and when they should be offered. Yet, though this priesthood honored God with sacrifice and prayer and united the people in worship, it could not bring salvation. Only the sacrifice of Christ would bring that about. The Church, however, sees in the priesthood of the Old Covenant a prefiguring of the ordained ministry that Jesus Christ himself established.

The rites of ordination for bishops, priests, and deacons include references to the priesthood of the Old Covenant. At the ordination of bishops, reference is made to God's plan for salvation from the beginning:

Holy Orders, Sacrament of ➤ The sacrament by which baptized men are ordained for permanent ministry in the Church as bishops, priests, and deacons.

God the Father of our Lord Jesus Christ, . . .
by your gracious word
you have established the plan of your Church.
From the beginning,
you chose the descendants of Abraham to be your holy nation.
You established rulers and priests,
and did not leave your sanctuary without ministers to serve you. . . .[1]

(*CCC*, number 1541)

When priests are ordained, the liturgy references the seventy wise men Moses chose to help him govern God's people and reminds us of the first high priest, Aaron. Addressing God the Father, we pray:

You extended the spirit of Moses to seventy wise men. . . .
You shared among the sons of Aaron
the fullness of their father's power.[2]

(*CCC*, number 1542)

At the ordination of deacons, the sons of Levi are referenced:

Almighty God . . . ,
. . . .
You established a threefold ministry of worship and service,
for the glory of your name.
As ministers of your tabernacle you chose the sons of Levi
and gave them your blessing as their everlasting inheritance.[3]

(*CCC*, number 1543)

As Abraham is our "father in faith" (Eucharistic Prayer I), our bishops, priests, and deacons inherit the spiritual blessings given to the sons of Aaron and Levi.

UNIT 5

Jesus Fulfills the Old Covenant

Jesus Christ fulfilled the priesthood of the Old Covenant through his institution of the Sacrament of Holy Orders. For Jesus Christ, our new High Priest, has entered not the earthly sanctuary of the Old Covenant but Heaven itself. His sacrifice was not the blood of lambs, but his own blood. This is the sacrifice of the New Covenant that conquered sin and brought salvation. This is the sacrifice we remember and celebrate, led by the ministry of the priesthood of the New Covenant, in the sacraments and especially in the Eucharist.

These young men are being ordained as priests. Ask your parish priest where and by whom he was ordained. Then trace the line of his and his ordaining bishop's ordination.

UNIT 5

The institution of the Sacrament of Holy Orders flows from Jesus' institution of the Church. We can see this in Scripture in such accounts as the naming of Peter as the rock upon which the Church would be built (see Matthew 16:18), the choosing of the Twelve Apostles (see Mark 3:14–19, Luke 6:12–16), and the command to make disciples by going out and baptizing and teaching (see Matthew 28:19–20). The priesthood is the sacrament of apostolic ministry. It is Christ's gift to the Church of his own authority and mission for the good of the whole Body of Christ. Through this sacrament, Christ's mission entrusted to his Apostles can be carried out in the Church until the end of time. ✳

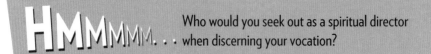

HMMMMMM. . . Who would you seek out as a spiritual director when discerning your vocation?

Article 43
The Priesthood of the New Covenant

Article 23 mentioned the priest Melchizedek, whose Old Testament offering of bread and wine prefigured the offerings of bread and wine at the Eucharist. Melchizedek's priesthood is also a prefiguring of the unique priesthood of Christ. The Letter to the Hebrews notes the connection between Melchizedek as high priest and Jesus as the new High Priest:

> In the days when he was in the flesh, he offered prayers and supplications with loud cries and tears to the one who was able to save him from death, and he was heard because of his reverence. Son though he was, he learned obedience from what he suffered; and when he was made perfect, he became the source of eternal salvation for all who obey him, declared by God high priest according to the order of Melchizedek. (Hebrews 5:7–10)

Later, in Hebrews 7:23–28, the connection between Christ and the priests of the Jewish people is compared. Unlike the Jewish priests, whose office lasted only as long as they were alive, Jesus' priesthood does not pass away because he will remain forever. In addition, Jesus will not have to offer sacrifices day after day like the high priests of the Old Covenant, because he offered himself once and for all as *the* sacrifice.

After the Resurrection of Christ, the Apostles understood that everything the priesthood of the Old Testament pointed toward found its fulfillment in Jesus Christ. He is the "one mediator between God and the human race" (1 Timothy 2:5), and, as High Priest of the New Covenant, gave himself as an offering "once for all" on the cross (Hebrews 7:27). Because we are baptized, we all participate in the one priesthood of Christ. Yet each bishop and priest participates uniquely in this priesthood of Christ, our High Priest and our "source of eternal salvation" (5:9). The uniqueness of the ministerial priesthood lies in its call and commitment to serve the entire Church and to help all Christians live a life of grace in union with Jesus Christ. Through this ministry, Christ builds up and leads his Church (see *CCC*, number 1547).

This unique participation in the priesthood of Christ and the leadership role that priests and bishops play in community life does not make them more important in the eyes of God than any other person. Nor does it mean they are holier than laypeople—God calls us all to lives of perfect holiness according to our vocation. However, the ministerial priesthood is different in its essence from the common priesthood of all the baptized. It isn't that bishops and

UNIT 5

priests have *more* priesthood than the laity; they have a *different* priesthood, one that gives them particular responsibilities that no layperson can fulfill. These responsibilities fall into three areas: teaching the faithful, leading divine worship (the liturgy, especially the Eucharist), and governing the Church.

Rather than being intimidated or feeling "not as important" as bishops or priests, we can try to think of it in this way: bishops and priests serve in ways that no one else can, but the same can be said for those who are called to married life or the consecrated life. We can move beyond thinking that those in different vocations have different levels of importance. Each vocation has its own responsibility, honor, and importance—none is more valuable than the next.

I DIDN'T KNOW THAT!

What do you do if you want to become a priest? The process has essentially four steps. Step one is internal discernment. This part may take years. Some people think about the priesthood from an early age, and others discover that calling later in life. Step two is the application process. To apply, a candidate must be a baptized and confirmed Catholic male. He must have completed high school or be within a year of graduating. He should be in good health and not married. He would fill out an application, submit sacramental certificates, academic transcripts, and provide references. He would need to have several interviews and go through a screening process. If the applicant is accepted, step three is seminary formation. Seminary staff educate the seminarians and guide them to become responsible and mature men who are ready to embrace the life of service that is the priesthood. Step four is ordination. After years of education, training, and preparation, the final commitment takes place in the Rite of Ordination. With family, friends, and priests from the diocese present, ordination is held within a Mass. The candidate makes promises to the bishop. He is vested in liturgical garments, and his hands are anointed. He is now able to celebrate the sacraments and is sent to a parish to begin his life of service to the People of God.

Representatives of Christ

Christ is the Head of the Church. He is the High Priest who has offered his life as a sacrifice, once and for all. He is the Good Shepherd who cares for his flock. He is the Teacher of Truth.

A parish priest is usually a "people person" who enjoys meeting with his parishioners, sharing their joys and sorrows. He finds that being Christ for his people, while burdensome at times, is also his greatest joy.

The ordained minister, through his service to God's people, makes the presence of Christ—as High Priest, Shepherd, and Teacher—visible. Through the Sacrament of Holy Orders, a priest is given the power to act "in the power and place of the person of Christ himself"[4] (*CCC*, number 1548). An ordained minister, especially a bishop or priest, is head, teacher, and good shepherd for his people. This does not mean that the bishop, priest, or deacon is perfect as Christ is perfect. Because the ordained minister is human, he is not always a perfect model of Christ. And because of their leadership roles, bishops, priests, and deacons can greatly help the Church and the spread of the Gospel. In the sacraments, however, as mentioned in article 7, the sins and imperfections of the minister do not impede the sacramental grace. For example, absolution granted in the Sacrament of Penance and Reconciliation is still valid and imparts God's forgiveness even if the priest granting the absolution is himself not in a state of grace.

UNIT 5

Bishops, priests, and deacons must always keep in mind that they were ordained not for privilege but for service. Acting "in the power and place" of Christ is a great responsibility. Christ himself warned his Apostles not to imitate the power of the authorities of this world, but to be servants as he himself came to serve (see Mark 10:42–45).

Christ's High Priestly Prayer

At the Last Supper, Jesus instructed his Apostles, "Do this in memory of me" (Luke 22:19). By saying this, he commissioned them to offer this worship until the end of time. After the supper, as recorded in the Gospel of John, Jesus offered what has been called his "high priestly prayer" of consecration for his Apostles and for all who would follow them. In this prayer, Jesus prays to the Father for those he has loved and taught in his earthly life. In the following portion of the prayer, he prays that they will be true to his word and his teachings:

> But now I am coming to you. I speak this in the world so that they may share my joy completely. I gave them your word, and the world hated them, because they do not belong to the world any more than I belong to the world. I do not ask that you take them out of the world but that you keep them from the evil one. . . . Consecrate them in the truth. Your word is truth. As you sent me into the world, so I sent them into the world. And I consecrate myself for them, so that they also may be consecrated in truth. (John 17:13–19)

Think back to the pre-read passage in the Gospel of John (17:13–26). Remember that in this passage, Christ is praying for you—for all who believe in him through the word of the Apostles and their successors. At the end, Jesus prays that the love of God the Father for his Son, Jesus, may be in us, and that Jesus himself may be in us.

UNIT 5

MAKE IT SO

How can you support priests? You can do some practical, tangible things to help support your priests whether they are newly ordained or have been priests for a long time.

1. Pray for your priests. Pray for wisdom, courage, and hope. Offer a Mass for them, pray a Rosary, or spend some time in adoration.

2. Invite your priests into your life. You can connect with your priests on a basic level in many ways. Talk to them after Mass, invite them over for a meal, or spend time with them at a parish event.

3. Offer solutions, not just complaints. If you want more opportunities for youth to participate in your parish, bring some options to the table. Rather than complain that there is nothing for you, suggest some ways to involve young people. Come to the conversation with some concrete ideas and people who would be willing to volunteer to bring your suggestions into reality.

Living Christ's Mission in the World

In the 1980s, the tiny country of El Salvador, in Central America, was torn apart by a violent civil war. Archbishop Oscar Romero (1917–1980) was the Archbishop of San Salvador.

Through weekly homilies broadcast by radio, he spoke out for peace and justice. Yet the violence continued. He told the people, "If some day they take away the radio station from us . . . if they don't let us speak, if they kill all the priests and the bishop too, and you are left a people without priests, each one of you must become God's microphone, each one of you must become a prophet."

They did not take the bishop's radio station. They took the bishop's life. On March 23, 1980, in his Homily broadcast throughout the country, Archbishop Romero challenged the army: "Brothers, you are from the same people; you kill your fellow peasant. . . . No soldier is obliged to obey an order that is contrary to the will of God." After he was interrupted by applause, he went

UNIT 5

on, "In the name of God then, in the name of this suffering people I ask you, I beg you, I command you in the name of God: stop the repression."

The archbishop received his answer the next day, when, as he was giving a Homily during Mass, he was killed instantly by a sharpshooter. The day before he had said to a reporter: "You can tell the people that if they succeed in killing me, that I forgive and bless those who do it. Hopefully, they will realize they are wasting their time. A bishop will die, but the church of God, which is the people, will never perish" (adapted and quoted from Renny Golden, "Oscar Romero: Bishop of the Poor," *U.S. Catholic* website, February 25, 2009).

Archbishop Romero was canonized as a saint on October 14, 2018. ✳

© Ken Hawkins / Alamy Stock Photo

Saint Oscar Romero (1917–1980)

HMMMMM. . .

Why do you think the responsibilities of teaching the faithful, leading divine worship (the liturgy), and governing the Church are unique responsibilities that only an ordained person can carry out?

Article 44
The Degrees of Ordination

The ordained ministry consists of three degrees, or orders: the order of bishop (the episcopate), the order of priest (the presbyterate), and the order of deacon (the diaconate). These three degrees are indispensable to the Church and its mission. Without each one of them, we would not be able to even speak of "the Church."

Elements of the Rites of Ordination

Each degree of ordination has its particular rite. However, these rites have certain elements in common:

- Bishops confer the Sacrament of Holy Orders in all three degrees.
- The essential elements of the Sacrament of Holy Orders are the laying on of hands and the speaking of the Prayer of Consecration. In this prayer, the presiding bishop asks God to grant the ordinand (the one to be ordained) the graces of the Holy Spirit required in his ministry as bishop, priest, or deacon.
- The Sacrament of Holy Orders imprints an indelible spiritual character.

During their ordination, these priests are experiencing the essential elements of the sacrament: the laying on of hands and the Prayer of Consecration.

UNIT 5

Requirements for Ordination

The Church ordains only baptized men who have been recognized as suitable for the ministry. Becoming an ordained minister (a bishop, priest, or deacon) is not a right or a purely personal decision but is based in the call of the Church. The Church alone has the right and responsibility to call someone to receive the Sacrament of Holy Orders. The Sacrament of Holy Orders is received as a pure gift.

Other requirements are a commitment to celibacy (in the Western Church, with the exception of permanent deacons), adequate education and formation, good mental health, a lifelong commitment to personal prayer and devotion, and a willingness to be a servant leader in the name of Christ.

Priests undergo extensive education and formation before being ordained. Candidates for the priesthood are usually admitted to a seminary. This is a house of formation in which candidates take college-level courses relevant to their future work. The program of study usually requires about five years of education beyond the college level. However, education for the priesthood is not only intellectual. Formation in three other areas—human growth, spiritual life, and pastoral practice—is equally important. Seminarians are given opportunities to help in parishes and other pastoral settings, especially in the summer. In this way, they are guided to greater self-knowledge and a fuller understanding of the vocation of the priest.

UNIT 5

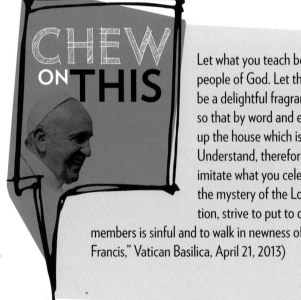

Let what you teach be nourishment for the people of God. Let the holiness of your lives be a delightful fragrance to Christ's faithful, so that by word and example you may build up the house which is God's Church. . . . Understand, therefore, what you do and imitate what you celebrate. As celebrants of the mystery of the Lord's death and resurrection, strive to put to death whatever in your members is sinful and to walk in newness of life. ("Homily of Pope Francis," Vatican Basilica, April 21, 2013)

The Role of the Bishop

When a priest is ordained a **bishop**, he receives the fullness of Holy Orders. This makes him a member of the College of Bishops (the word *college* here means "gathering" or "group") and also makes him the visible head of the diocese to which he has been appointed. Because bishops are the successors to the Apostles and members of the College of Bishops, their concern is not for their diocese alone. They have the responsibility of caring for the entire Church under the authority of the Pope, the Bishop of Rome and the successor to Saint Peter.

Each bishop ordained is in the line of Apostolic Succession that extends back to the Apostles and thus to Christ himself. This gives the bishop a place of chief dignity in the Church. The gift of the Holy Spirit, first given to the Apostles, is transmitted to bishops through the Sacrament of Holy Orders. Thus, through episcopal ordination, the bishop represents Christ himself as teacher, shepherd, and priest, and acts as Christ's representative (see *CCC*, number 1558).

The ordination of a new bishop must be approved by the Bishop of Rome, the Pope, as he is the visible sign of the union of all the particular churches. Since ancient times, as a sign of the unity of the Church and the unity of the College of Bishops, it has been a practice of the Church for several bishops to participate in the ordination and consecration of a new bishop.

The Eucharist celebrated by the bishop has special significance: With the bishop present, the complete local church is assembled in worship, and the representative of Christ—Good Shepherd and Head of the Church—presides.

The Role of the Priest

When a man is ordained a diocesan **priest**, he is ordained as a coworker of the bishop. He is united with the bishop in priestly dignity and looks to the bishop for guidance in his pastoral assignment and duties. These priests form a *presbyterium*, or body of priests, around the bishop, to help and advise him. It is the responsibility of the bishop to determine the pastoral assignment or other official responsibility for each priest in his care. Religious order priests belong

UNIT 5

---

bishop ➤ One who has received the fullness of the Sacrament of Holy Orders and is a successor to the Apostles.

priest ➤ One who has received the ministerial priesthood through the Sacrament of Holy Orders. The priest serves the community of faith by representing and assisting the bishop in teaching, governing, and presiding over the community's worship.

to a particular religious order, such as the Dominicans, Franciscans, or the Society of Jesus (Jesuits). Although all priests are required to respect their bishop, after ordination a religious priest is obedient to the superior of his religious community rather than to the local bishop directly and typically engages in a particular mission for which the order was founded.

During the Rite of Ordination, the unity of the priests is expressed by their laying on of hands, after the bishop, upon the head of the new priest. Every priest shares with the bishop in the authority of Christ himself in building up, making holy, and ruling his Body, the Church. This authority is given through the Sacrament of Holy Orders. At ordination, the new priest's bond with the bishop is expressed by the priest's promise of obedience to the bishop and by the Sign of Peace the bishop gives to the new priest. Together, these two actions mean that the bishop considers the new priest his coworker, his son, his brother, and his friend, and that the new priest owes the bishop his love and obedience in return.

By the anointing of the Holy Spirit and the character of Holy Orders, the priest is authorized to act in the person of Christ. He is consecrated to preach the Gospel, to guide the People of God, and to celebrate the liturgy of the Church as a priest of the New Covenant. Even though he is assigned to a particular ministry in a diocese, religious order, mission, or parish, he shares in the universal mission of Christ, to preach the Gospel to the ends of the Earth.

It is especially at the Eucharist, in the assembly of the faithful, that priests fulfill their priestly office, for at the Eucharist, acting in the person of Christ, they make present again the one sacrifice of Christ's offering himself for all: "From this unique sacrifice their whole priestly ministry draws its strength"[5] (*CCC*, number 1566).

The Role of the Deacon

The word **deacon** comes from the Greek word *diakons*, which means "service." The ministry of deacons is expressed in their title: They are ordained for service in the Church. Ordination bestows on them important functions in the ministry of the Word, divine worship, pastoral governance, and the service of charity and good works. These are all carried out under the authority of the bishop.

---

deacon ➤ Along with bishops and priests, one of the three Holy Orders conferred by the Sacrament of Holy Orders. Deacons are entrusted with various ministries, including baptizing, preaching, and witnessing marriages.

Deacons are ordained into a unique role of service in the Church. Do deacons serve in your parish?

For deacons, the character of the Sacrament of Holy Orders unites them to Christ, who came not "to be served but to serve" (Mark 10:45). Their service includes assisting at the liturgy (especially in the Eucharist) distributing Holy Communion, baptizing, assisting at and blessing marriages, proclaiming the Gospel, preaching, presiding over funerals, and serving those who are poor or in need.

There are two types of deacons: transitional deacons, who intend to be ordained to the priesthood in the future; and permanent deacons, who intend to remain lifelong deacons. Permanent deacons may be married or single. Deacons intending to be priests in the future, and deacons who are single, make a promise of celibacy at ordination. If a deacon is married, he promises not to remarry if his spouse should pass away. ✳

UNIT 5

HMMMMM. . . Which of the ordained ministries are you most curious about and why?

Article 45

The Graces of the Sacrament

The Holy Spirit gives those who receive the Sacrament of Holy Orders certain effects and graces. Like the Sacraments of Baptism and Confirmation, the Sacrament of Holy Orders marks the recipient with an indelible spiritual character. It is never conferred temporarily nor is it repeated.

There can be good and serious reasons for an ordained minister's being released from the obligations that he accepted at his ordination. Or, again for serious reasons, an ordained minister can be forbidden to exercise his ministry. However, even in such circumstances, an ordained minister never returns to the lay state. The character of ordination is forever. For example, in an emergency, when no other priest is available, a priest who has been relieved of his priestly responsibilities and is living as a layperson may still celebrate the Sacrament of Anointing of the Sick with someone who is dying.

CATHOLICS MAKING A DIFFERENCE

Cardinal Sean O'Malley felt a calling to the vocation of the priesthood from a very young age. When he was twelve, he began attending a boarding school for students who were considering joining the Franciscan order. He was ordained at twenty-six and was a professor at his alma mater, The Catholic University of America, and a pastor in the Washington, DC, area. He then became a bishop and eventually was appointed Archbishop of Boston. He needs every ounce of strength the grace of his ordained office provides him to serve immigrant communities, work with homeless people, care for people with AIDS, and take on dioceses affected by sexual abuse scandals. We need to look no further than Cardinal O'Malley when seeking a person who strives to live out the calling to their vocation most fervently. His motto, though brief, speaks volumes about his attitude toward serving his vocation: *Quodcumque dixerit facite*, "Do whatever he says."

The Grace of the Holy Spirit

The grace of the Sacrament of Holy Orders includes configuration to Christ as priest, teacher, and pastor, and enables one "to act as representative of Christ, Head of the Church, in his triple office of priest, prophet, and king" (see *CCC*, number 1583). The special grace of this sacrament for the bishop is the grace of strength—strength to govern and guide; strength to love all, especially those in need; and strength to proclaim the Gospel to all. The bishop is given strength to be a role model for his people, to walk the way of holiness ahead of them as a shepherd leads his flock, and to lead them to the life-giving Eucharist, in which he identifies with Christ. In this sacrament, the bishop receives strength to give his life, day by day, for his sheep. It can be hard to imagine the day-to-day life of a bishop. But certainly, a person in charge of the spiritual well-being of a large group of people would need the gift of strength. Not only do bishops have many administrative responsibilities, but they also celebrate Mass, assist and guide the priests and parishes under their care, and often have responsibilities for schools and diocesan outreach programs that serve the larger community.

UNIT 5

A prayer from the Byzantine liturgy expresses the grace of this sacrament for priests. In this rite, the bishop, while laying his hand on the priest, prays to the Father that the new priest may be filled with the Holy Spirit, saying the following:

> That he may be worthy to stand without reproach before your altar,
>
> to proclaim the Gospel of your kingdom,
>
> to fulfill the ministry of your word of truth,
>
> to offer you spiritual gifts and sacrifices,
>
> to renew your people by the bath of rebirth.
>
> (CCC, number 1587)

The prayer continues with the petition that the priest may, at the second coming of Christ, meet our Savior Jesus Christ and receive a just reward for "a faithful administration of his order"[6] (*CCC*, number 1587).

The sacramental grace for deacons is a wholehearted commitment to the People of God. In this commitment, deacons cooperate with the bishop and priests, offer service (*diakonia*) in the liturgy, proclaim the Word of God, and reach out in works of love toward those who are in need.

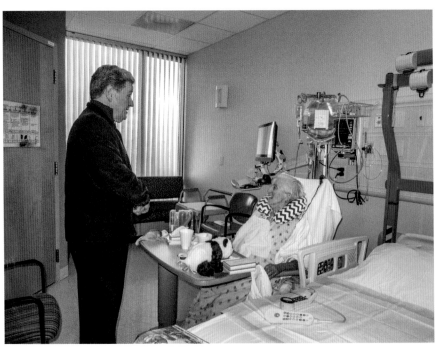

Care for the vulnerable (those who are poor or in need) has been a special grace and responsibility of deacons since the early days of the Church.

UNIT 5

The grace of ordination, as all graces, requires the cooperation and continual conversion of the one who receives it. Grace is a gift. It is not a thing but a relationship. The closer the bishop, the priest, and the deacon come to God, the more faithfully they will live out their commitment to serve God's people. The ordained clergy are ordained not as leaders alone, but as servant leaders, following in the footsteps of Christ. They are ordained to help the People of God follow their own baptismal call—to follow Christ in the path of their vocations. On this path, ordained ministers can have no greater model of service than Jesus, the Good Shepherd, who gave his life for his sheep. ✳

HMMMMMM. . . How do you see the priests you know exercising the grace of strength in the work they do?

1. What are the three orders of ministry to which men can be ordained?

2. Why do the Rites of Ordination for bishops, priests, and deacons include references to the priesthood of the Old Covenant? Select one Old Testament reference and explain its significance in the Rite of Ordination.

3. How does the priesthood of men called to ordained ministry differ from the common priesthood of all the baptized?

4. What are the three areas of responsibility for those in ordained ministry? Give one example of each.

5. To what vocation does God call each of us?

6. How did the priesthood of the Old Testament find its fulfillment in Jesus Christ?

7. How does a bishop or priest act in the person of Christ?

8. What are the essential elements of the Sacrament of Holy Orders?

9. What is the role of the bishop? the priest? the deacon?

10. Describe the special grace the Sacrament of Holy Orders gives to bishops, priests, and deacons.

UNIT 5

1. In what way does this drawing remind you of the role of a priest today?
2. What feeling does the medium the artist chose (pencil), bring out in you about the subjects of the artwork?

CHAPTER 12
The Sacrament of Matrimony

WHY SHOULD I GET MARRIED IN THE CHURCH?

SNAPSHOT

Article 46

Lifelong Covenant

Marriage is a calling to a particular person and to a particular way of life. Married life brings many joys to a husband and wife: the joy of devoted and caring companionship, a sharing of mutual goals, the nurturing and support of a loving spouse in times of challenge as well as times of celebration, and, for most married couples, the joy of raising children together. Of course, this does not mean that each and every day of married life is filled with boundless joy and no challenges. As many newly married husbands and wives might tell us, it is not long after the wedding, when the guests have gone, the honeymoon is over, and everyday life takes center stage once again that the idea hits home: A happy marriage takes *work*.

Your views on marriage and family life might have been initially formed by your impression of the relationship of your parents or other relatives. You may want to create a marriage similar to the ones found in your family. Or, for whatever reason, you might want to work to create a marriage different from those found in your own family. Although you might have an idea of what you

TAKE IT TO GOD

Dear God,
If my vocation one day is marriage,
Please help me prepare for it.
A cord of three strands is not easily broken.
Be the third cord in my future marriage.
Ensure that our covenant is not broken.
Open my heart to loving another selflessly.
Let me know what it means to humble myself
to serve you and my future spouse.
Remind me to never get so busy that there is no room for you in my
    marriage
 or to allow distance to come between my spouse and me.
More than anything else, God, please help me
discern my vocation and be present in my everyday life.
Amen.

UNIT 5

would like a future spouse to be like, where you want to live, and what kind of career you would like to have, many of these ideas might change and develop as you get older. The one thing that remains constant is that any healthy relationship takes work and must be nurtured with healthy communication, sacrifice, compromise, thoughtfulness, and deep commitment.

Marriage Is a Covenant

Through your previous study of religion, you probably became familiar with the importance of God's covenant with his people. The Old Covenant was a gift of God to the people of Israel, and it has never been dissolved. The New Covenant is a gift of God to us, in Jesus Christ, his Son, and we live by it today. We renew it at every Eucharist. Through the words and actions of the priest and the power of the Holy Spirit, the sacrifice of Jesus Christ is made present, and we participate in it by receiving, as did the Apostles at the Last Supper, his Body and Blood.

The union of a baptized man and a baptized woman in marriage is a sign and symbol of God's covenant with his people, a covenant of love and grace in Jesus Christ. In the wedding Mass, we may hear these words at the Preface:

> In the union of husband and wife
> you give a sign of Christ's loving gift of grace,
> so that the Sacrament we celebrate
> might draw us back more deeply
> into the wondrous design of your love.
> (*Roman Missal*, "Preface, Marriage B," page 1186)

Let's explore the meaning of the marriage covenant through the history of this sacrament and its scriptural sources.

God's Plan for Marriage

God created marriage, and it is part of his wonderful plan for human life. Because we are made in the image and likeness of God, we are made for love. Marriage is not a purely human institution, but is God's loving way of bringing happiness to his sons and daughters and assuring them that they need not be alone as they journey through life. Marriage has been planned by God to bring about two great goods: the good of the man and woman pledged to each other, and the gift and nurturing of children. In their intimate union in both body and spirit, the marital love of man and woman is an image and likeness of God's love for all of us. And if God blesses the husband and wife with the gift of a child, there is all the more reason to rejoice!

The cross is a symbol of Christ, who in Christian marriage, is joined with two individuals (symbolized by the rings) into an unbreakable union.

When Jesus taught about the divine plan for marriage, he went all the way back to the Book of Genesis and drew upon the following passage: "That is why a man leaves his father and mother and clings to his wife, and the two of them become one body" (2:24, see Matthew 19:1–12). Jesus concluded that this was the reason why marriages cannot be dissolved: "So they are no longer two, but one flesh. Therefore, what God has joined together, no human being must separate" (Matthew 19:6). It is here that Christ raised marriage in the New Covenant, marriage between Christians, to the dignity of a sacrament.

Marriage and the Old Covenant

In our society, relationships between men and women sometimes result in misunderstandings and conflict. This is due not to the nature of men and women, or to the quality of their relationships, but to sin. Within marriage, misunderstandings and conflicts can escalate into domination, jealousy, and infidelity. The first sin—the sin of the first man and woman—resulted in a break in the original communion between man and woman. The consequences of this Original Sin, the necessity of struggle and the pain of childbirth, became part of human life.

But God continues to offer us his mercy and healing. The consequences of the first sin also became a means of healing. In marriage, a husband and wife must support each other to sustain themselves and their families and to raise their children. The self-giving that this mutual support requires helps the married couple to grow in God's love and grace.

UNIT 5

CATHOLICS **MAKING**
A **DIFFERENCE**

On October 18, 2015, Louis and Azélie-Marie Martin were canonized as saints by Pope Francis. The Martins lived in the mid-1800s. They were immediately drawn to each other and married after just three short months. They enjoyed regular social activities as a couple, such as fishing, billiards, traveling, and parties. But they also attended daily Mass, prayed the *Angelus* every day at noon, and kept Sunday as a day of rest. They had nine children. Five of their daughters survived, and the youngest would become known as Saint Thérèse of Lisieux. The Martins were not martyrs and didn't found a religious order. They were canonized because they created a loving, family environment through their marriage that nurtured the growing sainthood of their youngest daughter. They are the first married couple ever canonized together.

Under the Old Covenant, the unity and indissolubility of marriage was a moral concept that developed gradually. The polygamy of kings and patriarchs was not explicitly rejected; however, the Law of Moses protected the wife from being at the mercy of her husband, even though it still permitted a man to divorce his wife.

The prophets, however, aimed at a higher standard. They saw God's covenant as one of an exclusive married love, with God as the Bridegroom and Israel as the Bride:

> For as a young man marries a virgin,
> your Builder shall marry you;
> And as a bridegroom rejoices in his bride
> so shall your God rejoice in you.
> (Isaiah 62:5)

In their prophetic teaching, the prophets prepared the people for a deeper understanding of the unity and indissolubility of married love between a man and a woman. The Book of Ruth and the Book of Tobit both describe a tender and exclusive married love. The Song of Songs—on the surface, a human love story—has traditionally been seen as a metaphor for God's covenantal love for his people. It was this abiding love of God for his people that prepared the way for the New Covenant in which the incarnate Son of God gave himself as the Bridegroom to all humankind.

The Book of Tobit

The Book of Tobit is a rather short book found in the Old Testament. It tells the story of a family consisting of Tobit, a faithful Jew who is afflicted with blindness; his wife, Anna; his son, Tobiah; and a young woman, Sarah. Tobit sends Tobiah on a journey to recover some money he had left behind in his home country. (Tobiah is not completely alone though; his dog follows him and is with him every step of the way.) His father also suggests that when Tobiah reaches the home of their people, he might look for a woman to marry. The angel Raphael joins Tobiah on his journey to help and guide him. When the young woman, Sarah, enters the story, Raphael's guidance becomes important indeed!

The Book of Tobit inspires us to be faithful to God's Law, to act respectfully toward parents, to honor marriage, and to value almsgiving, prayer, and fasting. The Book of Tobit is beautifully written and has a happy ending for all its characters.

The angel Raphael meeting with Tobit and his son, Tobiah.

The Wedding at Cana

The Church has always seen marriage as part of the divine plan, and sees in Jesus' presence at the wedding at Cana a sign of his blessing upon the state of marriage itself. At Cana, at the urging of his mother, Jesus came to the rescue of a newly married couple who had run out of wine for their guests. Through the miracle of changing water into wine, Jesus "revealed his glory" and announced that a New Covenant in himself had arrived (see John 2:1–11). Jesus' presence at the wedding affirmed the goodness of marriage and revealed that the Sacrament of Matrimony, from then on, would be a sign of his presence. (We might also recall that at the Last Supper, Jesus blessed the wine and made it the sign of the New Covenant in his blood.)

Jesus' affirmation of the goodness of marriage forms the background of his teaching on other issues related to marriage and family. For example, Jesus prohibited divorce and remarriage (see Matthew 19:1–12, 5:31–32). He taught that marriage is truly a covenantal relationship, like the covenantal relationship between God and his people, and therefore cannot be dissolved. God's plan for human relationship, for the majority of people, includes a lifetime of love to reflect, mediate, and witness his own deep and faithful covenantal love.

Jesus also demonstrated his love of children and stated that the Kingdom of Heaven belongs to them (see Matthew 19:13–15). "Children are the supreme gift of marriage"[1] (*Catechism of the Catholic Church [CCC]*, number 1652) and, as gifts, bring great good to their parents. In marriage, a man and a woman cooperate with God in bringing new life into the world.

Is Jesus' insistence on a lifetime commitment for married couples an impossible burden? Is it unattainable? Jesus said that with God's help, and with the grace and strength of the Sacrament of Marriage, faithfulness to one person for life is possible. This is, of course, with the understanding that there is no Christian life for anyone, married or not, without the cross. Marriage in Christ, in the New Covenant, is not trouble free, but, for those who follow Christ, it is not only possible but also loving and joyful. ✳

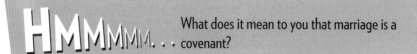

HMMMMM. . . What does it mean to you that marriage is a covenant?

Article 47
Witnesses to Love

Marriage is an exclusive, permanent, and lifelong contract between a man and a woman in which they commit themselves to care for each other and to procreate and raise children. When a marriage takes place between baptized persons who enter into a covenant modeled on that between Christ and the Church, it is recognized as the **Sacrament of Matrimony**.

© Rawpixel.com / Shutterstock.com

"Charity begins at home," but it doesn't end there. A loving marriage contributes to the stability of the entire family, and the influence of family love can reach around the world. How does your family share love with others?

We have already discussed the "lifelong contract between a man and a woman" mentioned in this definition. Let us move on to the next phrase, "a covenant modeled on that between Christ and the Church."

In the previous article, we briefly touched on Christ's love for the Church. In this article, we explore this reality in more depth, particularly in the writings of Saint Paul the Apostle, and consider its relationship to marriage.

Matrimony, Sacrament of ➤ A lifelong covenant, modeled on that between Christ and the Church, in which a baptized man and a baptized woman make an exclusive and permanent commitment to faithfully love each other and to cooperate in the procreation and education of children.

In his Letter to the Ephesians, Saint Paul makes the important point that married couples are signs of Christ's love for the Church:

> Husbands, love your wives, even as Christ loved the church and handed himself over for her to sanctify her. . . . So [also] husbands should love their wives as their own bodies. He who loves his wife loves himself. For no one hates his own flesh but rather nourishes and cherishes it, even as Christ does the church, because we are members of his body. (Ephesians 5:25–30)

Saint Paul goes on to quote the same passage from Genesis that Jesus quoted, ending with, "and the two shall become one flesh" (Ephesians 5:31). He concludes, "This is a great mystery, but I speak in reference to Christ and the church" verse 32).

TAKE IT TO GOD

Anniversary Prayer

Praying for parents, relatives, and friends who are married is an important way to support married couples. You might like to write this anniversary prayer in a card for the next wedding anniversary of a couple you know.

Dear God,
Bless _____ and _____ on their anniversary.
In their love for each other, they reveal your love to the world.
Give them grace to live out their marriage covenant,
provide them with strength when times are hard,
and shower them with joy in the company of family and friends.
Open their eyes to the gifts you have given them
in order to serve you by serving others.
May they enjoy many more years together,
growing closer to each other and to you.
May they love and honor each other all the days of their lives.
Amen.

Saint Paul states that he knows no greater union than that of Christ and the Church. The Sacrament of Matrimony is a sign of that union. In this sacrament, a man and a woman are given the grace to love each other with the same love with which Christ loves the Church. The Sacrament of Matrimony, through its graces, brings human love to fulfillment and to unbroken unity. The grace of the Sacrament of Matrimony joins a man and a woman and makes them holy as they journey together on the path to eternal happiness.

In the nuptial blessing, the priest prays for the married couple and refers to the wife in the following words:

> May her husband entrust his heart to her,
> so that, acknowledging her as his equal
> and his joint heir to the life of grace,
> he may show her due honor. . . .
> (*Roman Missal*, "Nuptial Blessing A," page 1182)

This prayer acknowledges the husband and wife as equal partners in their marriage relationship. Saint Paul also acknowledges this by writing, "Be subordinate to one another out of reverence for Christ" (Ephesians 5:21). At the very least, this means sharing ideas honestly and coming to decisions that both can live with. If married couples continually try to love each other as much as Christ loves the Church, they will form a true and lasting marriage in Christ and will be witnesses to his love their entire lives.

Preparing for a Catholic Marriage

Preparing for a Catholic marriage is more than just preparing for the wedding ceremony, but sometimes the two overlap. Here are some key considerations from the article "Getting Married Catholic," found on the For Your Marriage website, sponsored by the United States Conference of Catholic Bishops:

1. Meet with your parish priest as soon as you become engaged.
2. Prepare for your marriage. Set aside at least six months to have adequate time to arrange the practical wedding details and to reflect on your relationship and your plans for the future. Also give yourselves time for prayer—both individually and together.
3. Attend an approved marriage preparation program in your area. There are also national programs. Check for these by contacting your diocesan family life office.

What do you think are important topics to discuss during a marriage preparation program?

What does a marriage preparation program involve? Usually the engaged couple meets with a team consisting of a married couple and a priest or deacon. Sometimes, a parish may offer a mentor couple program, in which a married couple, especially trained for this work, meets with an engaged couple to discuss various issues related to marriage. Most preparation programs include a marriage preparation inventory taken by the engaged couple. In highlighting various areas of life, this inventory points to areas of agreement as well as areas that could benefit from further discussion between the potential spouses.

Some Frequently Asked Questions

Young people often have questions about the Sacrament of Matrimony, and it is important to have those questions answered before you are in a committed relationship. Consider the following questions and answers to see if this helps you understand some of the teachings on Catholic marriage:

1. What is the normal Catholic practice regarding getting married during Mass?

    When two Catholics marry, the Rite of Marriage is normally celebrated during the Eucharist. This is because all the sacraments unite us with the Paschal Mystery of Christ. Just as we celebrate, particularly in the Eucharist, that Christ gave up his life for us, so at a Catholic wedding, we celebrate the gift of life that the bride and bridegroom are and will be for each other. If celebrating the rite during Mass is not possible, then a Liturgy of the Word, followed by the vows of the Sacrament of Matrimony, may be celebrated.

2. What is a mixed marriage?

A mixed marriage is a marriage between a Catholic and a baptized non-Catholic. This kind of marriage is not forbidden, but it does present obstacles to complete unity in marriage. It can have consequences in the education of children, and tensions can arise, even to the point of abandoning the Catholic faith.

Another kind of mixed marriage is called "disparity of cult," which is a marriage between a Catholic and a

Your parish priest is one of the adults you can go to if you have questions about Church teachings.

person who is not baptized. In these cases, care must be taken on the part of pastors and the engaged couple to ensure that all misunderstandings about the life of faith are discussed before the marriage. Both kinds of mixed marriages require special permission from Church authority.

3. In a situation where one parent is Catholic and the other is not, and the children have been raised Catholic, how should they handle delicate conversations regarding religion that sometimes turn problematic?

Try talking with your parish priest. In many regions, a pastoral plan for families in mixed marriages has been worked out. It encourages families to nourish those things they agree on and respect those things on which they differ. If one parent has no faith at all, continue to love them and pray for them. We can never go wrong with love and prayer. ✳

UNIT 5

What are the biggest challenges to a husband and wife loving each other as Christ loves the Church?

© Ollyy / Shutterstock.com

Article 48
The Order of Celebrating Matrimony

Ann sat at the dining room table looking back and forth between her parents and her older sister. They were talking about her sister's upcoming wedding, and apparently the plans had hit a snag. "Mark wants to get married at the beach," Rachel said. "I told him it was important to get married in the church, but when he asked why, I didn't really know what to say." Ann really wanted to know the answer to that question because she wondered the same thing. "Rachel, when you and Mark have your Pre-Cana sessions with Father Felipe, I'm sure he will go over all your questions," said Ann and Rachel's mom. "But I can tell you that marriage is a sacrament, and because it is a sacrament, it must be celebrated within a sacred place—the church. When you profess your vows in front of the entire community that supports you, there is an understanding that your marriage is more than a party or celebration. You are making solemn promises on holy ground. I'm sure Mark will understand that." Rachel nodded and said, "Thanks, Mom. I just needed help putting it into words."

Marriage is a public vocation. Because of this, the Sacrament of Matrimony is usually public and in church. However, there are some places where permission or dispensations are granted by the local bishop for a marriage ceremony to take place outside of a church. The Sacrament of Matrimony

The matrimonial covenant is a covenant of mutual consent.

establishes the matrimonial covenant as a religious action, an act of worship, and emphasizes that in this action and as a result of it, God's love will be shared not only between the married couple but also with the community. Therefore, it is fitting that the ceremony be public, within a liturgical celebration, and before a priest (or deacon), two other witnesses, and the assembly. The presence of the minister and the witnesses is a tangible sign that sacramental marriage is a communal and ecclesial reality, not a private or secular matter.

Note that the priest or deacon is not the minister of the sacrament but a witness representing the Church. The actual ministers of the sacrament are the bride and the groom, who give their free consent to the marriage. (In the Eastern Churches, the priest witnesses the consent of the bride and groom, but in order for the sacrament to be valid, his blessing is also required. Thus, in the Eastern Churches, the priest is the minister of the sacrament.)

This consent, which must be freely given, is an essential element of the Sacrament of Matrimony. Consent is the will of the man and woman to give themselves to each other in order to live a lifelong covenant of faithful love, and to be open to sharing that love with children. This consent is expressed in the vows of Matrimony: "I, N., take you, N., to be my wife [or husband]" (*The Order of Celebrating Matrimony*, page 35).

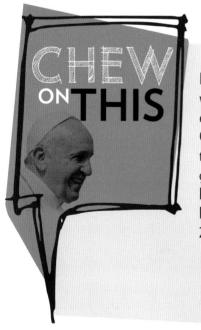

In marriage we give ourselves completely without calculation or reserve, sharing everything, gifts and hardship, trusting in God's Providence. This is the experience that the young can learn from their parents and grandparents. ("Address of Pope Francis to Participants in the Plenary Assembly of the Pontifical Council for the Family," October 25, 2013)

UNIT 5

The priest or deacon, as the Church's witness, receives this consent and gives the blessing of the Church with the following words: "May the Lord in his kindness strengthen the consent you have declared before the Church, and graciously bring to fulfillment his blessing within you. What God joins together, let no one put asunder" (*The Order of Celebrating Matrimony*, page 38).

If free consent is lacking on either side, there is no marriage bond. To be free when expressing consent means: (1) not being under any constraint (coercion or pressure, even if subtle) and (2) not being barred from marriage by any natural or Church law.

A *constraint* is an obstacle that prevents free and full consent to a marriage. Let us look at some examples of constraint. Pregnancy, mental illness, or a secret addiction could all be obstacles that prevent free and full consent. Where there is constraint, or obstacles to free and full consent, there is no

© Julio-FotoVideo / Shutterstock.com

I DIDN'T KNOW THAT!

What do you think are the essential elements to marriage? If you had to name three things, what would they be? fidelity? loyalty? the possibility of family? The Church considers the following three elements to be essential to every marriage:

- **Unity:** Marriage unites the husband and wife in an unbreakable and exclusive union. Adultery and polygamy are sins against the unity of marriage.

- **Indissolubility:** The marriage bond can never be dissolved. The husband and the wife make a commitment to lifelong fidelity. Divorcing one's lawful spouse and marrying another person is a sin against the permanence of marriage.

- **Openness to children:** Husbands and wives must be open to children and accept them as gifts from God. Artificial contraception is a sin against the openness to new life. It is intrinsically evil because it makes procreation impossible. The essence of conjugal love is total self-gift to the other, and using contraception, a refusal to be open to the possibility of new life, makes this gift a lie.

valid marriage bond. This is one reason the Church requires a period of preparation before the Sacrament of Matrimony, often with some kind of assessment to determine a couple's readiness. Free consent is important to a faithful and fruitful marriage.

"Not being barred from marriage by natural or Church law" means that one must be legally and ecclesiastically free to marry. For example, someone who has taken religious vows in the Church is not free to marry until they are released from those vows. Someone who is already married to someone else cannot contract a new bond of Matrimony. In some instances, natural law prohibits marriage, such as marriage between family members.

When a marriage has been entered into under constraint, or for other reasons, the marriage bond can be declared null and void by the Church. The Church's declaration of nullity is called an **annulment**. This declaration means that a true marriage bond, as a sacrament, never existed in the eyes of the Church. It does not mean that the children of that marriage are illegitimate or are now orphans. It simply means that for some reason, free consent to the marriage by one of the partners was never given.

An annulment declared by the Church is not the same as a civil divorce. Those who have been civilly divorced from a spouse still living, and have re-married without a Church annulment, have gone against God's Law as taught by Christ. They are still members of the Church, but may not receive the Eucharist. The Church encourages them to educate their children in the faith, to attend Mass and listen to the Liturgy of the Word, to pray, to do works of love and justice, to do penance, and to strengthen their relationship with God through prayer, asking for his grace for themselves and their families. ✳

UNIT 5

HMMMMM. . . What constraint would truly impede a person from entering into marriage completely?

---

annulment ➤ The declaration by the Church that a marriage is null and void, that is, it never existed as a sacramental union. Catholics who divorce must have the marriage annulled by the Church to be free to marry once again in the Church.

Article 49
Lifelong Journey

The grace of the Sacrament of Matrimony is the grace to bring the couple's love for each other to its fullness and to strengthen their bond with each other. This grace helps the husband and wife to live the responsibilities of married life, so that in their love and companionship they may help bring each other through this life and into the eternal and heavenly Kingdom prepared for them for all eternity.

The grace of the Sacrament of Matrimony prepares the newly married couple for a lifelong journey of fidelity. The gift of self cannot truly be made on a tentative basis: "Maybe I love you enough to stay with you, and maybe I don't." It cannot be a "Let's see how things turn out" proposition. That is not unconditional love, and it is an attitude and approach that undermines the stable commitment upon which a lifetime of happiness for both the spouses and their children is built. Unconditional love is the only foundation for a lasting marriage.

In addition, as we learned previously, Christian marriage is a symbol of the fidelity of Christ to his Church. Husbands and wives, strengthened by the grace of the Sacrament of Matrimony, are called to this same fidelity. In this fidelity, they proclaim the faithful love of God for all and can love each other because they share in God's love.

A married couple freely promises to love and honor each other all the days of their lives, in good times and in bad, in sickness and in health; to lovingly accept children, and to bring them up in the faith of the Church.

UNIT 5

The entire community must support those in the married state with their prayers and encouragement. Although there are some serious reasons for which the Church allows for the separation of a couple, a separated husband and wife are still married and may not contract another union. The ultimate goal of a separation is reconciliation and a renewed commitment to the matrimonial covenant. This may be accomplished through the guidance of a spiritual advisor and other counselors, as well as the support of trusted family members and friends. Most of all, it requires the firm and mutual resolve of the couple.

The grace of the Sacrament of Matrimony is a lifelong grace. Those who seek to cooperate with this grace find that at times, enriching their marriage through reflection and education is helpful. Retreat houses offer weekend retreats or days of recollection for married couples. Many husbands and wives find gathering with other married couples to reflect and pray together is a great support for marriage. Movements such as Marriage Encounter and Teams of Our Lady help support this. Dioceses and parishes often offer courses on human relationships and communication, taught from the perspective of faith. Many dioceses sponsor an Office of Family Life or Family Ministries and offer various resources on their diocesan websites.

Marriage and Family Life

In one of the seven themes of Catholic social teaching, the United States Conference of Catholic Bishops declares, "Marriage and the family are the central social institutions that must be supported and strengthened, not undermined" (USCCB website). The organization of society (in economics, politics, law, and policy) directly affects marriage and family. Think of the many obstacles to family life in our society: lack of affordable, quality childcare; issues of employment for parents (low-wage or part-time work); or the lack of any employment at all, resulting in poverty and hunger. Even economically stable families have difficulty scheduling family time due to parents' work demands, children's over-involvement in organized sports and other activities at younger and younger ages, and a lack of extended family nearby to help in times of need. All of us, whether married or not, have a right and a duty to care about families— others' as well as our own—especially families struggling with poverty and need. All of us have a right and duty to participate in society's decisions that affect the well-being of families.

The Domestic Church

The Sacrament of Matrimony is the foundation for the Christian family. The Christian family is the place where children first learn the love of God through the love of their parents. The family is the domestic church. It is "the church at home," where children first hear the faith proclaimed. The family is a domestic church because, as a community of grace and prayer, it fosters growth in human virtues and, especially, practice in Christian love.

Parents are children's first teachers in the faith. When children are young, parents—exercising their authority as members of the "common priesthood of the faithful"—should set a routine of family prayer and reading from Scripture. As children grow, parents should set an example of regular participation in the sacraments. Children should see their parents praying, helping those in need, serving others, and forgiving each other as often as the need arises. Children should learn the dignity and satisfaction of work, as they are gradually included in the daily chores of household living.

MAKE IT SO

Are You Ready for Marriage?

Marriage is a decision best made by mature and responsible people who have reached adulthood. However, how you handle friendships now is a good indicator of the way you might handle a married relationship in the future. The following questions might be helpful in assessing your attitudes on some aspects of friendship that will loom large in married life. Test yourself!

1. How well do I listen? Am I always looking to argue small points? Do I allow others to have their own choices and ideas in a friendship, or do I dominate the relationship?

2. How do I handle conflict? Do I fly off the handle, or do I find an appropriate time and place to discuss the issue with the other person?

3. How do I feel when my plans are upset for some reason? Am I angry? resentful? Or can I be flexible and look for ways to include the needs of others in a "plan B"?

4. Do I apologize when I am in the wrong? Even when I am in the right, do I seek to repair a misunderstanding? Do I constantly bring up past mistakes?

Families are the backbone and the lifeblood of the Church. Single people can make significant contributions to family life as aunts and uncles, godparents, or family friends. They certainly should not be left out of the love and support of the Christian community. Families should often include their single friends and fellow parishioners in their celebrations, particularly at important seasons of the Church year, like Christmas and Easter. Some single people, such as those living in senior residences or long-term care facilities, can easily be marginalized. Those who are homeless are in special need, as are those who are living alone in poverty. Pastors and families, as well as charitable organizations, should always seek to find ways to open the doors of the parish family to them.

Matrimony is the foundation for the Christian family. In what ways can parents pass on their faith and bring up their children in the Church?

The Gift of Children

As mentioned previously, a man and woman united in marriage must also be open to the gift of children and ready to take on responsibility for their growth and education, especially in morality and the spiritual life. For the parents, this is a cooperative work with God and his love. Each child is unique and comes with unique gifts and talents. As much as possible, parents are called to notice and nurture these gifts not only for the child's own good but also for the good of the world.

Parents are called to encourage each child, according to each one's particular gifts, in a suitable vocation. Parents are also called to encourage and nurture a religious vocation, should they discern that one or more of their children might be suited to this calling.

Those couples unable to bring children into the world can still support the gift of life as foster or adoptive parents, as active aunts and uncles, as mentors, teachers, or social workers, or as those who provide hospitality and love to friends, neighbors, and those in need. ✳

UNIT 5

HMMMMM. . .

In what way is openness to children an essential part of marriage?

© View Apart / Shutterstock.com

1. What is God's plan for marriage?

2. What is the definition of the Sacrament of Matrimony? Choose two key elements from this definition and explain why each is important in Christian marriage.

3. How did the idea of the unity and indissolubility of marriage gradually develop in the Law of Moses, the teachings of the prophets, and, finally, in the New Covenant established by Christ?

4. How do Saint Paul's words in Ephesians 5:25–30 relate to the union of husband and wife in the Sacrament of Matrimony?

5. Why is it important that consent in the Sacrament of Matrimony be free? What are some circumstances that may create constraint or pressure to marry, leading to a marriage contracted without free consent?

6. Who are the ministers of the Sacrament of Matrimony? What is the role of the priest or deacon in the Sacrament in the Latin Rite? in the Eastern Churches?

7. What three requirements are essential to marriage?

8. What are some ways those who are single can contribute to family life? How can married couples provide those who are single, especially those who may be isolated because of old age or illness, an opportunity to share in family life?

9. When might the Church issue a declaration of nullity, called an annulment, and what does this declaration mean?

UNIT 5

Marriage and Family

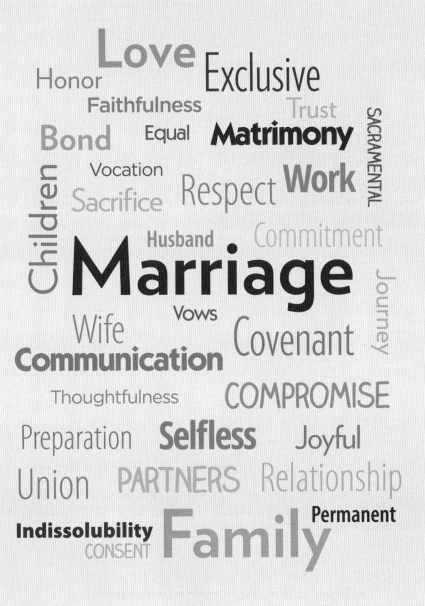

Love
Honor
Exclusive
Faithfulness
Trust
Bond Equal **Matrimony**
SACRAMENTAL
Vocation
Children Sacrifice Respect **Work**
Husband Commitment
Marriage
Vows
Journey
Wife Covenant
Communication
Thoughtfulness COMPROMISE
Preparation **Selfless** Joyful
Union PARTNERS Relationship
Indissolubility Permanent
CONSENT Family

UNIT 5 HIGHLIGHTS

CHAPTER 11   Priesthood of the Old Covenant

- Aaron, brother of Moses, was the first high priest.
- God chose the tribe of Levi to be priests, carrying out liturgical sacrifices and worship.
- Only the Levites were in charge of the Dwelling Place of God.
- The Dwelling Place of God was a tent that held the Ten Commandments and journeyed with the Israelites wherever they went.
- The priesthood honored God with sacrifice and prayer and united the people in worship.

- Jesus fulfilled the priesthood of the Old Covenant through his institution of the Sacrament of Holy Orders.
- Jesus, the new High Priest, didn't enter the earthly sanctuary of the Old Covenant but Heaven itself.
- His sacrifice was not the blood of lambs, but his own blood.
- We remember and celebrate this sacrifice, led by the ministry of the priesthood of the New Covenant, in the sacraments and especially in the Eucharist.
- Through the Sacrament of Holy Orders, Christ's mission is entrusted to the Apostles and carried out in the priesthood today.

Images: Shutterstock.com

Bishop

- The visible head of the particular diocese to which he has been assigned.
- Successor to the Apostles.
- Responsible for caring for the entire Church under the authority of the Pope.
- A bishop's ordination must be approved by the Pope.

Priest

- Ordained as a coworker of the bishop.
- Look to the bishop for guidance in assignment and duties.
- Religious order priests look to the superior of their religious community for guidance, and they usually engage in a particular mission for which their order was founded.
- Share the responsibility with the bishop of building up the Body of Christ.
- Consecrated to preach the Gospel, guide the People of God, and celebrate the liturgy.

Deacon

- Ordained for service in the Church.
- Ordination bestows important functions on them in ministry of the Word, divine worship, pastoral governance, and the service of charity and good works.
- All duties are carried out under the authority of the bishop.
- Service includes assisting at the liturgy, distributing Holy Eucharist, baptizing, blessing marriages, proclaiming the Gospel, preaching, presiding at funerals, and serving those who are poor or in need.

UNIT 5

CHAPTER 12   The Development of Marriage as a Sacrament

God's Plan for Marriage

- Unity and indissolubility were concepts that developed gradually.
- The Law of Moses protected women from being at the mercy of their husbands.
- Men could divorce their wives.

- The prophets prepared people for the unity and indissolubility of married love.
- The Book of Tobit, the Book of Ruth, and the Song of Songs all represent covenantal love.

- Jesus' presence at the wedding at Cana is a sign of his blessing on the state of marriage itself.
- Jesus' presence revealed the Sacrament of Matrimony and would forever be a sign of his presence.
- Jesus prohibited divorce and remarriage.
- Jesus taught that marriage is a covenantal relationship.

Saint Paul on Marriage

Images: © Renata Sedmakova / Shutterstock.com / Shutterstock.com

UNIT 5

"Wives should be subordinate to their husbands in everything" (Ephesians 5:24). This is reflective of the cultural context of that time.

"Be subordinate to one another out of reverence for Christ" (Ephesians 5:21). This means sharing ideas honestly and coming to decisions that both can live with.

"Husbands, love your wives, even as Christ loved the Church. . . . So [also] husbands should love their wives as their own bodies. He who loves his wife loves himself" (Ephesians 5:25,28).

"The two shall become one flesh" (Ephesians 5:31).

Sacrament of Matrimony

The Sacrament of Matrimony is public and held in a church.

The ceremony is public before the priest (or deacon), two other witnesses, and the assembly.

The bride and groom are the actual ministers of the sacrament, and they give their free consent to the marriage.

The priest or deacon, as the Church's witness, receives this consent and gives the blessing of the Church.

Three Essential Elements of a Marriage

Unity

Indissolubility

Openness to Children

UNIT 5

UNIT 5
BRING IT HOME

WHY ARE HOLY ORDERS AND MATRIMONY GROUPED TOGETHER AS SACRAMENTS?

FOCUS QUESTIONS

CHAPTER 11   Why can only men be ordained?

CHAPTER 12   Why should I get married in the Church?

MATTIAS
Seton Catholic Preparatory School

We are called by God to live out our vocation, whatever we discern it to be. The Sacraments of Holy Orders and Matrimony are grouped together because at the core, they are both about taking vows to serve God through our chosen vocation. Each sacrament has its own graces and challenges. We aren't born knowing if we will become a priest or a nun, a religious brother, a single person living a life consecrated to God, or a married person. However, the Sacraments of Matrimony and Holy Orders are both options for a living a life serving God in a way that is unique to each one of us.

UNIT 5

REFLECT

Take some time to read and reflect on the unit and chapter focus questions listed on the facing page.

- What question or section did you identify most closely with?

- What did you find within the unit that was comforting or challenging?

APPENDIX

Challenge Questions

The content of this course will raise some important questions for those who think seriously about their faith. This is especially true today when many people are asking hard questions about religious beliefs. We are not afraid of these hard questions because an honest search for answers will deepen our faith and understanding of what God has revealed. Here are some common questions with some key points for how to answer them. The references to paragraphs in the *Catechism of the Catholic Church (CCC)* are for further reading if you want to explore these questions more deeply.

QUESTION 1: Can't a person go directly to God without the help of the Church or a priest?

Of course, any person can always pray directly to God. However, God established the Church as a way for him to teach us and to enrich us with his grace. The Church is the sacrament of the Holy Trinity's communication with human beings. In every liturgy, especially the Seven Sacraments, we encounter God—the Father, Son, and Holy Spirit—in a unique and special way (see *CCC*, numbers 774–776).

How is this possible? It is possible because Christ is present to us in many ways in the liturgy. He is present in the priest, who acts in the person of Christ. He is present in the assembly because we are the Body of Christ. He is present in the Word of God, the Scriptures. In the Sacrament of the Eucharist, Christ is present in a special way when we receive Communion. So, yes, we can pray directly to God, and we should. Throughout the Liturgical Year, the Church reflects on the life of Jesus; his mission, his miracles, his teachings. And during this time, we have the opportunity, day by day and week by week, to know Christ better, to internalize his teachings and values as we encounter him in Word and sacrament. It doesn't matter if you are in the grandest cathedral or your local church, we encounter Jesus in every liturgy and through the sacraments celebrated within those liturgies. Each of the sacraments communicates the grace of Jesus and brings us into a deeper relationship with him.

The sacraments also bring us into a deeper relationship and unity with one another in the following ways. First, through Baptism, we become part of God's family, with many brothers and sisters. Saint Paul tells us, "We are members one of another" (Ephesians 4:25). Second, Saint Paul teaches that we grow in unity by sharing our spiritual gifts with one another: "To each individual the manifestation of the Spirit is given for some benefit" (1 Corinthians 12:7). He is explaining that we receive individual gifts, but together those gifts strengthen our unity and identity as the People of God. Third, we are each part of the Body of Christ, having our own role and responsibility, but these roles mean nothing unless we are functioning as part of the whole. Therefore, we are called together in worship and prayer to support one another in becoming the best Body of Christ we can be.

QUESTION 2: Can't God forgive us directly when we are sorry for sin?

Although God can forgive us whenever and however he wants, he knows what is best for us and has taught us through Jesus that he wants to forgive us through the Sacrament of Penance and Reconciliation. We know that Jesus, the Son of God, has the authority to forgive sins, and he passed this authority to the Apostles. Through Apostolic Succession, that authority has been passed down to the bishops and through them to the priests, and is administered through the Sacrament of Penance and Reconciliation. Jesus gave the authority to forgive sins and welcome back the sinner to the Apostles when he told Peter: "I will give you the keys to the kingdom of heaven. Whatever you bind on earth shall be bound in heaven; and whatever you loose on earth shall be loosed in heaven" (Matthew 16:19). Only God can forgive, and he has given that power to bishops and priests so that as servants of God, they can assure us that if we are forgiven on Earth in the Sacrament of Penance and Reconciliation, we are forgiven by God as well.

Confession is absolutely necessary so that mortal sins can be forgiven and the penitent can be reconciled with God and the Church. The Church also recommends confession of venial sins. By doing this, we help to form and strengthen our conscience, nip evil tendencies in the bud, open our hearts to the healing of Christ, and make progress in the life of the Spirit. When we receive the Father's mercy, we are encouraged to be merciful to others as well. The primary act of the penitent is repentance or contrition. If we are truly repentant, the sacrament assures us of forgiveness.

Honest conversations, in which we take responsibility for our actions and seek to make things right again, are a difficult but important part of human life. We need to confess our sins to face the reality of the wrong we have done. When we do this during the Sacrament of Penance and Reconciliation, we can be assured of forgiveness. Confession is an essential part of the Sacrament of Penance and Reconciliation. After our confession, when we receive absolution, we are assured of forgiveness and given the gift of pardon and peace.

QUESTION 3: Aren't the sacraments just celebrations to mark significant moments in our lives?

Although the sacraments are often celebrated at appropriate or significant moments or events in our lives, they are much more than simply a celebration of those moments. The sacraments are personal encounters with Christ, who acts through the sacraments to help us. The Holy Spirit works through the Church to make Christ present in the world and to be the instrument of grace and salvation for everyone. In every liturgy, especially the Seven Sacraments, the Church encounters God—the Father, Son, and Holy Spirit. Through these encounters and the outpouring of God's grace, we are justified, which means we are freed from sin, and we are sanctified, which means we are made holy and share in the divine life. And so, how then can we encounter Christ through the sacraments? Christ is present in the priest, who acts in the person of Christ. Christ is present in the assembly because we are the Body of Christ. He is present in the Word of God, the Scriptures. In the Sacrament of the Eucharist, Christ is present in a special way, in his Body and Blood, which we receive during Communion.

We should also remember that each sacrament gives us a special grace that strengthens us in our discipleship and vocation as a follower of Christ.

> The sacraments are efficacious signs of grace, instituted by Christ and entrusted to the Church, by which divine life is dispensed to us. The visible rites by which the sacraments are celebrated signify and make present the graces proper to each sacrament. They bear fruit in those who receive them with the required dispositions. (*CCC*, number 1131)

Efficacious means that they are *effective* and that they actually *work*, because Christ is at work in them. Given this reality, the sacraments are more than a celebration or a marker of a special time; they signify and make present the power of God.

QUESTION 4: Is there any difference between receiving Holy Communion in a Catholic Church and going to communion in a Protestant worship service?

The short answer is yes, there are differences. And those differences have to do in part with the fact that the reception of Holy Communion in the Catholic Church is a statement of belief in the Real Presence of Jesus in the Eucharist and the unity with all Catholics throughout the world (see *CCC*, numbers 1376, 1391, 1398). When we speak of the Real Presence of Christ in the Eucharist, this means that the mode of Christ's presence under the Eucharistic elements is unique. Christ is present in his Body and Blood in the fullest sense: "It is a *substantial* presence by which Christ, God and man, makes himself wholly and entirely present"[1] (*CCC*, number 1374). This presence is called the Real Presence of Christ.

Through Christ's Real Presence in the Sacrament of the Eucharist, we become more closely united to Christ and are strengthened for our life as his disciples. Christ becomes one with us so that we can become one with him, so that we can *become him* as the Body of Christ in the world. So, receiving the Eucharist encompasses our entire lives of faith: membership in the Church; belief in the teachings of the Church, including the Real Presence of Christ in the Eucharist through Transubstantiation; and a life lived according to the teachings of Christ. Gathering with others for Mass also gives witness to our union with Christ and with one another in the solidarity of faith and love that is shared by members of the Church. At the Eucharist, in word and action, we show that we are united in faith and love.

While all Christians are one in Spirit through our Baptism, we are not fully united in belief and practice. For example, other Christians do not acknowledge the Pope as the leader of the Church, and their leaders are not successors of the Apostles. Because of this, we are not ready to share a common table of the Lord in the Eucharist. This means that the reception of Holy Communion in the Catholic Church by non-Catholics is not allowed. Neither are Catholics permitted to receive Communion in non-Catholic congregations. Eucharistic intercommunion is not possible with those faith communities because they have not preserved Apostolic Succession through the Sacrament of Holy Orders. These include the faith communities usually described as Protestant. Churches without Apostolic Succession and the priesthood do not have the gift of Holy Eucharist (the Body and Blood of Jesus Christ).

QUESTION 5: How do we know that any of the sacraments really work? For example, if a person dies after receiving the Sacrament of Anointing of the Sick, does that mean it did not work?

The effects of the grace we receive through the sacraments are not something that can be seen or measured. Therefore, each of the sacraments works whether we feel it or not. However, the fruits (or effects) of the sacraments do depend on the faith of the one who receives them. The sacraments are *efficacious* signs of God's grace. This means they are *effective* and they *work* because God is at work in them. Their words and gestures carry the power of God. Sometimes, we can't recognize how Christ has touched us at the moment, but in looking back at a later time, we will be able to see how he has helped us through celebrating the sacraments.

Think about the Sacrament of Anointing of the Sick. It is God's gift for those who are suffering from a serious illness, old age, or dying. It gives spiritual healing and strength to a person who is seriously ill, and sometimes physical recovery is granted as well. But when death is near, it prepares us so that when our earthly time is over, we will look forward to meeting God. If a person dies after receiving the Sacrament of Anointing of the Sick, it does not mean the sacrament did not work. The grace of this sacrament renews the person's trust and faith in God and gives them the strength to accept death peacefully. This is in itself a grace of healing.

GLOSSARY

absolution ➤ An essential part of the Sacrament of Penance and Reconciliation in which the priest pardons the sins of the person confessing, in the name of God and the Church.

actual graces ➤ God's interventions and support for us in the everyday moments of our lives. Actual graces are important for conversion and for continuing growth in holiness.

anamnesis ➤ The Greek word for *memory*. In the Eucharist, this refers to the making present of the Paschal Mystery, Christ's work of salvation. The *anamnesis* refers also to a particular section of the Eucharistic Prayer after the words of institution in which the Church remembers Christ's saving deeds—his Passion, death, Resurrection, and glorious return.

annulment ➤ The declaration by the Church that a marriage is null and void, that is, it never existed as a sacramental union. Catholics who divorce must have the marriage annulled by the Church to be free to marry once again in the Church.

Anointing of the Sick, Sacrament of ➤ One of the Seven Sacraments, in which a gravely ill, aging, or dying person is anointed by the priest and prayed over by him and attending believers. One need not be dying to receive the sacrament.

Apostolic Succession ➤ The uninterrupted passing on of apostolic preaching and authority from the Apostles directly to all bishops. It is accomplished through the laying on of hands when a bishop is ordained in the Sacrament of Holy Orders as instituted by Christ. The office of bishop is permanent, because at ordination a bishop is marked with an indelible, sacred character.

assembly ➤ Also known as a congregation, a community of believers gathered for worship as the Body of Christ.

Baptism, Sacrament of ➤ The first of the Seven Sacraments and one of the three Sacraments of Christian Initiation (the others being Confirmation and the Eucharist) by which one becomes a member of the Church and a new creature in Christ.

bishop ➤ One who has received the fullness of the Sacrament of Holy Orders and is a successor to the Apostles.

catechesis, catechists ➤ Catechesis is the process by which Christians of all ages are taught the essentials of Christian doctrine and are formed as disciples of Christ. Catechists are the ministers of catechesis.

catechumen ➤ An unbaptized person who is preparing for full initiation into the Catholic Church by engaging in formal study, reflection, and prayer.

Christian Initiation, Sacraments of ➤ The three sacraments—Baptism, Confirmation, and the Eucharist—through which we enter into full membership in the Church.

Church ➤ The term *Church* has three inseparable meanings: (1) the entire People of God throughout the world; (2) the diocese, which is also known as the local Church; and (3) the assembly of believers gathered for the celebration of the liturgy, especially the Eucharist.

common priesthood of the faithful ➤ The name for the priesthood shared by all who are baptized. The baptized share in the one priesthood of Jesus Christ by participating in his mission as priest, prophet, and king.

concupiscence ➤ The tendency of all human beings toward sin, as a result of Original Sin.

Confirmation, Sacrament of ➤ With Baptism and the Eucharist, one of the three Sacraments of Christian Initiation. Through an outpouring of the special Gifts of the Holy Spirit, Confirmation perfects and strengthens the graces received in Baptism and gives a unique outpouring of the Spirit of Christian witness.

conversion ➤ A profound change of heart, turning away from sin and toward God.

D

deacon ➤ Along with bishops and priests, one of the three Holy Orders conferred by the Sacrament of Holy Orders. Deacons are entrusted with various ministries, including baptizing, preaching, and witnessing marriages.

discernment ➤ From a Latin word meaning "to separate or to distinguish between," the practice of listening for God's call in our lives and distinguishing between good and bad choices.

E

Easter ➤ The day on which Christians celebrate Jesus' Resurrection from the dead; considered the most holy of all days and the climax of the Church's Liturgical Year.

Eastern Catholic Churches ➤ The twenty-three Churches of the East, with their own liturgical and administrative traditions, which reflect the culture of Eastern Europe and the Middle East. Eastern Catholics are in union with the Universal Catholic Church and her head, the Bishop of Rome.

elect ➤ In the Rite of Christian Initiation, the title given to catechumens after the Rite of Election, while they are in the final period of preparation for the Sacraments of Christian Initiation.

Eucharistic adoration ➤ The practice of praying in front of the Blessed Sacrament, which is exposed in a monstrance or ciborium on an altar or in a church or chapel.

Eucharist, the ➤ The celebration of the entire Mass. The term can also refer specifically to the consecrated bread and wine that have become the Body and Blood of Christ.

evangelization ➤ The proclamation of the Gospel through word and witness.

examination of conscience ➤ Prayerful reflection on, and assessment of, one's words, attitudes, and actions in light of the Gospel of Jesus; more specifically, the conscious moral evaluation of one's life in preparation for reception of the Sacrament of Penance and Reconciliation.

H

Heaven ➤ A state of eternal life and union with God in which one experiences full happiness and the satisfaction of the deepest human longings.

Hell ➤ Refers to the state of definitive separation from God and the saints, and so is a state of eternal punishment.

Holy Orders, Sacrament of ➤ The sacrament by which baptized men are ordained for permanent ministry in the Church as bishops, priests, and deacons.

L

Liturgical Year ➤ The Church's annual cycle of feasts and seasons that celebrates the events and mysteries of Christ's birth, life, death, Resurrection, and Ascension, and forms the context for the Church's worship.

liturgy ➤ The Church's official, public, communal prayer. It is God's work, in which the People of God participate. The Church's most important liturgy is the Eucharist, or the Mass.

Liturgy of the Hours ➤ Also known as the Divine Office, the official, public, daily prayer of the Catholic Church. The Divine Office provides standard prayers, Scripture readings, and reflections at regular hours throughout the day.

Logos ➤ Greek word meaning "Word." *Logos* is a title of Jesus Christ found in the Gospel of John that illuminates the relationship between the three Divine Persons of the Holy Trinity. (See John 1:1,14.)

Magisterium ➤ The Church's living teaching office, which consists of all the bishops, in communion with the Pope, the Bishop of Rome. Their task is to interpret and preserve the truths revealed in both Sacred Scripture and Sacred Tradition.

Matrimony, Sacrament of ➤ A lifelong covenant, modeled on that between Christ and the Church, in which a baptized man and a baptized woman make an exclusive and permanent commitment to faithfully love each other and to cooperate in the procreation and education of children.

monstrance ➤ A sacred vessel, usually in the form of a cross, used for the exposition of the Blessed Sacrament for adoration and benediction.

mortal sin ➤ An action so contrary to the will of God that it results in a complete separation from God and his grace. As a consequence of that separation, the person is condemned to eternal death. For a sin to be a mortal sin, three conditions must be met: the act must involve a grave matter, the person must have full knowledge of the evil of the act, and the person must give full consent in committing the act.

mystagogy ➤ A period of catechesis following the reception of the Sacraments of Christian Initiation that aims to more fully initiate people into the mystery of Christ.

Oil of the Sick ➤ Blessed olive oil used in the Sacrament of Anointing of the Sick to anoint the forehead and hands of people who are seriously ill or near death.

ordained (ministries) ➤ Refers to ministries that require ordination, such as presiding at the Eucharist, hearing confessions, administering Confirmation, and so on. Ordained ministers may also perform other ministries that can be performed by laypeople, such as distributing Communion, reading the Scriptures at the liturgy, and teaching theology.

Original Sin ➤ From the Latin *origo*, meaning "beginning" or "birth." The term has two meanings: (1) the sin of Adam and Eve, who disobeyed God's command by choosing to follow their own will and thus lost their original holiness and became subject to death, (2) the fallen state of human nature that affects every person born into the world, except Jesus and Mary.

P

Paschal candle ➤ Also called the Easter candle, this is the large, tall candle lit at the Easter Vigil by a flame from the new fire; the symbol of the Risen Christ.

Paschal Mystery ➤ The work of salvation accomplished by Jesus Christ mainly through his Passion, death, Resurrection, and Ascension.

Passion ➤ The suffering of Jesus during his final days in this life: his agony in the garden at Gethsemane, his trial, and his Crucifixion.

Passover ➤ The night the Lord passed over the houses of the Israelites marked by the blood of the lamb, and spared the firstborn sons from death. It also is the feast that celebrates the deliverance of the Chosen People from bondage in Egypt and the Exodus from Egypt to the Promised Land.

Penance and Reconciliation, Sacrament of ➤ One of the Seven Sacraments of the Church, the liturgical celebration of God's forgiveness of sin, through which the sinner is reconciled with both God and the Church.

penitent ➤ Refers to the person who repents of wrongdoing and seeks forgiveness through the Sacrament of Penance and Reconciliation.

prayer ➤ Lifting up of one's mind and heart to God or the requesting of good things from him. The six basic forms of prayer are blessing, adoration, praise, petition, thanksgiving, and intercession. In prayer, we communicate with God in a relationship of love.

priest ➤ One who has received the ministerial priesthood through the Sacrament of Holy Orders. The priest serves the community of faith by representing and assisting the bishop in teaching, governing, and presiding over the community's worship.

Purgatory ➤ A state of final purification or cleansing, which one may need to enter following death and before entering Heaven.

R

redemption ➤ From the Latin *redemptio*, meaning "a buying back," referring, in the Old Testament, to Yahweh's deliverance of Israel and, in the New Testament, to Christ's deliverance of all Christians from the forces of sin. As the agent of redemption, Jesus is called the Redeemer.

reparation ➤ The act of making amends for something one did wrong that caused physical, emotional, or material harm to another person.

repentance (contrition) ➤ An attitude of sorrow for a sin committed and a resolution not to sin again. It is a response to God's gracious love and forgiveness.

Rite of Christian Initiation of Adults (RCIA) ➤ The process by which an unbaptized person, called a "catechumen," and those who were baptized in another Christian denomination, called "candidates for full communion," are prepared to become full members of the Church.

Rite of Election ➤ The Rite, which takes place on the first Sunday of Lent, by which the Church elects or accepts the catechumens for the Sacraments of Christian Initiation at the Easter Vigil. The Rite of Election begins a period of purification and enlightenment.

ritual ➤ The established form of the words and actions for a ceremony that is repeated often. The actions often have a symbolic meaning.

S

sacrament ➤ An efficacious and visible sign of God's grace, instituted by Christ and entrusted to the Church, by which divine life is dispensed to us. The Seven Sacraments are Baptism, the Eucharist, Confirmation, Penance and Reconciliation, Anointing of the Sick, Matrimony, and Holy Orders.

sacramental economy ➤ The communication or dispensation of the fruits of Christ's Paschal Mystery in the celebration of the Church's sacramental liturgy.

Sacred Chrism ➤ Perfumed olive oil consecrated by the bishop that is used for anointing in the Sacraments of Baptism, Confirmation, and Holy Orders.

sanctifying grace ➤ The grace that heals our human nature wounded by sin and restores us to friendship with God by giving us a share in the divine life of the Trinity. It is a supernatural gift of God, infused into our souls by the Holy Spirit, that continues the work of making us holy.

scrutinies ➤ Rites within the Rite of Christian Initiation of Adults that support and strengthen the elect through prayers of intercession and exorcism.

sin ➤ Any deliberate offense, in thought, word, or deed, against the will of God. Sin wounds human nature and injures human solidarity.

symbol ➤ An object or action that points to another reality and leads us to look beyond our senses to consider a deeper mystery.

T

Tradition ➤ The process of passing on the Gospel message. Tradition, which began with the oral communication of the Gospel by the Apostles, was written down in the Scriptures, is handed down and lived out in the life of the Church, and is interpreted by the Magisterium under the guidance of the Holy Spirit. Both Sacred Tradition and Sacred Scripture have their common source in the Revelation of Jesus Christ and must be equally honored.

Transubstantiation ➤ In the Sacrament of the Eucharist, this is the name given to the action of changing the bread and wine into the Body and Blood of Jesus Christ.

Trinity ➤ Often referred to as the Blessed Trinity, the central Christian mystery and dogma that there is one God in three Persons: Father, Son, and Holy Spirit.

V

venial sin ➤ A less serious offense against the will of God that diminishes one's personal character and weakens but does not rupture one's relationship with God.

vocation ➤ A universal call from God, rooted in our Baptism, to all members of the Church to embrace a life of holiness. Specifically, it refers to a call to live the holy life as an ordained minister, as a vowed religious (sister or brother), or in a Christian marriage. Single life that involves a personal consecration or commitment to a public, permanent, celibate gift of self to God and one's neighbor is also a vocational state.

INDEX

Note: Charts are indicated with "C" after the page number.

ACKNOWLEDGMENTS

Scripture texts used in this work are taken from the *New American Bible, revised edition* © 2010, 1991, 1986, 1970 Confraternity of Christian Doctrine, Inc., Washington, DC. All rights reserved. No part of this work may be reproduced or transmitted in any form or by any means, electronic or mechanical, including photocopying, recording, or by any information storage and retrieval system, without permission in writing from the copyright owner.

The excerpts marked *Catechism of the Catholic Church* or *CCC* are from the English translation of the *Catechism of the Catholic Church* for use in the United States of America, second edition. Copyright © 1994 by the United States Catholic Conference, Inc.—Libreria Editrice Vaticana (LEV). English translation of the *Catechism of the Catholic Church: Modifications from the Editio Typica* copyright © 1997 by the United States Catholic Conference, Inc.—LEV.

The excerpts marked *Roman Missal* are from the English translation of *The Roman Missal* © 2010, International Commission on English in the Liturgy Corporation (ICEL) (Washington, DC: United States Conference of Catholic Bishops, 2011). Copyright © 2011, USCCB, Washington, DC. All rights reserved. Used with permission of the ICEL. Texts contained in this work derived whole or in part from liturgical texts copyrighted by the International Commission on English in the Liturgy (ICEL) have been published here with the confirmation of the Committee on Divine Worship, United States Conference of Catholic Bishops. No other texts in this work have been formally reviewed or approved by the United State Conference of Catholic Bishops.

The quotation by Pope Francis on page 14 is from "The Light of Faith" ("*Lumen Fidei*," 2013), number 40, at *www.vatican.va/content/francesco/en/encyclicals/documents/papa-francesco_20130629_enciclica-lumen-fidei.html*. Copyright © Libreria Editrice Vaticana (LEV).

The excerpt on page 24 is from "Egeria's Description of the Liturgical Year in Jerusalem: Translation," based on the translation reproduced in Louis Duchesme's *Christian Worship* (London, 1923), found at *users.ox.ac.uk/~mikef/durham/egetra.html*.

The quotation by Pope Paul VI on page 24 is from *Universal Norms on the Liturgical Year and the General Roman Calendar* (Catholic Bishops Conference of England and Wales, 1969), number 21.

The excerpts by Pope Francis on pages 40 and 90 are from "General Audience" (Saint Peter's Square, November 6, 2013), at *www.vatican.va/content/francesco/en/audiences/2013/documents/papa-francesco_20131106_udienza-generale.html*. Copyright © LEV.

The excerpts on pages 88, 89, 90, 91, 91, and 91 are from the English translation of *The Order of Baptism of Children* © 2017, International Commission on English in the Liturgy Corporation (ICEL), numbers 76, 79, 97, 99, 100, and 105, respectively. All rights reserved. Used with permission of the ICEL. Texts contained in this work derived whole or in part from liturgical texts copyrighted by ICEL have been published here with the confirmation of the Committee on Divine Worship, United States

Conference of Catholic Bishops. No other texts in this work have been formally reviewed or approved by the United States Conference of Catholic Bishops. Used with permission.

The excerpts marked RCIA on pages 104, 105, 106, 108, 109, 109, 114, 114, 114, and 115 are from the English translation of the *Rite of Christian Initiation of Adults* © 1985, ICEL, sections 50, 53, 47, 11, 133, 141, 226, 230, 233, 244, respectively; the excerpts marked *Rite of Penance* on pages 245, 253, 261, 261, 261, and 261 are from the English translation of *Rite of Penance* © 1975, ICEL, sections 45, 46, 46, 47, 47, 47, respectively. The excerpts marked *Anointing of the Sick* on pages 278, 283, and 284 are from the English translation of *Pastoral Care of the Sick: Rites of Anointing and Viaticum* © 1982, ICEL, sections 117, 117, 124 in *The Rites of the Catholic Church*, volume one, prepared by the ICEL, a Joint Commission of Catholic Bishops' Conferences (Collegeville, MN: The Liturgical Press, 1990). Copyright © 1990 by the Order of St. Benedict, Collegeville, MN. Used with permission of the ICEL. Texts contained in this work derived whole or in part from liturgical texts copyrighted by the International Commission on English in the Liturgy (ICEL) have been published here with the confirmation of the Committee on Divine Worship, United States Conference of Catholic Bishops. No other texts in this work have been formally reviewed or approved by the United States Conference of Catholic Bishops. Used with permission.

The quotation from Benedict XVI on page 123 is from "Address of His Holiness Benedict XVI to Participants in a Meeting Organized by the Catholic Fraternity of Charismatic Covenant Communities and Fellowships," at www.vatican.va/holy_father/benedict_xvi/speeches/2008/october/documents/hf_ben-xvi_spe_20081031_carismatici_en.html. Copyright © 2008 LEV.

The excerpts on pages 130, 132, 132, 133, 134, 135, and 135 are from the English translation of *The Order of Confirmation* © 2016, International Commission on English in the Liturgy Corporation (ICEL), numbers 13, 22, 23, 25, 27, 13, 13, respectively. All rights reserved. Used with permission the ICEL. Texts contained in this work derived whole or in part from liturgical texts copyrighted by ICEL have been published here with the confirmation of the Committee on Divine Worship, United States Conference of Catholic Bishops. No other texts in this work have been formally reviewed or approved by the United States Conference of Catholic Bishops. Used with permission.

The excerpt on page 137 is from "Homily of Pope Francis" (Saint Peter's Square, April 28, 2013), at *www.vatican.va/content/francesco/en/homilies/2013/documents/papa-francesco_20130428_omelia-cresime.html*. Copyright © LEV.

The quotations by Pope Saint John Paul II on page 165 are from "The Eucharistic Church" ("*Ecclesia de Eucharistia*," 2003), numbers 5 and 8, at *www.vatican.va/content/john-paul-ii/en/encyclicals/documents/hf_jp-ii_enc_20030417_eccl-de-euch.html*. Copyright © LEV.

The excerpts by Pope Francis on pages 169 and 185 are from "Homily on Solemnity at Corpus Christi" (Basilica of Saint John Lateran, May 30, 2013), at *www.vatican .va/content/francesco/en/homilies/2013/documents/papa-francesco_20130530_omelia-corpus-domini.html*. Copyright © LEV.

The quotation on page 191 is from *Constitution on the Sacred Liturgy* (*Sacrosanctum Concilium*, December 4, 1963), number 52, at *www.vatican.va/archive/hist_councils/ ii_vatican_council/documents/vat-ii_const_19631204_sacro-sanctum-concilium_en.html*. Copyright © LEV.

The excerpt on page 206 is from *Called by Name*, by Peter G. van Breemen (Denville, NJ: Dimension Books, 1976), page 168. Copyright © 1976 Peter G. van Breemen.

The quotation from the T. S. Eliot poem "East Coker" on page 213 is from his book *The Complete Poems and Plays, 1909–1950* (New York: Harcourt, Brace and Company, 1952), page 129. Copyright © 1952 Harcourt, Brace and Company.

The excerpt by Pope Francis on page 219 is from "Address to the Participants in the Ecclesial Convention of the Diocese of Rome," June 17, 2013, at *www.vatican .va/content/francesco/en/speeches/2013/june/documents/ papa-francesco_20130617_convegno-diocesano-roma.html*. Copyright © LEV.

The excerpt on page 223 is from a Catholic Relief Services (CRS) brochure. Copyright © 2010 by CRS. Used with permission of CRS.

The quotation on page 227 is from "On the Progress of Peoples," ("*Populorum Progressio*," 1967), number 74, at *www.vatican.va/holy_father/paul_vi/encyclicals/documents/ hf_p-vi_enc_26031967_populorum_en.html*. Copyright © LEV.

The excerpt by Pope Francis on page 261 is from "General Audience" (Saint Peter's Square, November 20, 2013), at *www.vatican.va/content/francesco/en/audiences /2013/documents/papa-francesco_20131120_udienza-generale. html*. Copyright © LEV.

The excerpt on page 266 is from "Catechetical Meeting of the Holy Father with Children Who Had Received Their First Communion During the Year: Catecheses of His Holiness Benedict XVI," October 15, 2005, at *www .vatican.va/holy_father/benedict_xvi/speeches/2005/october/ documents/hf_ben_xvi_spe_20051015_meeting-children_ en.html*. Copyright © LEV.

The excerpt by Pope Francis on page 277 is from "Address to the Members of the Unitalsi on the Occasion of the 110th Anniversary of Its Foundation," November 9, 2013, at *www.vatican.va/content/francesco/en/speeches/2013 /november/documents/papa-francesco_20131109_anniversario -unitalsi.html*. Copyright © LEV.

The prayer on page 306 is from the USCCB website, at *www.usccb.org/committees/clergy-consecrated-life-vocations/ prayers-vocations.*. Copyright © USCCB, Washington, DC. All rights reserved. Used with permission of the USCCB.

The quotations on pages 315–316 are from and adapted from "Oscar Romero: Bishop of the Poor," by Renny Golden, at *www.uscatholic.org/culture/social-justice/2009/02 /oscar-romero-bishop-poor*. Copyright © 2009 *U.S. Catholic*. Used with permission of *U.S. Catholic*.

The excerpt on page 318 is from "Homily of Pope Francis" (Vatican Basilica, April 21, 2013), at *www.vatican .va/content/francesco/en/homilies/2013/documents/papa-francesco_20130421_omelia-ordinazione-presbiterale.html*. Copyright © LEV.

The quotations on pages 341 and 342 are from the English translation of *The Order of Celebrating Matrimony* © 2013, International Commission on English in the Liturgy Corporation (ICEL), pages 35 and 38. All rights reserved. Used with permission of the ICEL. Texts contained in this work derived whole or in part from liturgical texts copyrighted by ICEL have been published here with the confirmation of the Committee on Divine Worship, United States Conference of Catholic Bishops. No other texts in this work have been formally reviewed or approved by the United States Conference of Catholic Bishops. Used with permission.

The excerpt by Pope Francis on page 341 is from "Address of Pope Francis to Participants in the Plenary Assembly of the Pontifical Council for the Family" (Clementine Hall, October 25, 2013), at *www.vatican.va/content /francesco/en/speeches/2013/october/documents/papa-francesco _20131025_plenaria-famiglia.html*. Copyright © LEV.

The quotation on page 345 is from "Themes of Catholic Social Teaching," by the USCCB, at *www.usccb.org /beliefs-and-teachings/what-we-believe/catholic-social-teaching /seven-themes-of-catholic-social-teaching*. Copyright © 2005 USCCB, Washington, DC. All rights reserved.

To view copyright terms and conditions for internet materials cited here, log on to the home pages for the referenced websites.

During this book's preparation, all citations, facts, figures, names, addresses, telephone numbers, internet URLs, and other pieces of information cited within were verified for accuracy. The authors and Saint Mary's Press staff have made every attempt to reference current and valid sources, but we cannot guarantee the content of any source, and we are not responsible for any changes that may have occurred since our verification. If you find an error in, or have a question or concern about, any of the information or sources listed within, please contact Saint Mary's Press.

Endnotes Cited in Quotations from the *Catechism of the Catholic Church*, Second Edition

Chapter 3
1. *Unitatis redintegratio* 22 § 2.
2. Cf. *Lumen gentium* 10.

Chapter 6
1. *Lumen gentium* 11.
2. *Sacrosanctum concilium* 47.
3. *Lumen gentium* 11.

Chapter 7
1. Paul VI, *Mysterium fidei* 39.
2. Saint Justin, *Apol.* 1, 65–67: J. P. Migne, ed., Patrologia Graeca (Paris, 1857–1866) 6, 428.
3. St. Ignatius of Antioch, *Ad Smyrn*, 8:1, Sources Chretiennes (Paris: 1942-), 10, 138.

Chapter 8
1. St. Augustine, *Sermo* 272: J. P. Migne, ed., Patrologia Latina (Paris, 1857–1866), 38, 1247.

Chapter 9

1. St. Augustine, *Contra Faustum* 22: J. P. Migne, ed., Patrologia Latina (Paris, 1841–1855), 42, 418; Saint Thomas Aquinas, Summa Theologiae, I–II, 71, 6.
2. Cf. Council of Trent (1551): Denzinger-Schonmetzer, *Enchiridion Symbolorum, definitionum et declarationum de rebus fidei et morum* (1965) 1712.

Chapter 10

1. Cf. Council of Trent (1551): Denzinger-Schonmetzer, *Enchiridion Symbolorum, definitionum et declarationum de rebus fidei et morum* (1965) 1698.
2. Cf. Council of Trent (1551): Denzinger-Schonmetzer, *Enchiridion Symbolorum, definitionum et declarationum de rebus fidei et morum* (1965) 1694.

Chapter 11

1. *Roman Pontifical*, Ordination of Bishops, 26, Prayer of Consecration.
2. *Roman Pontifical*, Ordination of Bishops, 22, Prayer of Consecration.
3. *Roman Pontifical*, Ordination of Bishops, 21, Prayer of Consecration.
4. Pius XII, encyclical, *Mediator Dei, Acta Apostolicae Sedis*, 39 (1947) 548.
5. Cf. *Presbyterorum ordinis* 2.
6. Byzantine Liturgy, *Euchologion*.

Chapter 12

1. *Gaudium et spes* 50 § 1; cf. Genesis 2:18; Matthew 19:4; Genesis 1:28.